Phoenix to LA

A true story of one young man's journey out of the 1960's

Martin McMorrow

**Everything that has happened
creates a stage for whatever happens next...**

BookLocker.com, Inc.
2010

Cover Design by Christopher McMorrow

*Thanks to Steve Fessler for his editorial assistance on an earlier draft of this book.

To the extent of my efforts to remember clearly,
all of the stories and details in this book are true
and not embellished.
Of course, the names have been changed
to protect all of those who were so incredibly innocent.

For everyone who was there,
for the Mormon's friend,
for other people who were impacted by heroin in Vietnam,
and for my fine son, Christopher

Prologue – My Father's War

I finally got the call I had hoped would never come. I had just checked in at a nice downtown hotel where I was planning to get a little dinner and prepare myself to give a morning workshop on treating people with brain injuries at the prestigious Rehabilitation Institute of Chicago. I had yet to turn on the lights in the hotel room as I dropped my suitcase on the floor, plunked my briefcase on the dresser, and sat down on the end of the bed. My older brother's voice over the cell phone shattered my best-of-well-made plans for the evening.

"Dad has turned for the worse," my brother said. "He called me an hour ago as I was driving home and I got right over to the house."

"When I got there he was lying in his bed after having lost control of his bowels all over the bedspread and floor of his room. The place was a mess. I did my best to get him cleaned up. I put the bedspread in the wash. I threw out the green rug that was on his floor."

"Mom was just sitting in her wheelchair by the kitchen counter…I don't think she even realized that anything was going on. You have to get down here. Dad has got to go to the hospital. I can't do this anymore. One of these times, I know he's going to be dead by the time I get here."

After roughing my way through the workshop the next morning, I skipped the post-presentation luncheon and immediately took off for Peoria. When I arrived at the only family home I had ever known, my father was downstairs lying on the couch that my mother usually occupied. She was still upstairs in her bed in the middle of the afternoon. That made sense because, due to having lost her legs to peripheral artery disease, she required dad's help to get down the stairs.

"What are you doing here?" my father asked as if surprised. I told him about my brother's call. I said, "The family is concerned that you need help, dad. If you don't get any, we fear that we are going to have to watch you die right here in the living room."

"Don't you think I know that?"

Of course I knew my father knew that. He had been diagnosing and generally downplaying his physical deteriorization for many of his last eighty-nine years. Nevertheless, I knew it had gotten to the point that I couldn't support his treasured privacy and independence any longer. I told him that I felt it was time for him to go to the hospital. He gave me a few stern looks and tried to deflect the issue at first, but he eventually agreed to go. The ambulance arrived at the house around 4:30 that afternoon. My oldest sister came over to stay with mom. My older brother and I followed the ambulance to the emergency room.

When we arrived at St. Francis, the attendants moved my father to the ICU where he was surrounded by doctors and nurses who were assessing his condition. At one point, one of them turned to me and asked "What are your father's end-of-life instructions?" As if to come to my rescue, my father lifted his head from the pillow and said "What are you talking to him for? I'm still making the decisions around here. There's really no assessment needed. I've had prostate cancer for nearly 25 years, my renal system is shutting down, and you know as well as I do that there is nothing you can do about it."

One of the doctors turned to my father and said, "Dr. McMorrow, if you become unconscious, do you wish to be revived?" I thought I knew the answer to the question because my father had shown me his Living Will a couple years earlier. However, at this moment of truth, he unexpectedly altered the instructions. "If I am not going to live for some time, then let me go. Otherwise, revive me, but absolutely no supports no matter what." I was surprised and pleased to see that dad still had a little fight left in him.

We checked into the hospital on the night of June 2, 2005. Others in the family were alerted. I stayed with him for two days straight until my sister from Oregon arrived. Then I hustled five hours south to my home to get some fresh clothes and turn in my rental car. I got back to the hospital in time to relieve my sister the following night. I slept when I could in a chair next to his bed. For the next seventeen days either my sister or I was with him continuously. That is all he had asked for.

What he gave was so much more. I watched and listened as my father welcomed my mother, his peers from the hospital, each of his children, his grand children, and his great grand children to his bedside. Between counting the sparse drops of urine that fell from his catheter and his drifts in and out of consciousness, we shaved, repositioned, opened and closed the curtains to introduce day and night, and kept the room as presentable as possible for all the well-wishers.

But during most of our time I just sat by the bedside holding my father's hand and occasionally giving him prolonged kisses on the forehead. Every so often he would awaken and provide me with another seemingly important piece of information that he must have recalled in his sleep. He told me where to find his checkbook and the important papers in his antique desk. He informed me that he had named me as his Power of Attorney and Executor of his Will. He filled me in on where to find the key for the gray lockbox that he kept in the closet next to his shoes and where to find the little stash of cash that he kept in a dresser drawer under his socks.

More importantly, in the days before his death my father shared what I believe were the most important gifts he had ever given to me. On one special occasion, he awakened suddenly and signaled for me to come closer. When I did, he whispered "Do you know that I have prayed the same way every day for as long as I can remember?" As if taking his cue I asked, "What do you pray for?" He said, "First, I give thanks for my wife and each of my seven children, nineteen grandchildren, and eleven great grand children. After that I give thanks for the life I have been given. Then, I make requests if I have any, but lately I have had only one – that I outlive your mother so I can take care of her." Momentary treasures that they were, none of these things was that surprising to me. As much as anything else, my father was a family man.

Then he hesitated. I wasn't sure if he was done talking or not, but he shifted around in the bed as if he had something else on his mind. I asked if there was anything else he wanted to say. He looked at me as long and as hard as he could. Then I noticed tears welling up in his eyes. As he burst into tears, my father said, "I pray every day that there will be an end to war."

A few days later my dad passed away in the presence of most of the immediate family. Gratified as I was to have been there when he shared some of his deepest thoughts; shortly thereafter I made up my mind that I would not wait until I was dying to tell others what's been on my mind.

Michael (Row the Boat Ashore)
(Folk lyric popularized by The Highwaymen)

Back in grade school, when we were kept busy learning how to practice the Catholic faith, there was an enthralling ritual that would take place in our classroom on the First Friday of each month. First, all of us boys in dark brown pants and light tan shirts and all the girls in short-sleeved white blouses and plaid jumpers would lower our heads to our wooden desktops and close our eyes. Then, Sister Mary Grace or one of her impeccably groomed, black and white counterparts would ask us to listen very carefully as she meticulously reviewed each of the ten commandments and instructed us to ask ourselves how any of our actual, venial, or mortal sins might relate to them. I was never sure whether actual sins were considered to be more serious than venial sins, but everyone understood that mortal sins represented the top of the ladder.

I learned a lot from this painstaking, yet enlightening little exercise. In particular, it provided me a glimpse of what the world was purported to have been about in the late 1950's...honoring one's parents and a single God, not killing anybody, not stealing, not committing adultery, not talking nasty about other people, not coveting other people's stuff, and not even tinkering around with the idea of messing around with another man's wife. As my inquisitiveness began to blossom, I often wondered if it was somehow okay for one of the girls to think about fooling around with another woman's husband. Strangely, none of the Sisters ever said a word about that, but the rules already appeared a bit one-sided to me.

While I was pleased to hear that the Commandments included a few positive directives about what we should do, most of them just added to an already endless list of what we young boys and girls were not supposed to do as we went about

1

our course of growing up. During the moments of silence as I rested there looking at the insides of my eyelids, I wondered how the Sisters knew so much about all this stuff since I had been told they never had kids and were not known for getting out much. I wished I could find whatever book it was that helped them understand so much about what not to do in life.

Although I had been hearing about coveting, jealousy, adultery, and other equally mysterious terms from an early age, for the longest time I had little idea what they actually were or how they related to sinning. I was always very curious to find out more about these things, so I looked forward to First Fridays. With my head down on the desk I'd consider which of my friend's mothers I could possibly have any interest in coveting, let alone adulterating. As if to comply with the Sister's instructions, I'd cautiously gauge my potential attraction to every mother on the block. I suppose the closest I came to a possible target was my friend Jake's mom. She used to spend entire summers tanning in her back yard covered only by her strapless one-piece bathing suit and slippery-looking, iodine-infused baby oil. However, I was confident that the thoughts I had about Jake's mom could have never constituted a sin.

After the Sister's exhaustive review of the possible sins, all of us kids would raise our heads, walk in single file over to the church, confess to one of the Priests in the dark little rooms at the back of the church, and do our penance. I found it fascinating that the confessionals were specially designed with golf-ball-shaped red and green lights above the doors so that everyone outside would know when some other kid was kneeling in front of the Priest disposing of his or her wrongdoings. I thought the stalls in the boys' school bathrooms should have lights like that. It seemed like some kids stayed in there forever.

I rarely had much to say when I finally got into the confessional. I'd typically report the same old worn-out offenses, usually in the category of saying bad words or nasty things about other people. Once I confessed that I had taken some empty soda bottles from behind our neighborhood florist shop and cashed them in for nickels and dimes so that I could buy more Hank Aaron and Mickey Mantle baseball cards. Mercifully, I let myself off the hook a bit on that one by acting as though I wasn't sure if taking empty soda bottles actually constituted stealing.

It seemed that no matter what sins I would eventually own up to, I always got the same penance – three Our Father's, two Hail Mary's, a Holy Be, and an Act of Contrition. The punishment was no big deal because I knew all those prayers by heart before the third grade. Sometimes, after confessing, I'd wonder if this time I'd done something bad enough that I'd have to climb up three hundred rugged stone steps on my knees or one of the other medieval penances I had been told about, but it never happened.

I never saw any other kids traversing stone steps on their knees, either. I figured that if anyone had ever warranted this sort of penance, it would have been Bird Dew. After all, it was Bird Dew who explained to the fourth grade boys how to use a condom after someone discovered a soggy one on the school playground. He was the one who tore out some of the wiring on the control panel of the school bus that we were supposed to have been cleaning as restitution for fooling around in the hot lunchroom. He was also the one who was threatening some little kid's life every time we turned around. But I never saw Bird Dew going out of his way to atone for any of these obvious sins. I chalked it up to the fact that he must have had to struggle pretty hard to live with the social and emotional turmoil caused by his barely treated cleft palate. I figured that the Priests were giving him a break due to all the interpersonal hardships he already had to bear.

Although I never noticed anyone doing anything out of the ordinary to make up for their sins, one time when we were kneeling in the church pews after our confessions and all of the other kids were presumably busy trying to remember their penance prayers, I heard a loud thump on the back of my pew. Several of us turned around to see Peach Fuzz with his chin on the backrest like a vase setting precariously on the edge of a shelf. His face had turned pale white and his eyes were rolled back in his head, as if the devil had gotten into him or something. Then, to our astonishment, his mouth opened really wide and he puked all over the seat behind us splashing little chunks of vomit all over the backs of our dark tan pants. After everybody got cleaned up, I speculated for a long time about whatever it was that Peach Fuzz must have done to deserve such a penance.

Today I wonder sometimes about how my life might have turned out had I somehow remained within the gentle simplicity of the 1950's that cuddled the earliest years of my life. If so, I suppose I could be sharing hardy "Good morning" greetings with some of the same kids I went to kindergarten with at the old church on Sunday mornings. We guys might be getting together on weekends to reminisce about our school pranks over chicken wings in each other's backyards. Who knows? I might have married one of my grade school sweethearts. I might have even watched our kids play little league or venture out on dates for the high school proms.

But of course, it didn't turn out that way. For better or worse, we all became children of the sixties.

Blowing in the Wind
(Bob Dylan)

My dad was a Catholic pediatrician who always drove Fords. He was a private man, who used to type out sweet little poems and stories for the family every Christmas on his Smith-Corona typewriter. He usually taught by example, not direct instruction. My mother grew up in a poor coal mining community called West City that is now under the water of man-made Rend Lake in Southern Illinois. A beautiful, orderly, and articulate woman, my mother taught her children how to sit up straight and smile, no matter what. My parents met at the hospital where my father was an intern and she was studying to become a Registered Nurse. They eventually raised a family of seven kids in which I was usually described as being "in the middle." I had three older sisters and one older brother, as well as a younger brother and sister. I reasoned that being the fifth born of seven was somewhere close to the middle.

To me, being in the middle meant that by the time my age finally reached the double digits my parents were probably a little tired out from raising children. I always felt as though I was pretty much left alone. For instance, I don't recall my parents ever having read books to me or helping me with my homework. My favorite book as a child was "The Little Engine that Could." I understood the story long before I could read the words. As I grew, my parents always let me stay out later than the other kids in the neighborhood and I could ride my bike to the Sheridan Village Shopping Center almost any time I wanted.

By the time I finished grade school I had already made an unchaperoned overnight bike trip to Canton, which was about thirty miles southwest from Peoria. A friend and I had planned to ride only as far as Farmington, but when we got there before

9:30 in the morning and discovered nothing of interest, we decided to pedal on another ten or so miles down the two-lane highway to a bigger town. That night we slept on the wooden bleachers at the town baseball park after having been disappointed by one of Elvis Presley's "B" movies that was showing at the Canton movie theatre. Considering that we were twelve-year-olds out on our own, we had hoped Elvis would teach us a bit more about the serious sins we had been hearing about all the way through grade school.

It truly was a beautiful childhood. My older brothers and sisters were off doing their things and typically I was off doing mine. That was just the way things were around my house. Except for my mother's involvement in preparing meals, doing all the laundry, determining when haircuts were due, making our beds, laying out our school lunch money, reviewing our report cards, planning summer vacations at the lake, and organizing holidays that were always fantastic and always exactly alike, all of us kids were pretty much expected to take care of ourselves. I respected my parents for what they taught us and didn't mind at all that they left us alone to find our way when we were away from the house.

As I gradually moved toward self-sufficiency, I did an awful lot of grass cutting. One summer I had four neighborhood lawns on my weekly grass cutting route including Ernie Snarl's place. Ernie Snarl was the only person on the block who drove a Cadillac and of particular interest to all us kids was that he didn't leave the house to go to work like all of the other men. Although I had heard that he was able to afford a Cadillac because he didn't have any children, somewhere along the line I learned that he was actually at home playing the stock market. The person who filled me in on this little tidbit made it sound like Ernie was betting the horses, playing poker, or some equally scandalous thing. I didn't care where he got his money.

He was the only person on my route who gave me a crisp five dollar bill for doing a two dollar lawn job with my push mower. Sometimes I didn't even have to do the trimming or sweep up.

Although no one ever really knows for sure, I felt like I had it pretty good compared to other kids on other blocks and I assumed the other kids on my block probably felt the same way. We knew that most of us were Catholics because whether we believed the teachings or not, we saw each other at St. Philomena's school and church. As a good show of our faith, most of us boys served as altar boys at one time or another. Most of us figured that our families must have been doing okay because all of our mothers stayed at home and all of our fathers worked. And, of course, we all had lots of brothers and sisters.

I suppose there were a few things that I considered might have made me a little different though. For some reason, I typically had the feeling that I thought about things a little more or a little harder than most of the other kids. Whether or not it was true, I was confident others didn't think about things exactly like I did. I frequently considered the relations between different things that would happen around me and the way people reacted to them. In the fourth grade for example, while most kids were cheering for Gretchen Winters to beat up Jimmy Williams on the school playground, I was busy thinking how badly Jimmy must have felt and thanking my lucky stars that it wasn't me getting pounded by a girl.

I also recall that I was alert not so much about being included in stuff, but rather about not being excluded from anything. Whenever I found myself among the last guys picked for an after-school baseball game, it wouldn't stop me from showing up for the next game, but I did spend time pondering my social stature as I stood alone chasing honey bees off the clover just short of the four-lane highway in deep right field.

It seemed that I spent large portions of my youth honing my social skills to make up for what I surmised was my general lack of prowess in virtually everything else. Inviting kids to play Whiffle ball in my backyard or basketball on my driveway not only assured me a spot in these games, but also that I would be less likely to be excluded from other things that the kids were up to. Providing banana-flavored Popsicles or little six-ounce bottles of Coca Cola from my parent's icebox didn't hurt in that regard either.

Besides working hard to keep from being excluded, I also tended to ignore or sometimes even stick up for other kids that I viewed as being a little like me. Despite having to do Confessions every month, the tough kids at St. Philomena's could be vicious. The nicknames they ascribed to those who were out of the "in" group told it all. Although my nickname, Moose, was really a joke because I was short and skinny, it was nothing compared to kids who grew up with brandings like Bird Dew, Peach Fuzz, Stinky, Barn Smell, Air Head, Fatso, Booger, and No Neck. Although I could empathize with the branded kids, when they were not around I would usually play along with the tough guys. At times I noticed that I could be as unkind as any of them.

But when the tough guys were not around, I would do what I could to make sure I saved my spot among the lepers. I just didn't care to risk being excluded by anyone. I was pretty sure that Stinky, Barn Smell, and most of the others understood that about me and sometimes appreciated it. As a result, I noticed that I got pretty good at playing on both sides of the social fence.

They were remarkable times...the late 1950's and early 1960's. As a youngster I had no way of knowing just how remarkable they were since I had nothing to compare them to. I would hear little bits and pieces about worldly things at our evening meals, but I never figured anyone suspected I was actually listening. I probably appeared to be absorbed in the all the regular things that tended to absorb most young boys in those days. Baseball, basketball, cross-country running and even golf provided good cover for a kid who was equally fascinated by the "Nudist News" and early "Playboy" magazines on the upper rack at the Sheridan Village Book Emporium.

In fact, one of the first "issues" that I recall listening to around our family dinner table had to do with the upcoming Presidential election in 1964. My parents had great concern as to whether we would be eating hot dogs and baked beans if the Democrats, Lyndon Johnson and Hubert Humphrey, were elected that year. My folks feared increased government oversight of health care, believing that my father would lose a big part of his income if "socialized" medicine ever caught on in America as it had in other parts of the world. Although this issue seemed really important to my parents, I remember thinking that it might not have been so bad if I had to eat beans and weenies every day for the rest of my life…as long as we had ketchup and pickle relish, of course.

Social issues beyond the family dinner table and the borders of the street where I lived didn't matter a great deal to me until after I completed my first year in high school. In those days there was no middle school…just grade school, high school, and whatever happened after that. No one I knew ever thought very far ahead.

At summer's end, 1965, my attention was drawn to something other than sports, my fear of being excluded, forbidden magazines, fear of tough girls, and the intricacies of sin for the first time. The event showed up on the coffee table in our living room, on the cover of my parent's "Life" magazine: the riots in the Watts district of Los Angeles. Watts moved me in a way I had not been moved to that point in my life. For the first time, I really wanted to understand how and why.

Somewhere in the midst of the emerging War in Vietnam and Civil Rights movement, and directly in the aftermath of what people, black people, believed was the unjustified arrest of a young black man for drunk-driving, the Los Angeles neighborhood of Watts had exploded into five days of rioting. Thirty-four people were killed. More than a thousand people were injured. Almost a thousand properties were damaged or destroyed by fires, looting, or both.

I was fascinated by the photos of National Guardsmen, burning buildings, and hoards of people emerging from shattered store windows carrying clothing, food, television sets, and anything else that they could get their hands on. Watts stood in stark contrast to all of my previous experience. People on my block didn't do things like this. On my little block in Peoria the milk truck still made morning rounds and we looked forward to the ice cream man on hot summer evenings. Watts seemed so different, so mysterious, and so far away. I figured that mortal sins must have been taking place in clusters of two, three, and four at a time. It was all a bit troubling, but I couldn't get enough of it. I began to understand that the world was bigger than the block where I lived.

However, it seemed to me that few other kids got very interested in what had happened in Los Angeles that summer. I didn't notice many adults who were particularly moved by it either. I got a low "C" grade on the paper I wrote about the Watts riots for my sophomore year social studies class at the new Catholic high school I attended. Though I had gotten many "C's" that I understood, this one was really hard to swallow since I had done my research and I even included a collage of cut-out pictures from the magazines with my paper.

For a long time I couldn't figure out why this event that meant so much to me seemed to mean so much less to so many of those around me. The teacher put my paper in a stack with all the other social studies papers when I really thought it ought to have been in a special stack all by itself. I tried not to let my disappointment show. It was hard for me to understand how everything else just seemed to go on as if nothing important had happened in Los Angeles. My sense of feeling different from my friends magnified. I tried not to think about it. Around that time I realized I had always tried not to think about things like that, though I often did.

My attention was captured like this again almost exactly one year later by an event that I considered to be similar to the Watts riots. Once again the photos in the Life magazine were startling. Once again the authorities were everywhere. Once again the event stood in contrast to my experience. At the University of Texas in Austin, Charles Whitman, an ailing twenty-five-year-old ex-Marine, shot and killed his mother and wife, climbed to the observation deck of the Administration Building Tower, and opened fire. By the time he was eventually shot dead by the local police, fourteen people had been killed and thirty-two others had been wounded.

I wrote another school paper about this event in which I covered details and speculated about the how's and why's behind the killings. Did anyone care that what the news reported as Charles' "history of mental illness" could have been the effects of a deadly brain tumor that impacted his decision making? Did anyone consider that there may have been other, more tangible reasons why Charles did what he did other than just *being distraught*? Did people know that he had been trying to find help for the problems he was having? Would any of those things have been suitable explanations for such an outrageous act anyway? I didn't understand why it mattered so

11

much, but the relations between the things that might have influenced Charles, the things that he did, and the way people portrayed him consumed me for a time. But once again, it seemed that few of those around me got very concerned about Charles Whitman, Austin, or the people who were killed, injured, or affected there.

Questions 67 and 68
(Chicago Transit Authority)

I was pretty much washed up in what most kids considered to be the *real* sports by my junior year in high school. As people began paying attention to my actual skills at playing baseball, football, and basketball, my social skills in those arenas mattered less and less. As a result, I started to lose touch with many of my athletic friends and began spending more time by myself. I still spent a lot of my time playing golf and running cross country, but most didn't consider these to be real sports. At the time, knocking around a little white ball and running barefooted through the countryside were sports that most of the *real* athletes bypassed. Being included or excluded in these things didn't matter that much because no one paid attention to them anyway.

My favorite times to play golf were in the waning hours of the day when the sun was dropping down behind the trees and everyone else had already packed up their Sammy Snead clubs and gone home. It was so still, so peaceful, so conducive to thinking about things that were going on around me. I hit the ball, walked toward it, and hit it again. In these special moments of solitude I began to play around with thoughts that were unlike any I had ever had. In particular, I noticed myself (as if I was not myself) contemplating whether I was driving the ball or whether it was actually driving me. I noticed that this odd sort of inquiry began to show up in other aspects of my life as well.

Aside from giving me time to think, playing golf so many nights until after dark also resulted in two of the most special accomplishments of my youth – tying for Medalist Honors at the 1968 Peoria Jaycees Junior Golf Tournament with a three under par sixty-eight, and winning City Medalist's Honors the next day in a three-way playoff against two of the best known players in town. Even so, because other things began to drive me, these were about the last times I ever played competitive golf.

I graduated from high school in 1968. Although I hadn't given the matter much thought, I wasn't sure I'd get into college because I hadn't gotten very good grades at my college-prep high school. After each report card I ever got I would hear someone say that I "had not applied myself." I was never sure those appraisals were very accurate. At seventeen, I didn't even know what it meant to apply myself. There were times I thought that perhaps I had applied myself, but not in what others would have considered the normal way. No matter. It was now the time to think about college. I had to think about college because, just like following a golf ball, all the kids in my family were expected to go to college after they graduated high school.

Depending on who you talked to, Peoria was either the second or third largest town in Illinois. It was home to the Caterpillar Tractor Company, a Hiram Walker Distillery, a Pabst brewery, Bradley University, the World's Most Beautiful Drive, and a minor league baseball team called the Chiefs. But everyone knew that Peoria didn't rival Chicago. Chicago was always "the City" in Illinois. Not only did Chicago have the Museum of Science and Industry, the Natural History Museum, Marshall Field's, Trader Vic's, the Ham and Egger, and the coordinated subway and elevated train system, it also had professional sports teams like the White Sox, Cubs, Blackhawks, Bulls, and Bears. I knew about all these things because my family would occasionally ride the Illinois Central "Rocket" to the city for us kids to experience them first hand.

With my father's gentle prompting I applied to Loyola University in Chicago. It was a mid-sized Jesuit school with campus locations downtown near Old Town, where musicians and hippies had begun to replace the beatniks, and on the north side just short of Evanston by Lake Michigan. I'd always enjoyed visiting Chicago and I liked lakes, so the idea of going to Loyola began to appeal to me. At the time these reasons were good enough because I had no idea what I would actually study in school.

However, I still had to get accepted. With a bit more prodding from my folks, I finally completed and sent in my application materials somewhere around the middle of summer. I was concerned that my application was late and that my grades might not have been good enough to get into a private school like Loyola, but I was relieved when my letter of acceptance came back not more than a week after I'd sent in my stuff. I concluded that the fact that my father was an alumnus of the Loyola Medical School had something to do with my getting in, "B minus" high school average and all. That was a good thing too since I hadn't applied anywhere else.

Almost any child of the sixties would recall that late August of 1968 appears to have constituted the crescendo of a string of monumental events that occurred during this pivotal year. Following the assassinations of Dr. Martin Luther King on April 4th, and Robert F. Kennedy on June 6th, and in the midst of the monstrous TET offensive in South Vietnam, the Democratic National Convention and a "Festival of Life" were scheduled to take place simultaneously in Chicago.

As I quickly learned, the Chicago Festival of Life was not unlike gatherings in other big cities that had begun to attract the attention of many young people in the late 1960's. At the time, I was way behind the curve in terms of understanding how the Convention and the Festival might interact, but similar to my fascination with Watts and Austin, I was eager to find out more. Public sentiment regarding social issues ranging from race relations to human rights and war was about to collide with the political leadership of the country. And with the advent of on-

15

the-spot live television reporting, it seemed that the "whole world was watching" to see what would happen.

Inside the convention, the Democrats were in the process of nominating Humphrey for President and Edmund Muskie for Vice President, since Johnson had removed himself from consideration on the ballot. Just outside, the Festival of Life and other barely-coordinated events had attracted an estimated ten thousand people to the streets of Chicago. On Day Three of the convention, the Festival and the Convention converged in a way that will likely hold a significant space in social history for decades to come. For me, the collision was even more enthralling than Watts and Austin because, with the television reporting, I could watch the events unfold on the evening news. This time, I noticed that I definitely did not feel alone. If anything, still sitting in Peoria, I had already begun to feel left out.

The crowds swelled in Lincoln Park to the north and throughout downtown Chicago. By evening, the largest gathering had formed in Grant Park, which was just across Michigan Avenue from the International Amphitheatre and hotel where many of the delegates, politicians, and reporters were staying. Then it happened. Under Mayor Richard J. Daley's direction some of the Chicago Police and National Guard troops, who had been poised nearby at Soldier's Field for "immediate action if necessary to maintain order," entered Grant Park. I was glued to my television as lines formed with young people on one side and the Chicago Police and most of the cameras on the other.

Finally, it seemed to me, the rioting ensued. I watched as kids no older than me got whacked with billy clubs and dragged through the streets into Police vans. Cameras on the tops of buildings showed the crowds scattering like ants. The commentators and politicians spoke faster and more emphatically than before. It seemed that I could almost smell the tear gas and mace that spread through the Park and into the downtown Loop.

Over the remaining days of the Convention and in those that followed, more than a hundred fifty officers were reported to have been wounded and hundreds of demonstrators were treated in the streets and hospitals around Chicago. Remarkably, no one was reported to have been killed. Remarkably, most people nationwide seemed to support Mayor Daley's decisions related to controlling the crowd. I didn't. To me, such an aggressive response to the young people's restlessness and discontent seemed to be a gross overreaction. It was one of the first times I noticed that I had begun to form a clear opinion about anything like this.

Crossroads
(Cream)

The Democratic National Convention of 1968 ended just before my mother, father, and older sister from Milwaukee dropped me off at college. That day sticks out for me, in part because I had to attend a private orientation session at the school while the rest of the family went out for breakfast at the Ham and Egger restaurant. I also recall it because just moments after he introduced himself, my guidance counselor informed me that I had "better than a sixty percent chance of flunking out of Loyola during my sophomore year." His comment might have been intended to fire me up about going to school, but I already suspected his crystal ball was probably right, particularly when I got to the dormitory.

I don't think anyone in my family had considered that the scene fueled by the confluence of the Convention and the Festival of Life was still going to be right there for me to step into once I arrived in Chicago. In early September of 1968 I exited the family station wagon and moved into the old Edgewater Beach Hotel in lieu of the brand new dormitory that was supposed to have been completed by that time on the lakefront campus just up Sheridan Road at Loyola. Nobody shed any tears as I took my bags into the hotel. On the contrary, I was excited to see what was in store for me. For the first time I felt as though I had a chance to become a real participant in big city events like those which had been grabbing for my attention since 1964. After hanging up my golf clubs, I was thoroughly ready to be moved in a different way.

The famous Edgewater Beach Hotel had closed to the public in 1967, but it was still as grand a place as I'd ever seen. I easily visualized the hotel as it had been in its heyday...playing host to Frank Sinatra, Marilyn Monroe, Perry

Como, visiting baseball teams, and all those famous big bands that my parents used to listen to on Sunday mornings over breakfast. When I walked into the hotel lobby for the first time the place looked as though it was still open to the public, except on this day the patrons were all college students who were schlepping their own bags.

I checked in with some older students who were positioned as if they were clerks at the registration desk. In a small room off to the side I noticed that several long-tailed doormen's coats were still hanging on shiny brass hooks. Rolled- up banners welcoming the Phillies, Cardinals, and Dodgers were tucked in an old umbrella stand in one of the corners. Stacks of hotel stationery and note pads were strewn on the floor. I was struck by the contrast between the new path my life was about to take and all the vintage stuff that surrounded me at the hotel.

To my surprise and delight, there was not a great deal of organization or University oversight of the new students at the old Edgewater Beach. Though we were assigned roommates in alphabetical order and the guys and girls were placed on different floors, most of us just occupied whatever rooms seemed to suit us best. Some students even moved into the fancy corner suites in the towers at the ends of the hallways. As alphabetical order would have it, I wound up with a sandy red-haired kid, who was quickly labeled as "Cowboy," in an odd-shaped room on the fifth floor by the elevator. Cowboy was from Colorado, but he didn't look or act like any gun-slinger I had ever seen on television. He was soft-spoken, humble, and ready to go to school. The room didn't have a highly preferred view, but after we rearranged the furniture, it was a good place to be - mostly because Cowboy was there. We became friends immediately.

Within a month of my arrival in Chicago I had already begun smoking Salems, had already consumed more cheap

beer, Ripple and Boone's Farm wine than in my entire previous
life, and had already been carried away by the Moody Blues'
"Days of Future Passed," and Cream's "Sunshine of your
Love." I had also been exposed to a small array of chemical
accompaniments that helped this music sound much different
from my older brother's Gene Pitney and Johnnie River's
records. Guys from Chicago and the other big cities introduced
me to pot before I had cracked my first book.

In a process similar to natural selection, which I was
actually paying attention to in my Natural Sciences class; I
found myself pretty well inseparable from Cowboy and an
increasingly homogeneous group who seemed to be attracted to
the same things that I was. My other new friends included
"Joon" from Bloomington, "Skip" from Buffalo, and "The
Cork" from South Chicago. Our little group gravitated together
quickly over dinners in the Hotel restaurant, late night pizzas
from Napoli's, bus rides to and from campus, and special events
that took place around town and in the hotel ballroom. Of
course there were many others with silly nicknames like
Jewelie, Blimpie, Blumpy, Cosmo, and Rose. I was sometimes
called "Boy" as I had been affectionately tagged by Skip. One
girl actually held onto the name she had been assigned at birth.
Kathy and I spent a lot of nights sitting around an off-lobby
hallway at the hotel studying the music of Tim Buckley,
Sergeant Pepper's era Beatles, Bob Dylan, Janis Joplin,
Melanie, and others who we listened to on her portable box
record player.

Music was a huge influence on our lives that first year, and
each of our years, at college. To me, music in college was a lot
like sports had been in grade school. I noticed that as long as
people were filling their heads with music it didn't seem
necessary for them to talk very much. I sometimes wondered if
people listened to music so they wouldn't have to talk to each

other. Perhaps everyone just assumed that the music was moving all of us in the same way. Yet, I noticed that whatever a person listened to pretty much defined what team they were on. I suppose it was a good thing that there were different types of music, otherwise we all might have turned out just alike.

For me, music provided a great way to find out what other, seemingly enlightened people were thinking and it also helped me stay in tune with what was happening in the world. I noticed that my tastes skipped from high school favorites like "Louie Louie," "Gloria," and "Wooly Bully," to "Over, Under, Sideways, Down" and "Eight Miles High" over night. This was partially the result of selecting a dozen free albums when I joined the Columbia Record Club the summer after my senior year in high school. I didn't know it at the time, but these random selections actually helped define who I would become. The Yardbirds, the Byrds, and others on my selection list carried me away to a deeper, more interesting place than the Kingsmen, Shadows of Knight, or Sam the Sham and the Pharaohs ever had.

As I noticed myself and others beginning to transform, musical preferences provided solid clues as to which way each of us was headed. For example, I was amazed to see Ray Steven's "Gitarzan" climb the popular music charts in 1968. With all the serious things going on in the world at the time, it seemed odd that this song would have attracted any attention whatsoever. At least I was clear that I wouldn't have had much to talk about with anyone who was actually into it.

This same dynamic held true, but to a lesser extent, regarding those who preferred groups like Tommy James and the Shondells, the Young Rascals, Diana Ross and the Supremes, the Cryin' Shames, and the Monkees. Of course, this music was around and no one would have been embarrassed if they got caught listening to it, but for many of us it only

21

constituted a short phase until we got on to something more inspiring. I never even mentioned to my new college friends that I had seen the Monkees play live at Chicago Stadium a few years earlier because I felt like I now understood how little they had to say about anything that mattered. They hadn't even played their own instruments.

It was more confusing to determine where big fans of musicians like the Turtles, Aretha Franklin, Three Dog Night, or Blood Sweat and Tears were coming from. Of course our group listened to them, but mostly early on and mostly when we were after a more inclusive party atmosphere. Before long, I was pretty well convinced that music either had something to say or it didn't. And I noticed that I began to leave what I considered to be the "soft stuff" behind as I became more attracted to musicians that had something to tell me about what was going on around us. Even so, I felt like I was in an identity crisis at times when so many different albums popped up in a stack of records on a turn table in late 1968. Shifting on a dime from "R-E-S-P-E-C-T" to something like "Mr. Spaceman" or "Tuesday Afternoon" was no easy feat.

Around Loyola, I considered myself fortunate to have the chance to see a lot of good live music. Most of us got into the local groups like the Siegal-Schwall, Baby Huey, Virgin Dog, and one of Kevin Cronin's early bands. However, when those shows were done we were increasingly consumed by the message of early Simon and Garfunkel; Crosby, Stills, Nash, and Young; and Cat Stevens. When these guys were on somebody's record player, nobody had to say a thing.

In time, I completely lost track of what was changing more quickly…the music or me. Similarly, as I read a bit of Darwin, I couldn't tell if I was choosing what to listen to or if it was somehow selecting me. All I knew was that, at the time, it was a very compelling attraction. Things were happening so quickly. I gradually began taking less time to try to sort them out.

Considering that those of us at the Edgewater Beach were physically isolated down the road from the main campus, before long it seemed as though we constituted our own distinct group in our own separate neighborhood. I felt it was a special place to be. At Christmas time, I watched rush hour traffic come around the corner from Lakeshore Drive onto Sheridan Road for hours at a time. I thought the six-lane throng of white headlights and red taillights looked beautiful from my window at the Edgewater Beach. In the late afternoons and evenings I also enjoyed walking out to Lake Michigan. I found myself out by the water frequently, even as the crush of the Chicago winter set in, watching the ice-tipped waves, guarding myself from the piercing wind, and admiring the fishermen who perched along the shores.

Similarly, the surrounding Bryn Mawr neighborhood still held much of its 1920's flavor. I enjoyed watching the hoards of people enter and exit the elevated train station there and I frequently wondered where they were coming from or going to. The diner under the elevated tracks became a regular hangout for ninety-nine cent breakfasts on weekends and the liquor store just up the street didn't even card the girls.

I was learning a lot in Chicago, but not as a result of my studies. Living up to my reputation as one who did not apply himself, I just didn't work very hard at them. In fact, only one class stands out in my memory of that entire first year at school. It was a warm and sunny afternoon. Kids were sitting on the lawns by the Lake and tossing footballs back and forth on the intramural field in the middle of campus. The big windows in the old classroom building were cracked open to the first signs of spring. I was watching and listening to my elderly English professor in the midst of all the potential distractions.

The old professor was a theatrically-inclined man who had been reading something from Shakespeare. After twenty or thirty minutes of his reading, several of us began to notice that he had become absolutely engrossed in portraying the characters. He was fascinating to watch, but as he read his lines on and on, it became clear that he was increasingly oblivious to the fact that anyone else was even in the room.

I was enthralled as his face flushed bright red, his hands waved expressively, and he stared deep into the bare ceiling. I suspected that students walking by the open windows could have heard his voice rise above the beautiful afternoon. His motions accelerated and he began to pace around the room like a much younger man. Finally, as the class-change buzzer sounded, someone attempted to interrupt him just to see if he was actually still with us. Apparently, he wasn't. Maybe he was overcome by the combination of the beautiful day and his obvious infatuation with the literature. For all I knew, maybe he had gazed beyond the ceiling and into some blissful Shakespearian paradise. He joyfully continued on with his part as students silently filed from the room. I might have been the last to leave.

The next English class, my fascination and concern for the old English professor turned to a bit of disappointment and confusion when a new instructor announced that he would be taking over the class for the rest of the semester. Sadly, we never heard anything more about the old Professor, but shortly thereafter I decided I would change my major from "Undecided" to English.

In a Gada da Vida
(Iron Butterfly)

I returned home to Peoria the summer after my freshman year at Loyola, although I didn't stay at the family house very much. Even though we were a little older (I was eighteen), my remaining high school friends continued to be impressed at how my parents let me be when I was at home. I guess my friends didn't recall that this was the same as it had always been for me. And besides, my folks knew I was pretty much on my own in Chicago, so why should they treat me any differently when I was back in Peoria? I regarded it as their way of helping prepare me for a future that didn't involve living under their roof.

Most nights at the start of that summer I would venture out with my hometown buddies, Jake and Tingsly, driving around town looking for something to do. I had known Jake since before Kindergarten, but I had only hung out with Tingsly since high school. Jake was one of my few truly life-long friends and I was familiar with his penchant for finding himself at the center of attention. When we were little kids I watched as he fell forty-five feet from the neighborhood climbing tree and walked away. Later, I was fascinated as he entertained the sixth grade class by sticking a lead pencil into an open wound on his arm all the way up to the eraser. I listened as he claimed to have been kidnapped after he had turned up missing at least two times in his life – once as early as the fifth grade and once during our sophomore year of high school. I also heard him tell about how he'd been coaxed into having sex with the only good-looking single lady on the block who often mowed her tiny lawn in a two-piece swimming suit and sandals. It was Jake who stole a copy of the final senior English exam so he could give the answers to everyone else, then got expelled and did not graduate with the class, yet threw his own mock graduation party at a local hotel.

And it was Jake who got arrested that night at the Howard Johnson's in the oversized bathtub with two underage girls.

Jake had probably endured more grief and jokes at his expense than anyone I had ever known or heard of. I suspected that he'd been beaten up, teased, poked, or prodded by more than half of the people he ever knew. And from outward appearances he just kept laughing which tended to entertain the other half. Most times Jake seemed to take my mother's "sit up straight and keep a smile on your face" lesson to the extreme.

The three of us were getting bored with driving up and down Peoria's Main Street one night when Jake came up with the idea that we should head over to the nearby town of Pekin where he had been hanging out some of the time while Tingsly and I were away at school. As always, I was driving in my folks' 1964 and a half, baby-blue Mustang convertible with fake wire wheel hubcaps.

The six or eight mile drive from Peoria to Pekin seemed to take forever that night, probably because I felt like we were just killing time. We passed the muddy pond at Twin Lakes on the way and I reminisced a bit about the times I had been swimming there as a kid. I remember thinking that Pekin girls had always seemed a bit more mature and seasoned around the edges than the ones at our high school...in fact, some of the girls from my school frequently referred to them as sluts. I suspected that appraisal might have been mutual.

We got to Pekin around midnight. Jake directed us to an old two-story house at the end of a dark block where at least every other house looked as though it had been deserted. Then he announced that this was usually a good place to hang out, get high, or find some fun girls to hook up with. Tingsly and I weren't quite sure what that meant coming from Jake. As far as we knew he didn't have much of a history of hanging out, getting high, or hooking up with particularly attractive girls. We thought of him as the kind of kid who didn't or couldn't hold his attention on any one thing for that long.

Jake asked us to wait in the car while he walked inside the house to see if anything was going on. Tingsly and I sat in the convertible looking at the abandoned cars in the side yard and wondering what in the heck we were doing there. We had a good laugh and sat in anticipation of whatever would happen next.

Fairly soon, Jake came strutting back out of the house holding hands with a girl that Tingsly and I had never seen before. We were surprised to see that she was really attractive, more like a full-fledged woman than a girl, probably in her mid-twenties, and well dressed for a hot summer night in a lime green tube top, silky mini-skirt, and fairly high heels. She greeted Tingsly and I enthusiastically as she and Jake squished into the back seat, but didn't pay much attention to anyone but Jake after that. Tingsly and I were a little baffled that she appeared so happy to be with Jake, although it was possible that her judgment might have been impaired by whatever substances she'd been into earlier in the evening. Then, amid the laughter and giggles of their initial interaction, Jake quietly tapped me on the shoulder and asked me to put up the convertible top and start driving around town. I asked him where he expected me to go, but he didn't respond.

I quickly realized that our itinerary didn't matter as my first vivid exposure to casual sex began to unfold before my eyes. The laughter from the back seat instantly turned to giddiness as Jake pulled the woman's tube top up over her head and willingly outstretched arms, revealing a pair of the biggest breasts I had ever seen. There she sat, outrageously topless in the back seat of my parent's car, as Jake noisily fondled and kissed her. Tingsly and I pretended to look other ways.

As we made slow rounds through a local cemetery Tingsly and I couldn't resist snatching glimpses in the rear view mirror as Jake and this free-spirited woman carried on. I watched as he skillfully reached up the side of her skirt, slipped off her underwear, and then blocked her view with his body as he dangled his dainty little prize between the bucket seats for Tingsly and I to see. A moment later the panties were floating through the air onto the deserted cemetery road. Jake had tossed them from the passenger side window.

Shortly thereafter, with her saliva-soaked breasts naked to the streetlights and her slippery little mini-skirt pulled up to her belly button, the woman playfully began to let Jake know that it was probably time for him to stop. She actually started acting bashful and coy as if she was all-of-the-sudden surprised to find herself in the buff in a Mustang with three much younger guys. Unbelievably, she sat there virtually naked as the four of us casually discussed whether the two of them should continue. Although she was a really pleasant sight and I might have tried to extend the conversation a bit, Tingsly and I eventually agreed with her. I don't believe either of us cared to see Jake's white ass and, besides, it was clear how ridiculous this whole thing had become. After some convincing from the three of us, Jake reluctantly ceased his foreplay, but it took some moments for him to catch his breath.

As I drove the car back toward the house, the woman carelessly yanked her skirt back in position and pulled her top back over her head to its rightful place. When we turned onto the gravel drive, she suddenly appeared more intoxicated than when she first joined us. Stepping out of the car she didn't even seem to notice that she was now without underwear and her mini-skirt was turned around backwards. She walked back toward the house adjusting her tube top with one hand and waving goodbye with the other. At that point, Jake announced that he knew her boyfriend and suggested that we get out of Pekin as quickly as we could. We didn't argue with him.

If You Come to San Francisco
(Scott McKenzie)

Later that June of 1969, Tingsly and I decided to get out of Peoria for a while. Like so many others were doing that summer, we planned on hitchhiking across country to San Francisco. By that time, hitchhiking was not new to either of us. In fact, I used to hitchhike rather than walk the mile or so to high school almost every morning before I raised $125 for my 1956 Ford Sedan at the start of my senior year. In addition, during freshman year at college I had made several trips back and forth between Chicago and home to visit my family and between Chicago and Northern Illinois University to visit Tingsly and my sometimes high school girlfriend, Sadie. Hitchhiking had already become a whole lot more than just a cheap way to get around. I viewed it as a ticket to instant adventure.

Hitchhiking had rarely resulted in any problems for me. In high school I'd been propositioned by an old guy who asked me if I wanted to look at some girlie playing cards while he drove me toward my home. But he let me go without much fuss. Then there was the time when I went out to Dekalb unannounced only to show up at Sadie's apartment late one night and interrupt her while she was sleeping with another guy. It was about that time when she finally stopped trying to conceal her infidelities from me. But that little setback wasn't really related to my hitchhiking. As some of my old friends from high school told me later, that had more to do with my tendency to trust someone who never should have been trusted in the first place. I eventually took their word for it, but I'm not sure that part of me ever changed. I have usually trusted someone until it smacked me in the face that I couldn't. This tendency probably resulted in my fair share of disappointment along the way.

There was also that chilly day heading out of Chicago for Peoria on Route 66, which was being transformed into Interstate 55 at the time. I had made it smoothly from Roger's Park on Lakeshore Drive through downtown, but out on the open highway I was having a little trouble getting a ride.

I suppose it could have been that I was beginning to look a bit more like a hippie, which probably turned some people off to the idea of picking me up. Although I never considered myself to *be* a hippie, I guess I must have looked the part in my extended bell-bottom jeans, half-boots, flannel shirt, and sheep-lined suede coat with a scarf around my neck and a small backpack over my shoulder. I hadn't cut my hair since I had been away from home and it was so thick it often tended to resemble an Afro, especially when the wind was blowing.

Though some may have been taken back by my looks, I noticed that my appearance had a different impact on others...especially on the road. Families tended to drive by, while hippies tended to make room where there wasn't any for other hippies. Appearance seemed a lot like musical choices: I felt that you could tell a lot about someone just by looking at them. Clearly, others felt that way too. Nevertheless, I thought that I looked like one of the "good guys" and often wondered why everyone wouldn't think so.

Unfortunately, what seemed so sensible to me was more likely to make most others drive by, without even entertaining the idea of letting me sit with their kids in the backseats of their station wagons. Sometimes standing on the side of a road watching drivers look the other way as they passed me by made me bitter, especially when it was cold outside. How could people just roll on with their pretty little lives, I wondered, while so many of us young people were getting bumped around by all the crazy things that were happening in the world? Why were they not more understanding?

On this day, as I was standing next to southbound Route 66 kicking rocks, an Illinois State Trooper decided to stop and check me out. It must have been too cold for him to talk to me outside the cruiser, so he put me next to him on the front seat passenger side as he examined my identification and listened to my story. I didn't mind the diversion because it gave me a chance to warm up.

While the trooper and I were talking, he suddenly reached over and, with the thumb and middle finger of his right hand, picked out the soft pack of Tarreytons I was carrying in my shirt pocket. I watched as the pack moved in his fingers through the air between us. Then, just as neatly, he cupped the pack in his left hand, removed one of my cigarettes, put it between his lips, and with his right hand returned the pack to my pocket without ever turning it around.

It was an amazing visual. It was also pretty fortunate considering that on the backside of the pack, inside the cellophane wrapper, were two joints I had stored away for my weekend trip home. All I got from the trooper was a written warning, which was about all I ever got from the police for hitchhiking. I continued on my way, as he knew I would, immediately after he drove off.

With our experience and fearlessness in tow, Tingsly and I took off for San Francisco that summer of 1969 without much more than two space blankets and some Payday candy bars. Space blankets looked like quilted tin foil, and from what we had read, we expected them to keep us as warm and protected as we would need to be on the sunny west coast. We also had about $50 each and our scattered anticipation of what San Francisco might be like. We had no particular course in mind other than to get to the freshly completed Interstate 80 which would eventually take us there.

Thumbing out of Illinois and through Iowa was no trouble at all, but Nebraska quickly became a different story. No sooner had we crossed the eastern border of the Cornhusker State than we started getting stopped by the Nebraska State Police every time we set foot out of a car. Each time, we would hop in the back seat of a cruiser while the trooper called in to see if we had caused any trouble or if anyone was looking for us. And each time after the check came back clean we would get a pink copy of a written warning and a lecture about the rules of the road in Nebraska.

The fourth or fifth trooper we met in this way must have heard some sort of radio bulletin to stop giving us pink slips for hitchhiking. He looked back over the seat and said, "I know you boys have already been warned about hitchhiking in Nebraska." Of course, we replied, "Yes sir, we have." Then, to our momentary delight, he said, "Well, I have received approval from my higher-ups to take you someplace where it is okay for you to hitchhike," and pulled the cruiser back onto the Interstate.

About five miles down the road, the trooper zipped off the highway at an exit ramp. We assumed that he was going to drop us off at the exit, instruct us to stay at the top of the entrance ramp that headed back on, and be on his way. But unfortunately, he didn't stop. He continued driving north. Before too long we were cruising down a two-lane back road with paint markings that were barely visible, corn fields on either side that were already way taller than "knee high by the Fourth of July," and nightfall rapidly approaching. Then, out in the middle of Nebraska nowhere, the cruiser rolled onto the shoulder of the road. Just as he had before, the trooper leaned back over the seat and said, "Well, here we are boys...it is okay for you to hitchhike here."

Tingsly and I both echoed, "Thanks a lot," and stepped out of the car onto the gravel shoulder of that lonely country road. We watched the cruiser make a quick u-turn and head back into the night. There we stood, with whatever thoughts we might have had about the trooper's good intentions rapidly fading. We hadn't seen a car on that road the entire way out there and we knew we were unlikely to see one anytime soon. We had been ditched at night in the middle of Nebraska.

"We're screwed," said Tingsly. "Look at this place, the damn corn is so high; you can't see or hear a fucking thing." He was right, but I tried to make light by saying, "It's like we are inside a room without any windows or ceiling." We paced around in circles for a while in disbelief and then Tingsly shouted, "How could anyone be such a jerk?"

After a few more minutes of pacing around Tingsly's eyes lit up when we heard the sound of a train somewhere in the distance. We looked back and forth along the road until we saw the red lights of a railroad crossing about two hundred yards to the north. Tingsly immediately declared, "We're taking the train!" We grabbed our things and ran toward the crossing as fast as we could.

We reached the crossing before the train. Coming through the tall corn as it was, we weren't absolutely sure which direction it was actually going to be headed when it arrived at the crossing. However, as the bright spotlight on the front of the engine became visible, Tingsly said "Good news, Moose, it's heading our way."

The bad news was that it was huge and it was traveling much faster than either of us had imagined. We practiced running next to it several times to see if we could grab onto something and hop on, but neither of us had the nerve to try. What if one of us made it and the other didn't? Finally I called out, "There's no way, Man. It's going to rip our arms off."

Worn out from running, we watched the lights from the caboose recede down those tracks just as we had watched the taillights from the cruiser leave us behind on that deserted back road.

Several hundred yards down the tracks, in the pitch dark without other options, Tingsly and I decided it was probably best to follow the tracks until we could find our way back to civilization. We walked. The sense of isolation created by the corn was haunting at times and Tingsly was concerned that another train might appear out of nowhere. "This is just great," he said factitiously. "We're gonna' get squished by a giant train in the middle of nowhere and we'll be lost forever."

About two miles down the track, in a grassy gap in the corn, we noticed bright lights on the horizon to our left. We guessed that these lights were from a truck stop back by the interstate, so we decided to go "as the crow flies" straight through the corn in that direction. Unfortunately, this created an even greater sense of isolation because the walls around us had now closed in considerably. As we were plowing through the corn, I recall asking Tingsly, "I wonder how Cornwall Jackson got his name?" I kept trying to make light of how uncomfortable we were as we trudged on.

Just as we thought we might need to hunker down for the night, we came to another small clearing in the corn. Barely visible in the dark about a dozen feet in front of us was a ten foot high, solid wall. The glow of lights we had seen was coming from the other side of the wall. Energized by the possibility of seeing human life again, I clasped my hands together so that Tingsly could use them to reach the top of the wall, pull himself up, and find out what was on the other side. Once he'd gotten up there he said, "You're not going to believe this." I waited for him to explain.

"We've landed at an airport – there's a terminal building on the other side of two runways."

After a short discussion about our lack of options, we decided that the most direct route back to civilization was to go over wall and head directly for what Tingsly thought was the terminal. He helped me up on top of the wall and, after catching our breath; we hopped down and bolted for the building.

Our dash to reconnect with mankind lasted all of about fifteen seconds before we were corralled by the bright spotlights of two security vehicles that appeared out of nowhere. We dropped our stuff on the ground as instructed by a voice on a loudspeaker and stood there with our hands in the air as security personnel made their way toward us through the glare of the spotlights. Once again, Tingsly proclaimed, "We're screwed."

It could have been a lot worse. As it turned out, we had leaped the wall onto some sort of military base near Lincoln, Nebraska. We had no trouble convincing the security people about how we happened to get there and I was pretty sure they might have even sympathized with us about the shitty trick the State Trooper had played on us. They had to know that we couldn't have made that stuff up. After a stop at the security office for a little more questioning, two of them drove us back down the road and dropped us at a truck stop beside the interstate. When they left, we hung around by the door of the building until a young trucker agreed to take us with him as far as the State line.

After the night we'd had in central Nebraska, we decided we deserved a rest and a night in a cheap motel in North Platte. When we weren't sleeping we spent time at a highway honky-tonk bar where we had a few beers and talked with a pigtailed young country girl in a long cotton dress who told us about a big music festival that was going to be taking place in Denver that weekend. Apparently, she wasn't able to go, but I suppose she gathered by our appearance that we might have been interested.

I must have had a notion that Tingsly and I might wind up somewhere around Denver on our trip because I had gotten my Uncle Mac's address and phone number from my mother just in case. We called the number from the bar and he immediately invited us to come down to his place for as long as we cared to stay. The Wednesday afternoon trip down to Denver was quick and easy because virtually everyone leaving Nebraska for Colorado was headed to Denver. Between the Nebraska border and the mountains there didn't appear to be anywhere else that people might have wanted to go.

In Denver, we got dropped off on Colfax Avenue where we learned more about the upcoming Denver Pop Festival. It looked like it was going to be a really big deal, so we each spent $15 of our trip money on tickets for the entire weekend of shows. Later, we made our way out to Uncle Mac's. When he answered the front door of his early suburban house in his plaid shorts, sandals, and t-shirt, I realized how long it had been since I had seen him. He must have been in his seventies, but he had clearly held on to his youth. He was short, thin, spry, tanned, and very happy to see us. We stayed with him until Friday morning. Although neither of us understood just why, Tingsly and I figured that it would be difficult to be full participants at the Festival if we commuted to and from Uncle Mac's.

Actually, Tingsly and I thought it was nice staying at Uncle Mac's for a couple days mostly because it didn't cost us anything and he toured us around Denver, Central City, Golden, and some other beautiful mountain places in his bright red 1965 Mustang fastback. Though we weren't quite sure at that point in our lives, we also enjoyed staying with Uncle Mac because, unlike our perception of many older people, he seemed to have a pretty good idea who we were. After spending time with him, he was more like a friend or kindred spirit who treasured his own adventures and wanted to share in ours. For example, I had heard that in his early twenties, he left Peoria on his own to work in the ore mines of the Rockies. So, one night while he was sharing a couple bottles of beer around the kitchen table with his underage visitors I asked him about it. In the midst of his long and winding explanation, Uncle Mac kept winking at me, but almost had Tingsly convinced that he had come to Colorado for the Gold Rush. He was a funny little man and we respected him for living alone that far away from family with a Mustang in his garage and cold beers in his fridge. Tingsly and I were so touched by all of his kindness that we left a thank you note on the nightstand in his spare bedroom before we moved on.

Most people never heard of the Denver Pop Festival because it was overshadowed by Woodstock. Yet, Denver attracted many of the same musicians that played in upstate New York just a month and a half later. Although there was surely more involved, it seemed as though popular bands showed up at big events like this for the opportunity to play in front of such large crowds. We even heard rumors that the Rolling Stones had flown into Aspen and were going to make a surprise appearance at Denver, but it never happened. To us, it seemed ironic that this early rock concert was held at Mile High Stadium, because it seemed that almost everyone was.

Acts on the first day of the Festival included Big Mama Thorton, a Chicago-based band called The Flock, Three Dog Night, Iron Butterfly, and Frank Zappa with the Mothers of Invention. Tingsly and I watched and listened as Zappa encouraged different sections of the crowd to make movements and sounds as he conducted from the stage. But his impromptu choreography dragged on so long that we actually got a little bored. Perhaps we would have been more excited if we had realized that this performance was subsequently credited as having been the start of the "wave" craze at sporting events.

Zappa was probably creative beyond my comprehension at the time, because most of the other stuff he did went over my head as well. Other than for the thrill of the crowd and Three Dog Night's drummer playing a fantastic solo with his bare hands, we weren't knocked out by any of the shows that night.

When the music was over at the stadium, Tingsly and I walked to a nearby city park along with the thousands of other people who had set up camp there for the weekend. We located a small spot by some trees, spread out our space blankets, and watched some more. Though we had nothing to share, we graciously accepted hits off an endless string of joints that showed up on the fingertips of strangers. I got as high as I had ever been and in a short time both Tingsly and I were romping around to spontaneous displays of acoustic music, checking out the smattering of anti-war activities, and feeling very much a part of the action.

However, later, as our highs began to wear off and others' apparently didn't, the atmosphere started to change. Two wild-eyed girls wearing nothing but bib overalls jammed flyers in our faces, started going on about some unfamiliar cause, and pleaded for some of our money. Before we even had a chance to explain our situation, one of the girls got knocked to the ground by a shirtless guy who was running around between campfires, wielding a bowie knife, and shouting crazy, unintelligible stuff about the upcoming end of the world. A small crowd gathered around us and the girl to see what had happened. The shirtless guy was so wiped out he didn't even seem to notice what he had done. Fortunately, the girl wasn't hurt beyond a bloody lip and, after we helped her up, she and her friend just went on with their panhandling.

In the midst of the sudden pervasive chaos, Tingsly and I retreated to our little spot by the trees. I recall telling him that I felt like we were just kids compared to most of the others in the

park. Some of the people had children with them and appeared
to be carrying everything they owned. Others looked like as
though they were street thieves who were quite accustomed to
the rough and tumble atmosphere. We were probably as old as
many of the people, but not quite as experienced at being so
wild, reckless, and free. I wasn't sure that I cared to be even
though it represented the status quo in the park. Tingsly didn't
understand. He told me that I was just tired. We curled up in the
tenuous security of our blankets somewhere around the middle
of the night.

By the second day, the disarray we had witnessed at the
park started to spill over into the parking lots outside of the
Stadium. A number of protest groups had now shown up and
those who did not have tickets to get inside constituted a ready
made audience for them. Everyone seemed to be angry about
something. Eventually, Tingsly and I made our way into the
stadium with the other ticket holders.

Saturday featured another Chicago-based group called
Aeorta, a local band called Zephyr, Poco, Johnny Winter,
Credence Clearwater Revival, and our hero Tim Buckley all by
himself on guitar. Although all the bands were great and
Tingsly and I marveled at Tim Buckley's ability to bang his
twelve-string solo in front of fifty thousand people, Zephyr
turned out to be the highlight of the show.

Before that night Tingsly and I had never heard of Zephyr,
but we could sense the enthusiasm of those who had as we saw
them move to the edges of their seats. Candy Givens, who we
had heard was a wild Joplin-esque lead singer, was assembling
the band. Just as most of the group was coming together on
stage, it seemed to become clear to everyone that their lead
guitar player was not there. Candy, in her bare feet, three-
quarter sleeves and little dress, began calling out over the
stadium public address for "Tommy" to come to the stage. Time

passed and more tension ensued as Candy ran her hands through her frizzy crop of hair and kept calling out for Tommy.

Finally, after the crowd was getting tired of entertaining themselves during the long break between acts, we spotted nineteen or twenty-year-old Tommy crawling up the side steps to the stage. Tingsly grabbed the sleeve of my t-shirt and said, "Wow, Man, is he screwed up or what?" Gradually, Tommy made his way to his feet and to his guitar and awkwardly pulled its giant leather strap over his head. However, instead of leaping into the first song with the band, he bowed his head over his guitar and began wrapping his long hair in the strings. Half the crowd was now getting downright irritated, whereas it seemed the other half was totally into whatever he was doing. Moments later, with everyone's attention glued on the stage for one reason or the other, Tommy flung his head back, ripped his hair through the strings of the guitar, and created a bellowing chord that shook the entire stadium. Then, he and the band launched into the most incredible live version of "Cross the River," the most incredible version of almost anything, I had ever seen or heard to that point in my life. I looked at Tingsly and suddenly felt right at home again.

Zephyr brought down the house. People in the stadium abandoned their reserved seats and pressed through the fences onto the field for a closer look at the stage. People outside, who had expected to see the concert for free, began pressing harder too, tipping over police cars and attempting to topple the chain link gates that kept them out of the stadium. I wasn't sure how I felt about them being excluded from the event. Because we often could in those days, young people sometimes expected to hear music for free, regardless of where it was happening. Before the end of the night, the tear gas used on those rioting outside had affected most of the thousands of people inside as well. But somehow Zephyr played on. And somehow the pervasive smell of the tear gas seemed almost fitting.

Tingsly and I eventually made it back to the park that night, but we couldn't sleep. Zephyr had been too good and everyone, including myself, was just too hyped up. We feared that if we were to lay down in our space blankets we might get trampled, run over, set afire, robbed, or something equally lousy. Tingsly had a plan and, considering the situation at the park, I was game for just about anything. Around three or four in the morning we made our way up the street and parked ourselves next to a drive-up motel with an outside entrance to each room. Initially, I thought Tingsly planned to pay for a room at the motel, but I knew we would never make it to San Francisco and back home if we spent any more of our money on another motel room, particularly when the park, albeit virtually out of control, was free.

In those days when guests checked out of a motel they would often leave their doors cracked open so that the maids would know that the room had been vacated when they arrived for their morning cleanup. Tingsly's plan was to spot an open door, slip in, sleep, clean up, watch a little TV, and be gone by check-out time, refreshed and ready to go. It worked perfectly our last two nights at the Festival.

The final day at the Denver Pop Festival included groups called Aum and Sweetwater, the physically-electrified Joe Cocker, and...The Jimi Hendrix Experience. Tingsly and I already knew that seeing Hendrix and the Experience play all their hits including "Fire," "Hey Joe," "Foxy Lady," "Purple Haze," and the "Star Spangled Banner," was going to be something special to remember. We might have savored it even more had we known that this would be Hendrix' last performance with the Experience and that he would die shortly thereafter of a drug overdose.

More exciting to us was that Zephyr was brought back to close the Festival on Sunday night. This time there was no need for anyone to tear down any fences. Paying fans were simply allowed to come through the gates up to the stage and, since some people had already gone home, the non-paying fans left in the parking lot were finally allowed in. The Sunday night show was also great, but less moving than the day before. Perhaps everyone was little tired by that time or the enthusiasm was dampened because the stragglers couldn't find any more rules to break.

Rumors related to the upcoming rock festival at Woodstock circulated widely around the Denver Pop Festival. In fact, Tingsly and I were so intrigued about it that we considered changing directions and heading to New York, but finally decided to stay the course for San Francisco. We encountered many more novel events along the way including: getting a police escort out of Grand Junction, Colorado for loitering; cashing bad checks under the coercion of a band of roughnecks who were transporting us part of the way through Utah; eluding the hard sell of a Native American prostitute and her tribe of teenage pimps in Reno; surviving several more nights of fires and collective chaos in an abandoned apartment building next to People's Park in Berkeley; and adopting a skinny little puppy from a cardboard box on the campus at the University of California. However, after our Denver experience, none of this seemed particularly special.

As we left San Francisco and started to head back across country taking turns hiding the puppy inside our coats, Tingsly and I agreed that we had probably gotten there a little too late and should have turned around for Woodstock. Haight-Ashbury appeared mostly deserted. The people we saw there looked old and seriously drugged out. North Beach was empty, miserable, and cold even in July. We found nothing going on at the

Fillmore and Sausalito was uncomfortably upscale. We saw little sign of anti-war resistance or excitement anywhere we looked. I don't think we noticed anyone with a flower in their hair.

Boom Boom (Boom Boom)
(John Lee Hooker song made more famous by The Animals)

We arrived back in the Heart of Illinois just a few weeks before it was time for me to leave again for my sophomore year at Loyola. I left the hyper little dog we had named "Berkeley" with my parents, younger sister, and brother and headed back to Chicago considerably more experienced than before. By that time the old Edgewater Beach Hotel had been demolished and was lying in a heap at the corner of Sheridan Road and Hollywood. It looked something like my recollection of the previous year at school. After the summer I'd had, I was ready to move on.

Almost everyone else from the Edgewater was assigned a room in the brand new high-rise dormitory on campus. However, for reasons I never understood, I was assigned a room and a new roommate in the Campion Hall Dormitory just across the street. I remember thinking that this might be okay since my friends would still be nearby and I was trying to convince myself that I might like meeting some new folks. After sleeping in my tin foil blanket by the side of so many highways, I was more durable than before and felt I could now deal with just about anything. But I was wrong.

I lugged my stuff into Campion Hall, got the key to the room I was to share, and headed up the steps to my new year at school. I set my things down in the hallway, inserted the key, and pushed open the door to the room. Before I'd even stepped across the threshold I saw that there was going to be a problem. On the wall, much bigger than life right in front of my face, was an enormous poster of an M-16 rifle. As I scanned the room, I saw that the bed and desk I'd be using was surrounded by military paraphernalia including: team shots of military troops; little Army pins; and a photo of my new roommate standing at attention in his Reserve Officers Training Corps (ROTC) uniform. I couldn't help thinking that he probably had an erection.

I hadn't expected anything like this and, until that moment, I'm not sure I realized how much I was repulsed by the military and most everything associated with it. I thought of it as a kind of club that no one would mind being excluded from and I noticed that I had started to make judgments about those who were part of it. For a few minutes I moved around the room in angry disbelief. Then suddenly, it seemed as though I stopped thinking and went on autopilot. I left my things lying in the hallway, marched myself back down the stairs, and told the older student in charge that my room assignment wasn't going to work for me or my roommate. To that point in my life I don't think I had ever been so clear about anything.

But what was so incredibly obvious to me was not yet clear to the person in charge. He gave me a bewildered look and asked, "Well then, why don't you think this assignment is going to work?" After stumbling around for a moment waiting for my rationale to show up, I said, "Have you ever seen the person who has been designated as my new roommate?" He said, "Yes, I believe I have." I couldn't hold it any longer, so I let loose, "Do you know that this guy's photo is probably in the student handbook under Rabid ROTC Person?" My comment wasn't particularly polite, but he laughed. "Look at me," I said. After he took a good look at my increasingly seasoned, hippie-like appearance, he continued to laugh and said, "Okay, I think I get your point."

Of course, nothing could be settled at that moment. I would have to wait a few days until all the other students got back to campus before it would be known if and where another bed would be available. I settled down some by convincing myself that I could probably do just about anything for a few days if there was no other option. I went back upstairs, slid my stuff against the bed, and ventured off to distract myself with a Little King's submarine sandwich.

Over the next few days, I saw my new roommate for only moments at a time. I had already seen him more than I ever cared to. Everyone had seen him parading around in his military garb like he was some sort of campus commando. We looked at each other, but I don't recall that we ever spoke. I suspected that he felt as strongly about me as I did about him, although I never took time to ask. He probably got angry when I put my mattress on the floor as a place for Jake to sleep when he came up unexpectedly from Peoria to visit, but we never said a word about it. Jake and I spent as little time as possible in the room. I was content to leave it as the commando's space and always locked the door behind me when I left, even when he was still in there.

Fortunately, I was able to move over to a new dormitory room close to most of my old Edgewater Beach friends just a few days later. Since I hadn't unpacked anything at Campion Hall it was an easy move. Neither the commando nor I ever said "hello" or "goodbye" to each other. Our separate worlds remained intact.

After hitchhiking across country to San Francisco and after learning more about myself in my first few days back on campus, I became more alert to what was happening around me at Loyola, in the Roger's Park neighborhood, in Chicago, and in the world. Though I seldom read papers or watched TV in those days, somehow I felt better informed than I had been before. Events and experiences seemed to be changing me from moment to moment. Many times I felt as though it was a challenge to keep my perception of who I was consistent with whoever I was becoming.

In Chicago, Abbie Hoffman, Tom Hayden, Jerry Rubin and other constituents of the "Chicago Eight" were at the front and center of the protest activity and public attention. These guys, who everyone acted like they knew on a first name basis, had been indicted and were being tried for their alleged part in the Convention rioting a year earlier. The trial started on September 24th, my nineteenth birthday.

The Picasso-adorned pavilion in front of the Cook County Courthouse had become a fairly regular stop for some of us who, by that time, viewed ourselves as regular participants in the anti-war demonstrations and related activities that were taking place around the city. At least one time, after a group of us had reenacted a Convention protest walk from Lincoln Park to the Loop, part of our group constituted the bulk of the action on the pavilion.

As it happened, the walk and the subsequent demonstration at the Courthouse had gone without incident...Chicago police where everywhere of course, but despite consistent taunting from the rest of us, very little tense interaction had taken place. By this time I suppose we might have been disappointed about that. It was easy to feel that a protest was worthless if it didn't result in something exciting to talk about later.

Jake was still hanging around Chicago, working part time at the Sir Whoopee's fast food place near campus, storing his little travel bag in my room, and crashing on the couches in the social areas on our floor at the dorm. I learned that he too had begun to stray beyond Peoria and Pekin in the thirteen months since high school. Apparently, he had also spent a little time in places like Champaign, Oklahoma City, Berkeley, and Los Angeles. I didn't see what Oklahoma City would have had to do with it, but partially as a result of his travels Jake now felt that he knew a thing or two about anti-war protesting. Jake typically presented as if he knew a thing or two about a lot of stuff which turned out to be true as often as it was not. That afternoon he was bored with the lack of action at the Courthouse and wanted to go back to campus to chase girls. He had not changed at all in that department. Jake always wanted to chase girls no matter where he was.

Just as there was a break in the more formal protest agenda, Jake signaled for several of our group to come closer. As we huddled around him in a circle, he said, "Don't you think this is really boring?" Before we had a chance to answer the question, in his matter-of-fact way he said, "Watch this...I am going to create a disturbance and get myself arrested." Then he explained, "...after I get arrested, I bet you I will be back at the dormitory before any of you can get there." When Jake used to say things like this, there wasn't much else anyone could say about it except, "Okay." Trying to talk him out of something he had fixated on often just seemed to make him more resolute.

Jake began to move away from the rest of us. I watched in my characteristic apprehension, amazement, and childlike amusement as he methodically moved through the crowd, walked up on the stage, approached the speaker's podium, chatted with a couple organizers, and worked his way up to the microphone. Once he had it in his hand he immediately began shouting into the crowd. At that moment I got the distinct impression that he was telling the truth about having done this sort of thing before. He ranted about Nixon, Vietnam, and his ideas about how to address the problem which didn't seem consistent with what people had been hearing to that point. Then, because he was so loud and it was difficult to tell which side of the political fence he was on, some of the organizers attempted to pull him away from the microphone and remove him from the stage.

A scuffle ensued between Jake and the organizers which prompted the Chicago Police to intervene. Sure enough, we all watched as he was handcuffed and dragged into one of the blue and white paddy wagons. And sure enough, by the time the demonstration had ended and the rest of us got back up to the campus about an hour and a half later, there was Jake sitting with two nice-looking neighborhood girls on the front steps of the dorm.

We reconvened in a small group around him in an effort to understand how he had pulled off this remarkable stunt. After building up some suspense, Jake told us that while riding in the paddy wagon he convinced the Police that he'd been repulsed by "all the anti-war movement crap" and that he was trying to undermine the group's effort at the Courthouse. As a result, he said the Police treated him like a hero and that they wound up giving him a ride all the way back to the dorm. "And to think," Jake said, "The hippies call these guys Pigs." The rest of us would-be hippies stood there looking bewildered as Jake laughed out loud by himself.

Although I was temporarily baffled by Jake's seemingly outrageous comments and he eventually tried to pass them off with my friends as if he was just joking, I began to consider that maybe this was what he truly believed. Maybe he was opposed to the war, but perhaps he was even more opposed to the manner in which people were expressing their discontent. I had not thought about it so clearly before that day. Yet, there I was taking serious lessons from someone who virtually everyone else had always taken as a joke.

Perhaps the length of our friendship was an indication that I had always been learning from watching Jake navigate his crazy world. After all, I had always stood by him during times that I suspected had to be difficult for him. And judging by his pattern of consistently showing up in my life at times that I might have needed it, it appeared that he was actually doing the same thing for me.

Late that night as I was falling asleep on the upper bunk in my comfortable new dormitory room, Jake entered with his blanket and curled up on the thinly-carpeted floor beside the bed. This wasn't uncommon, so neither of us said anything to each other. Moments later I heard Jake sobbing underneath his blanket. I had never heard Jake cry, not even as children back on the block. As far as I knew, he had always been immune to pain. I laid there in the dark, not sure what to say to him. Finally, I asked him what was wrong. His crying stopped. Then, as seriously as I had ever heard Jake speak, he said, "You know my life isn't as fun as it looks." After another long hesitation, I said, "Yes, I do," and we both went to sleep.

Spinning Wheel
(Blood, Sweat, and Tears)

By December of 1969, I'd become involved with Sunshine, who had just entered college that year as a freshman. Sunshine was exactly that…vibrant, fresh, energetic, and with yellow-blonde frizzy hair to boot. Although I figured every sophomore guy at Loyola must have noticed her arrival on campus, I think the fact that she looked so delightfully hip and I had already hitchhiked to San Francisco probably sealed the deal for us. Since the day we met by the dorm's back entrance, we found reasons to be around each other almost all the time.

From the start of my sophomore year at school things were noticeably different than they had been before. I wondered at times if things had actually changed so much or if I was now interpreting them differently than I had in the past. My feeling wasn't just because I was seeing a lot of Sunshine, but that probably had something to do with it.

It also may have had something to do with the fact that my group of friends was now a little less isolated than we had been down at the Edgewater Beach Hotel. Mertz Hall, the new dorm, also housed the Student Center, the Student Government Offices, and the Student Activity Office, so there always seemed to be lots of people around. Many students who lived in Chicago commuted to campus and between classes the Student Center was a prime spot for them to hang out. In addition, the new dorm had a bit more supervision than the Edgewater, although there still wasn't much. I frequently found myself bouncing back and forth between the extremes of political discontent on the one hand and mindless fun on the other. Once again my studies took a back seat to just about anything else that showed up.

My friends who lived in the six-room dormitory suite next to mine set the pace in terms of flirting with trouble and authority. As a result, I spent most of my time with them. We were attracted to anything that might have been considered rebellious or absurd. From goofy things like jumping in unison on the elevator to try to get it to stop, to risky things like abducting the expensive fiberglass clown that covered the garbage can at the Sir Whoopee's or walking out of Marshall Field's with a giant plastic Santa Claus, our appetite for excitement might have appeared insatiable. Sometimes we viewed the craziness as our defiance for rules and authority, but mostly we just thought of it as fun. About the only things that seemed predictable were the times I spent with Sunshine and the shifts that Skip and I worked in the dish room at the dormitory cafeteria.

One day, a friend we called "Doolie" introduced a very feisty squirrel monkey into the little alternative community that had formed on the dormitory's seventh floor. Of course we all knew that pets weren't allowed, but considering that a vacant single room had become available when someone had dropped out, it certainly seemed like another good reason to bend the dormitory rules. All was well with the monkey until a few week's later when it became lethargic and then obviously very sick. Doolie surmised that it must have had something to do with the emptied tray of rat poison that had been left in the vacant room until a new tenant came.

Within twenty four hours of becoming sick, someone discovered that the monkey was dead. While it was a bit sad to see it lying in a wad on the floor of its private room, no one would really miss it very badly. Most of us were tired of finding tiny monkey turds in our clothes, books, and nightstands. Still, we had to figure out what to do with a dead animal in the dormitory. There was no way we would just toss it down the trash shoot.

When opportunities like this arose, my friends and I had a tendency to plan a little and act very spontaneously. We decided to have a funeral ceremony that night. Doolie drew up announcements for a "Monkey Funeral," and by dinnertime we'd posted them by the entrances to the building and cafeteria. Blimpie pulled out the beanie that he had snatched off a priest's head late one night during our freshman year. It would help make him appear as a perfect host for the ceremony. His roommate, Blumpy, took charge of the background music. Cowboy and I wrote eulogies that we volunteered to read in front of everyone we knew would show up. Joon and Skip prepared the burial site.

By 8:00 that evening a crowd filled the suite's social area and had overflowed into the foyer by the elevators. Blimpie looked authentic conducting the formal part of the service in his beanie and bathrobe. The hundred or so people who were there fell silent during the eulogies. Everyone thought the monkey looked good, flat on his back with a pillow case pulled up to its neck and an evergreen sprig in its hands. My footlocker served as the casket.

At the end of the ceremony Blimpie instructed all the attendees to go downstairs and reconvene at the building's main entrance for the procession to the burial site. When they were gone, he gently lowered the lid of the footlocker. Then he led our group of pallbearers from the suite, packed us into one of the elevators, and marched us out of the building to the front steps of the dorm. By this time, the monkey's funeral had begun to attract more and more people and we organizers were completely in our element. Blimpie then guided the crowd down the main campus sidewalk, between two of the small women's dorms, and slowly down Columbia Street to Lake

Michigan. We carried the casket on our shoulders to add to the drama. People were hanging out their windows trying to see what was going on. Many more joined the procession along the way.

When we arrived at the small patch of sand at the east end of Columbia Street, Joon and Skip were already there. They had constructed a raft from a wooden shipping skid, plastic sheeting, and a big pile of dead branches they'd collected from the beach. People gathered around as Blimpie instructed the pallbearers to remove the monkey from the footlocker and place it onto the branches. He gave some final words and doused the pile with gasoline. He instructed Doolie, Joon, Skip, Cowboy, and I to push the raft down the sand so that it floated at the water's edge. Doolie held it as the rest of us stepped away. Then, as Blimpie called for the crowd's undivided attention, which had probably tripled in size, Doolie gave the raft a push and flicked a match into the stack of branches beneath the monkey.

While many of the onlookers clapped and laughed or feigned mourning, the sight of the burning raft dancing on the moonlit water instantly transformed the moment into a solemn event for many of us, as though it captured the contrast between our ability to find levity in almost any situation and the seriousness of the times in which we were living.

Aside from extracurricular activities like the monkey funeral, it became increasingly common for people to get together at anti-war events and then wind up the day at a party. Like Jake, who had moved on by that time, I had begun to feel that events I'd taken so seriously often turned out to be not much more than excuses for everyone to get high and listen to the music. Neil Young's "After the Goldrush" album was everywhere. Sometimes it didn't even seem to matter whether or not you knew whose party it was or where a person stood on the issues. It seemed that everyone simply assumed that they knew where everyone else stood. There were times I wondered if anyone truly cared about the War anymore. It only seemed important to appear as if you cared.

Although others in our group had long since begun to sit out, Skip, Sunshine, and I were still almost always sitting in, whenever there was a protest, whenever there was music, whenever there was the potential for a new experience. Sometimes I wondered if I was doing these things just for the opportunity to be with Sunshine.

Because we got involved in other things around campus that did not involve protesting, I sometimes thought that the three of us might have been viewed as being a little less informed or passionate than others when it came to anti-war issues. It was true that we rarely ever talked out loud at the events. There were so many things I didn't understand and I knew it. But an equal number of times I felt that those who did speak out loud didn't really know what they were talking about either.

No matter how deeply you thought about things, how strongly you felt, or how excited you got, there were always others who appeared deeper, stronger, or more excited. Usually, these folks christened themselves with the speaking roles because they had a hand in organizing the events. In general, I didn't believe that anyone understood very much about whatever it was that got everyone so excited. In any case, I suspected that others thought Skip, Sunshine, and I just went for the music, the experience, and whatever else was being served. I didn't want to believe that was the case. I had a nagging sense that I needed to convince someone that I could be as passionate about my disdain for the War as anyone.

Late one of those nights after a day full of protest activities, I wound up under a blanket on someone's floor with Sunshine. Sleeping away from the dorm was still new to both of us, as was finding ourselves together under the same blanket. Given the circumstances it appeared to be the time to move our relationship to some next level.

Sunshine often wore white, loose-fitting tops with either her regular bell-bottom jeans or Oshkosh coveralls. That night, I was pleased that she had worn her jeans because it was easier to access things that previously had been private about her. As we carried on under a borrowed blanket in a strange living room full of sleeping friends and strangers, we cracked up laughing a few times as we stirred the joy and silliness of being together with the seriousness of the issues that we had been attempting to address.

Fooling around with Sunshine was sweet, but we wound up getting distracted somewhere along the way. Although we spent many nights together, that year we always wound up shifting our attention somewhere along the way. It seemed that we would always find some reason to pause at the height of our excitement: too many people, no place to go, something else occupying our thoughts…in the days that followed I kept thinking that flirting with sex and falling in love with Sunshine was a tad out of context. We continued to do things together, but I started to feel that the two of us were supposed to be part of something bigger, deeper, and more socially relevant than falling in love. Talking about it didn't change anything. My confusion about our relationship was as strange as everything else taking place around me at the time. There were moments with Sunshine when I feared I had gotten distracted from whatever course I'd been on before we met.

December of 1969 was different for other reasons as well. The Vietnam Moratorium protests were said to have brought a million people to the streets across the country. Buffalo Springfield's "For What Its Worth" filled the air. Richard Nixon declared that the War would end, somehow, in 1970. A few might have believed it. But then, just as things might have been looking up, it was announced that a Draft Lottery would be reinstated for the first time since WWII.

On the evening of the first of December, 1969 all of us gathered in the suite to watch the results of the Lottery on television. The event started out like an early Super Bowl party or as if we were members of the audience on some stupid television game show. The Lottery show was set up so that the Selective Service officials on TV would match guys' birthdates with their order of selection for induction into the military and presumably all expense paid trips to Southeast Asia. The first date picked would be the first to be inducted in 1970 and so on.

Most of us wanted to go on believing that we would avoid 1-A Draft status because of our college deferments and the "oldest first" draft rule that had existed previously. However, news of the Lottery left no one convinced of anything. Many thought the rules would keep changing if it turned out that there were not enough troops available. Some were concerned about their ability to stay in school. Others were fearful that the War and the draft would continue for years to come, so ultimately no one would be safe. We'd been told that the War was supposed to be ending, but the reintroduction of the Lottery seemed to make it clear that more young people were needed to carry it on.

It was a disconcerting experience when guys heard their birthdates called out early in the selection show. September 14th was the first date called. At first, we clapped and cheered because no one in the room was born on September 14th, but that little routine came to a rapid halt after a few more numbers were called out. Like an unexpected slap in the face, everyone quickly realized that there wasn't anything to cheer about.

While there were a few more attempts to turn the event into another party, the selection show turned out to be a pretty sobering event. Guys made a lot of eye contact with each other which seemed unusual. The girls made angry statements about the government, Nixon, and the military industrial complex as if they were soon to become widows to the War. Eventually, it became clear to everyone that the Lottery was likely to have an impact on a lot of lives...not just the guys in the room who happened to be in school.

By the end of the night, all of the birthdates had been matched with Lottery numbers. No one had a sense of winning, but some numbers were cause for a little relief and others for more obvious distress. Joon had the lowest number in our group. Guys with the highest numbers tended to stay quiet for the sake of those who were selected earlier in the process.

Life became more serious during the remainder of that sophomore year after the Lottery. After all the selecting was done, the fear wasn't gone because no one knew what would be the highest number called or when. Perhaps more importantly, no one knew how many guys would be needed to fight the War. So, although no one wore their numbers on their shirts, everyone kept them in mind. And although few said it, I was pretty sure most of the guys began studying more earnestly for fear of losing their college deferments. I remember that I wasn't that concerned about it, even though my number turned out to be 195 and I was barely making it in school.

The distraction that Sunshine and I may have been for each other began to end on a night near the end of the spring semester. We had planned to travel downtown to eat, go to a movie, and come back for a big off-campus party later that night. We were going to see "Johnny Got His Gun," based on Dalton Trumbo's 1939 classic anti-war novel, which was showing at an artsy theatre near the Berwyn subway stop. Although we had both read the book, we must not have recalled its power. Instead of warming ourselves up for what we were about to see, we rushed from the diner where we ate just in time for the show to start. In our rush, we skipped the movie popcorn we had been looking forward to.

The story "Johnny Got His Gun" was about a soldier who came home from WWI as a quadruple amputee, a mute and faceless torso of flesh. Johnny's survival was considered something of a medical miracle. He was also believed to have been brain dead until one compassionate nurse discovered that he was still able to communicate by thrusting his head back on his pillow in response to the inquiries she tapped out in Morse Code on his chest. The Chicago Daily News called it a "smooth, savage, and brilliant tale"...and declared that it would be hard to imagine a more persuasive argument for staying out of war. As Sunshine and I became engrossed in the film, it became clear to us that the Daily News hadn't stated it strongly enough.

By the end of the movie when Johnny was pounding out his wish to be paraded on the streets to showcase the horrors of war, our clasped hands were sore and sweaty. Our eyes were red and swollen from all the tears we had stopped trying to hold back. Although others jumped up and left, we sat frozen through the credits until the theatre lights came on. What would we do now?

I suspected that we both imagined bursting from the theatre and screaming up and down the streets about the atrocity of war and the impact that U.S. involvement in Vietnam was having on our generation. Instead, we walked slowly and quietly into the night locked in our fear, anger, and rapidly emerging guilt. So many people had already died and so many people were continuing to die in Vietnam. Our protesting wasn't making any obvious impact on anything. Simultaneously, I had already been feeling that my budding relationship with Sunshine was something to be embarrassed about. How could we be falling in love? How could we not devote all of our time to trying to change the world? We didn't show up at the party that night.

Although we continued to hang around with the same group of friends at most of the same old events, my relationship with Sunshine faded away somewhat uncomfortably after that night. I just didn't care to be with her anymore, but I never really told her that. I definitely did not tell her that I felt the War was pulling us apart because we were supposed to have been on the same side. I was told that it upset her when I didn't call on her to come around or when I avoided her if she did. Others talked about it, but we didn't. I think I was becoming less fun to be around. Our relationship, mutual and fresh as it had been, went away. Our friends began to wonder what was wrong with me. I began to avoid them too because I couldn't explain what was happening.

Ohio
(Crosby, Stills, Nash, and Young)

Events that spring took their final twist just after Nixon announced that the U.S. was sending troops into Cambodia. This news was interpreted by many as an escalation of the War in Vietnam at a time when many people hoped and wanted to believe it was winding down. After all, that was what we'd been told as far back as Nixon's election platform in 1968. Coming on the heels of the Draft Lottery, the invasion of Cambodia intensified the confusion and anger around many college campuses, including Loyola, where students feared that the escalation would increase their chances of getting drafted. Then, just a few days after Nixon's announcement, the War really began to hit home.

Four young people were killed and nine were wounded by National Guard troops during an anti-war rally at Kent State University on May 4, 1970. In those days I wasn't getting much information from newspapers or other media. I just picked up what I felt I needed to know by word of mouth. Based on what I had heard, I pictured the tragedy as being similar to the campus or park rallies I had been attending around Chicago. All I could envision were sunny days, students gathering to see what was going on, and faculty members communicating the latest facts and opinions, while police or National Guard troops stood around a perimeter as if waiting for things to spiral out of control.

To me, it was not surprising that a campus rally could suddenly turn ugly. But who would have expected it to happen in Ohio on a sunny Monday afternoon in May? The Kent State massacre, as many quickly labeled it, not only reenergized attention to the War, it seemed to further accent differences between people here at home. Kids were viewed as either enlightened leaders of a critical movement or vigilant, hippie, militant, radical, revolutionary, anti-government hoodlums that needed to be controlled and stopped. And, it seemed that those who supported the government generally understood only one way to get that accomplished – with force. In my view, that style had been playing out unsuccessfully in Vietnam and now it was playing out more intensely than ever on our own soil. Some students withdrew from the action, while most became angrier and more impulsive than ever. Some continued to attempt to address the root problem, which to me was the same as it had been for years - finding an end to the War in Vietnam.

Hundreds of college campuses were temporarily shut down as part of a national Strike to protest the War following the announcements of the Kent State tragedy and subsequent deaths at Jackson State. To the surprise of some of us, Loyola University participated in the activity after more and more of its religious faculty began to side with the growing number of protesting students. During the Strike, there were "teach in" lectures by faculty and local dignitaries and a memorial Mass on the intramural field in front of the old gym. There was talk of burning down the ROTC building on campus as students were said to have done at Kent State on the Saturday before the shootings, but despite all the rumblings, that didn't happen at Loyola.

By Memorial Day things seemed to have settled down a bit, so the long weekend presented an opportunity for several of us to get away from campus for a while. It didn't take long to figure out where to go since there had been news circulating about a big protest event (called the "Incident at Kickapoo Creek") that was supposed to take place in conjunction with the Kickapoo Creek Outdoor Rock Concert on someone's farm in tiny Heyworth, Illinois. Heyworth was just slightly over a hundred miles south of Chicago.

A notice posted in the Student Center indicated that anybody with an interest in going to Heyworth should show up for an organizational meeting. When our crew arrived at the meeting, I was a somewhat surprised to discover that there were only about a dozen people from Loyola who planned to make the trip. The small group included Joon, whose home was only a few miles from Heyworth, Cowboy, Skip, Doolie, me, and a few campus organizers I still didn't know very well.

Strangely, although the organizers did talk about getting together once we got to Kickapoo Creek, there was no discussion about how anyone was going to get there. I suspected that this may have been because one or two of them might have actually had cars but didn't want to say so for fear of having more riders than they wanted. Or perhaps they felt they knew us better than we thought and just didn't want us coming along on whatever important business they might have had.

No matter. I wasn't going to concern myself with the group dynamics since I had hitchhiked on Interstate 55 so many times and, as was becoming more typical for me, I didn't mind if I made the trip by myself. Before we disbanded, everyone agreed that I would take my orange bandana and that when I got there I would put it on the end of a long stick so others could meet up with me in the same place...just in case the event drew a big crowd. Lame as it was, that was about all the planning we did.

I don't recall what my friends intended to do, but the next afternoon they seemed to be moving a little slowly, so I went ahead and set out for Heyworth by myself. The short journey went pretty smoothly until I got off the interstate and onto the small country road that led to the farm. At that point I realized how seriously we had underestimated the size of the event. Vehicles were lined up on the entrance road for what seemed like ten miles. The people who had given me my last ride decided to park and walk in, even though no one seemed to know how far that actually was. Walking was better than sitting still in the car.

After a few hundred yards I separated from the others and found myself walking alone down the dark, car-lined gravel road. So far, it had been a peaceful night and I was looking forward to whatever the weekend might have in store. Although it was not a particularly common thing for me to do, I swallowed one of the tabs of Mescaline I had brought along and walked on.

As I neared what I thought was the main entrance gate, it finally dawned on me that people had been walking toward me in the other direction for some time. Despite the early effects of the Mescaline I recognized that this was a bit weird, so I finally stopped someone and asked what was going on. I was told that people were being turned away at the gates, in some cases whether or not they had tickets for the event. I was told that the Festival had been taken over by a motorcycle gang and that they were giving people a really hard time, particularly if they were not carrying a ticket.

I had two strikes against me. I had always been leery of motorcycle guys and I didn't have a ticket. Neither did any of my friends. We had figured we would get them at the gate if it turned out we needed them. How crowded could it get on a sixty-acre farm in the middle of Illinois? Nevertheless, I approached the gate area cautiously in light of all the violence that had been occupying our thoughts that spring.

From about twenty-five yards away I saw several Andy Frain ushers in their oversized blue suits with yellow trim standing by the makeshift ticket booth at the main entrance to the Festival. Their presence made it look just like concerts and other public events I had attended around Chicago. I began to wonder if the people walking in the other direction were playing some sort of organized trick on me until I noticed all the people standing around outside. No one was approaching the ticket booth or the gate.

By then I had come so far that my feet just kept walking me toward the ticket booth. About the same time that I caught a glimpse of the line of choppers inside the freshly-constructed gate, a biker came rushing out of nowhere, blocked my path, and got up in my face. Loudly, as if putting on a performance for all those looking on, he asked "What in the hell are you doing?" I tried to act like I wasn't intimidated by looking right back at him. Very softly, I said "I'm just here to check out the Festival and lend my support to the anti-war movement." He came back at me quickly. "Where in the hell are you from?" I said "I hitchhiked down from Chicago, but my real home is just up the road in Peoria." Changing his tone, he quietly asked why I was there alone. I said I had separated from my friends somewhere along the way from the city. He looked at me up and down for a long time. I wasn't sure if he was about to beat me to a pulp. Then he said, "Go up to the gate and tell the usher that the Nice Biker sent you."

Of course, I followed his instructions. What else was I going to do? Strange as it seemed, I walked right up to the uniformed Andy Frain usher, sheepishly looked him in the eyes, and said, "The Nice Biker sent me?" He smiled, handed me a ticket stub, and signaled me through the gate.

I wish the rest of the Festival had turned out as nicely as my entrance. Within an hour of my arrival, the place had already taken on the look and feel of the park in Denver, Peoples' Park in Berkeley, and every other chaotic place I had been bumping into since high school. I learned quickly that there were no police anywhere close to the grounds because the event had not been sanctioned by the State or local authorities.

The authorities apparently had no intention of having it appear that they were welcoming young, violent people anywhere near this community. Instead, the promoter who owned the farm had handed over "security" to the motorcycle gang. This was evident at the gate and throughout the grounds every time a small band of Harleys would carve its way through the mass of humanity that the gang had allowed to come inside.

Although the music was not scheduled to start until Saturday morning, I worked my way through some of the sixty thousand people toward the stage, which was close to an old barn where "security" had set up its headquarters. Around the barn, tough looking bikers were giving rides to innocent-looking, teenie-bopper girls who were lined up for a thrill. It appeared that if a biker liked a girl, he would invite her inside the barn to join the rest of the gang. I couldn't help thinking that some of the girls were headed for disaster, but I just sat and watched. I did that a lot at these kinds of events, but it usually wasn't a good thing for me to be doing. It typically brought me down...kind of like watching a pretty girl at a strip joint.

Within a short time, the rain started and the Mescaline had fully kicked in. I broke a long dead branch from a lonely tree and raised my orange bandana among the hundreds of other bandanas that waved along the hillsides near the stage. Yet I realized pretty quickly that I wasn't very likely to hook up with the Loyola contingent even if they got there and somehow managed to get in.

After all the walking and because it was now almost too crowded to move, I eventually planted my flag and hunkered down at the peak of one of the rolling hills about a football field away from the stage. For several more hours I just sat, watched, and listened to the now-familiar sounds of thousands of young people partying into the night. After the speedy side of the Mescaline finally wore off, I wrapped my soaking wet body in my handy space blanket and stretched out on the bumpy bare ground in the rain. Thoughts about my childhood, my parents, and Sunshine crossed my mind before the tapping of raindrops on my tin blanket eased me to sleep.

The next time I opened my eyes, there was a strange quiet as compared to when I had closed them. I stayed still for a while in my cocoon to relish the silence and the smell of wet campfires in the distance. Through a crack in the blanket I could tell the sun was beginning to shine. I felt like I knew what the crowded fields would look like so there was no big hurry to move.

After a little while though my peace was interrupted by the recognition that I was still wet to the bone and, worse than that, I had to pee like a racehorse. I eventually untangled myself from my blanket and sat up facing the stage. I stretched my neck and my arms, pleased that all my parts were still there and that I had not been run over by a stray Harley in the night. The sight and feel of the rising sun was comforting. Then I turned my head to the left to begin scoping out my newly adopted neighborhood.

It is difficult to convey how amazed I was to wake up in a field of sixty thousand strangers, look to my left, and see my younger cousin Smiley sitting up on his blanket right next to me. I had not seen Smiley in a couple years and remembered him best from the Christmas Eves our families used to spend together in the basement at my house. We greeted each other as if Santa Claus had just arrived with our presents. I almost peed in my pants.

After checking in with each other, and realizing that neither of us could find the people we were supposed to have met at the Festival, we decided to hang together at least until we found someplace to pee. We rolled up the few things we had in our blankets and started walking toward a wooded area down by the creek. Unfortunately, Smiley and I got separated somehow before we even got to the trees. Our parting was almost as strange as our meeting. In fact, since I was still shaking off the morning-after effects of the drugs, there were moments when I wondered if it had been a part of my dreams.

When I finally made it to the trees down near the Kickapoo Creek it turned out that I had to urinate in an area that hundreds of people were using as an open toilet. Although it felt really good to empty my bladder, the sight of so many human beings shitting and pissing in the middle of an otherwise beautiful place suddenly struck me as sickening.

From there everything went downhill. Since it had been raining off and on and everyone had seen the pictures from Woodstock, the creek side had already become a giant muddy playground. While it looked and sounded like all the naked people were having a really great time sliding their flabby bodies down the hills in the mud, I sat at the top wondering how many of them might have friends or family members in Vietnam who would be disappointed to see them now. I wondered if any of them cared about anything other than the crazy moment they were in. Then, when I saw a couple in the nearby trees making what might have been love, I became lonely, disappointed, and angry again.

I got back on my feet and went searching for some evidence of protest activity. After all, that was what we had heard at least part of the Festival was supposed to have been about. And that was the main reason I had come. I wasn't looking to slide in the mud or get involved with some freed-up seventeen-year-old hippie chick. I was still looking to get to the heart of the issue.

All I actually got was mad.

Aside from Ted Nugent's stupid "F-U-C-K" cheer at the start of the show that everybody else seemed to think was really cool and a bit of Country Joe and the Fish, I don't recall anything at the Kickapoo Creek Outdoor Rock Concert that even remotely resembled protest or anti-war sentiment. The music was equally disappointing. For all his talent, I couldn't see what B.B. King would have to do with a protest event. REO Speedwagon? Maybe Canned Heat might have moved me on another day, but at times like this "Going up the Country" was not nearly enough.

I left the bikers, the teenie-boppers, the party, the farm, and Heyworth later that Saturday afternoon and headed back to Chicago feeling horribly alone. At the time, I concluded that the Festival represented about the worst that young people had to offer.

Light My Fire
(The Doors)

When sophomore year ended in the spring of 1970, Joon, Cowboy, Skip and I had already decided that we were going to stay in Chicago for the summer. We were a bit concerned that this might create a problem because, at that time, out of town Loyola students were still required to reside in campus housing through their junior years at school. We suspected it was going to be difficult to find an apartment that did not entail an annual lease. But it wasn't. We found a perfect, basement apartment in a three-story walkup just two blocks from campus with no lease requirement. We moved in immediately after the last day of class.

Our new apartment on Lakewood consisted of a long, extra-wide hallway with two bedrooms and a bathroom on the right hand side and the kitchen at the end. Joon occupied the first room in from the front door, Cowboy the second. There was another small bedroom off one side of the back of the kitchen which I occupied. After laying down our $125 deposit and first month's rent, we also discovered that there was another door off the back of the kitchen which led to an open, garage-sized room with a door onto the alley. Skip occupied a back corner of this room by hanging tye-dyed sheets from the pipes to define his little space. Although we tried to make it different at times, the rest of the back room and the huge front hallway were good for only one thing – more parties.

I worked full-time downtown in the Loop that summer in the "Clubroom" clothing section of the Montgomery-Wards store. This entailed daily showering and making myself presentable in a shirt and tie and something other than my blue jeans. I might have even topped off my fresh appearance with some English Leather or Jade East cologne that I had left over

71

from high school. Working downtown provided me some new scenery that didn't involve the college or the neighborhood and I discovered that I could not only get to work on time, I actually enjoyed it. People downtown didn't seem so preoccupied with the War or partying. Many of them seemed to have other things on their minds, like surviving. It was a healthy break for me.

One slow morning while I was folding pants, Cassius Clay (not yet Muhammad Ali) came strolling through our section of the store. He was impeccably dressed in a suit and tie, and stood out like some sort of god among all the other shoppers at the Montgomery Ward's store. I followed him out of the building and caught up with him in a throng of people who were standing in awe of him on State Street. I got him to sign an autograph for me when I told him I wanted to take it back to all his fans at Loyola University. I remember thinking how odd it was for me to be so interested in getting Cassius Clay's autograph at that time. I guess it was some sort of assurance, like being downtown, that the rest of the world was still going on. I had begun to forget that at times.

It might have been that same afternoon when Tingsly visited from Dekalb for a summer concert that was taking place in Grant Park. Since it was only a short walk from the store, I told him I would meet him there somewhere around the stage. After Kent State and Kickapoo Creek, I was having a hard time getting excited about much of anything in those days, but winding up on stage, sitting on Jefferson Airplane's speakers with my old friend Tingsly, and listening to Grace Slick belt out "Somebody to Love" picked me up a bit. Even so, I found it surprising the band didn't even stir as much attention as the Sly and the Family Stone concert which had taken place at the park a few weeks earlier. I couldn't even motivate myself to show up at that one.

At Montgomery Ward I worked the floor with an older salesman named Roy. Roy was an easygoing black guy who didn't seem particularly concerned about anything but his sales commissions and women. Whenever a pretty black lady would walk into the Clubroom, Roy would say "Can I show you something in black pants?" as he gestured to himself. Whenever a pretty white lady would walk in, he would say, "Can I show you something in a blue shirt?" as he gestured in my direction. His style was cute, but it never actually worked for either of us. I remember telling Roy that I appreciated his effort on my behalf, but I didn't really care if it worked.

That summer I took the example of others who fascinated me and learned how to sleep on the train to and from the apartment. It was so incredibly loud when it was underground near the Loop and so scorching hot when it emerged onto the elevated tracks past Wrigley Field and the neighborhoods. One time on the way home I actually slept through the Loyola stop and woke up at Howard Street, the end of the line. It didn't bother me. I felt I was fitting in quite nicely.

Aside from working all day and our nightly routines of macaroni and cheese with peas, ninety-nine cent six packs of Weideman's, Stroh's, or Ballantine, and gatherings of people at the apartment, there were really only two other events that stood out for me that summer of 1970. One involved nearly falling into a serious relationship with a beautiful, slightly older, married woman with a child who lived in Rogers Park. Nikki and I met in public while walking on Sheridan Road near the Granada theatre, but she said we needed to get together at my apartment so her husband would be less likely to see us about the neighborhood. We spent nearly a month's worth of nights in a row there listening to music on my bedroom floor, talking endlessly, and playing around with the idea of falling in love.

Without question, it was the closest I'd come since being in Chicago.

As our evenings together began to add up I watched Nikki become younger right in front of my eyes. It was a beautiful transformation. Whereas she'd worn a skirt and jacket with her long hair pinned up when we met, within a short time she was showing up at the apartment unabashedly braless in bell-bottom jeans with beaded tassels dangling from her belt loops. Nikki looked so natural compared to many girls I'd met, even Sunshine. And she was having no trouble whatsoever letting her hair down with me. Although I knew that I was messing around with another man's wife, I rationalized that I was doing her some good, which also felt special to me.

I surmised that my youth attracted her and, after her disillusionment with her early marriage and childbirth, she was looking to start over again. Nikki was always interested to hear what I had to say…everything I thought about anything. She was the first person in a long time who seemed so interested in me and I appreciated it very much.

One hot summer night, as we were kissing and gently sharing her breasts through the thin fabric of her t-shirt, it became clear that Nikki was ready to know me even better. She stood, slipped off her rose-tinted glasses, threw back her hair, neatly unzipped her tight fitting jeans, and began to wiggle out of them as I sat, speechless, on the floor in front of her.

It was a beautiful vision…a young man's wildest dream. However, it was also another moment of choice for me: I could either welcome her to my bedroom floor as I had already imagined endless times or I could interrupt our steamy moment of sensuality by reminding her that she was still married and explaining that I wasn't ready to take a true lover's leap with her.

I found myself taking the latter course, which didn't go over particularly well. She quickly stopped her undressing motions and began to cry profusely as she dropped to her knees and covered her pretty face with her hands. With her jeans still wrapped around her ankles she explained that it would be okay, that she was ready. I needn't be concerned about her motorcycle-riding husband. She really cared for me. In turn, I told her that she was absolutely beautiful, I truly enjoyed being with her, I loved the little painted rock she had done for me, and so on, but I was uncomfortable making love with her. That was, after all, what having sex with Nikki would have been.

Although we talked each other through it and everything seemed alright by the end of that evening, I guess we both knew it really wasn't. As was becoming something of a pattern for me, I grew less interested in our meetings and she eventually stopped coming around. It was a clumsy breakup, but generally I felt I had come to my senses not a moment too soon. My roommates agreed, though they rubbed it in by going on and on about how incredibly attractive she was. Comforted by the indelible memory of my vision, I was sure they couldn't picture the half of it.

If I had declared a best friend at the time, it surely would have been Skip. He had morphed quickly from whoever he was when he came to Chicago into one of the cooler, more legitimate hippie types on the Loyola campus and I looked up to him for it. He always spoke softly and stayed calm even when things got tense. He was the kind of guy who had a good time whenever he could help everyone else have a good time.

It seemed like I had always known Skip in his carpenter style jeans, salt-soaked suede chugga boots, oversized knitted sweaters, and long blue overcoat that he lived in during the winter months. He was more adaptable than most of the others, as he'd demonstrated by creating his small room out of the open space in the back of our apartment. Furthermore, although he never seemed to have very much in the way of possessions, he always managed to get by without complaining much.

Skip was well-known on campus partially because he hung around with Heart, who had become President of Student Government. I suspected they stuck together because they were both from the east coast and that geographical proximity must have cemented some type of bond between them. Though they were actually very different, it sometimes sounded as if they were from the same neighborhood. Skip was also well known because he was typically involved in planning student activities and spent almost as much time in the Student Activities office as he did at our place.

Although we were really good friends, I did have a few reservations about Skip. For one, we didn't actually spend as much time together as people seemed to think we did. I always wished that we had more common interests or that Skip had fewer interests, so we could hang out more. For another, he usually referred to me as "Boy," which was a nickname I never really cared for. It seemed to imply his superiority and added a competitive feel to our relationship. Perhaps most importantly, I was unsure why Skip gave me so much grief about walking away from my relationship with Sunshine. I didn't understand this because I often suspected that he was as interested in being with her as I was and our breakup could have provided the opportunity for him to move in. As a result, I wondered what he was up to when he would hang out with her and then tell me all the stuff she was thinking about me. But as with everything else, Skip and I just talked around these things.

That summer Skip and I befriended an older Loyola sometimes-student named Morrie who lived by himself in the backroom of a storefront a few blocks to the north of campus. It was a neat old place, sort of like our apartment, but with a big front room directly off of a nicely shaded street. The building had been used for some sort of business in the past, but currently was not being used for anything. One night when we were singing along with Skip's conga drum at Morrie's place, someone came up with the idea that we should open our own coffeehouse in the front room.

Neither Skip, nor I, nor Morrie knew much of anything about running a coffeehouse, except that we had been to a few. To us, it was just a matter of dragging in every piece of old furniture and interesting junk we could find in the alleys, creating some spaces for people to sit, lighting some candles and incense, putting up a sign in the window, and showing up. Once the place had begun to take shape, for no clear reason we decided we would call it "How Do You Spell Munchkin's?" or "Munchkin's" for short.

We scheduled our opening night for the first weekend that students would be back at school that fall. We put up flyers around campus, borrowed a big coffeepot from the Student Activities Office, and invested in a small stock of coffee, beer, and Boone's Farm apple wine. Skip and I planned to sit up front with our nylon-string guitars, strum some A and E-minors, and recite a few of our poems to provide "entertainment" for anyone who showed up.

Sunshine, most of our friends, new students, Nikki, and several high-schoolers from the neighborhood piled in. We started selling cups of beer, coffee, or wine like crazy for fifty cents each. People congregated around the big wooden wire spools we used for tables. It looked like things were off to a great start. Even the music that Skip and I plunked out didn't sound too bad. Munchkin's was taking off with a bang.

Just as things might have been looking up, two Chicago Police cars rolled up outside the building with their blue lights flashing. Four officers got out and quickly blocked the front door to the building. A few of those who probably had something to hide hustled out the back through Morrie's little apartment, but everyone else just sat there wondering what had gone wrong.

The officers requested to speak with the owner of the building. Owner? Of course, there was no owner present. None of us could recall ever having seen an owner. Then they asked for the Manager. Manager? We hadn't considered who was going to be the Manager, but by default Morrie, Skip and I all stepped forward at the same time to meet the Police. There was no hiding from it. It was our place. If a Manager was needed, then we would all be Managers.

After trying to answer the question, "What is going on here?" (Which was not easy) we were ordered to produce our business registration and liquor license. Business Registration? Liquor License? Of course, we had no business registration or liquor license. We hadn't even considered that these things might be necessary to open the doors and light the candles at a place like Munchkin's. We just wanted to start a coffeehouse; it hadn't crossed our minds that we'd be starting a business.

Within about five minutes, only about an hour and a half after its opening, Munchkin's was cleared of all of its patrons. We Managers were instructed not to reopen the place until we had obtained the appropriate business registration and licenses. At that moment the contrasts between whatever we had been thinking and the realities about the way things were supposed to be showed up in an important way in our lives.

Munchkin's never reopened and we saw a lot less of Morrie after that night. However, Skip and I did move a couple of the wooden spools and some of the other old stuff down to the back room at our apartment. We could put it to better use there without having to have a license.

The rest of the fall and winter of 1970, we took care of ourselves the best we could in the midst of erratic local and national attention to the War. As it turned out, Joon, Cowboy, Skip and I helped change University rules regarding off-campus living that year. When the fall semester started we simply told the bursar's office that we would have to quit school if we were forced to give up the apartment and move back into a dorm. The administration gave in and we scored one for the good guys.

Like many other days, Saturdays that fall were reserved for what seemed like twenty-four hour parties. On many of them our rag-tag campus group called "the Organs" would show up at a nearby neighborhood park in support of Loyola's fledgling Club Football team. Initially, the Organs simply took it as their role to arouse the few fans that were in the stands and let the team know that they had a following. However, Skip, Cowboy, Joon, and I could never just keep things that simple. Before long we were standing out front of the bleachers, leading bizarre cheers that we made up, and conducting halftime shows that featured a pre-adolescent neighborhood girl in a sequenced outfit twirling her baton. Of course the shows were never much good, but that didn't matter – it was a very consistent part of our shtick.

Win or lose, after the games we would retreat to the apartment with as many, primarily female, fans as we could muster. I had always loved sunny afternoons in the fall and this ritual consistently carried me away. I recall many times when the Organs would march a group of people from the game to the apartment and I would hurry down the steps and through the front door to get Grand Funk Railroad's, "Aimless Lady" cranking before everyone packed inside for the evening. We spent our Sunday's chasing people away and getting the place back in some sort of order.

Although it was becoming increasingly common to forget about it, the War dragged on. There were so many other important and seemingly frivolous or contradictory things going in the world, I frequently gave up on trying to stay focused...from the trial related to the massacre at My Lai to the first Earth Day; from the invasion of Cambodia to Black Sabbath's debut album; from the aftermath of the Kent State shootings to putting a man on the moon; from all the Marches on Washington to Nixon's signing of a bill lowering the voting age to 18; and from a thousand-plus air strikes on Hanoi on the day after Christmas to the last studio performance of the Beatles.

Sometimes I felt there was just too much happening to try to keep up. Sometimes I felt that nothing made any sense anyway. Many times I felt that too many people continued to use the issues that should have mattered most as an excuse to get together and get wasted. I often second-guessed it even more when we got together and got wasted without any pretense...as if it was okay to go on having a good time when so many others were in harm's way. As I noticed my own emerging apathy, I started to get concerned that I was shallow and hypocritical and I became increasingly troubled by it. I wasn't sure what depression was, but I began to suspect that I may have had a touch of it.

I was a long way from my high school interests in Watts and Austin. Back then I'd felt on the cusp of something like a social conscience. Now, when I wasn't high or drunk or otherwise off in my own little world, I was troubled by just about anything that came along. By winter I had begun to spend a great deal of my time lying on my bedroom floor with my head jammed between my cheap stereo speakers blasting Hendrix' "Electric Ladyland," It's a Beautiful Day, and Fuse into my brain. Though I was probably doing it to escape the discomfort, the music actually might have fostered the loneliness, confusion, and anger that seemed to be building in me. I had been changed so much by so many different things in such a short period of time that very little made good sense, although now I seemed to be sensing just about everything in one way or another.

Bring it on Home to Me
(A Sam Cooke song made more famous by the Animals)

By year's end 1970 I probably should've noticed that I was on the brink of something, but I was not at all clear about what it was going to be. Tingsly, Jake, and I were all visiting our homes in Peoria for another round of holidays. Tingsly and Jake continued to be like magnets that attracted unusual things to happen. I went after the distractions they created because I was concerned that I was thinking too much and thinking just brought me down.

One beautiful winter night just after Christmas Jake had the idea that we should crash a party taking place off Main Street by the old Steak and Shake drive-in that almost nobody drove in anymore. Tingsly and I stood outside the apartment building as Jake attempted to talk our way into the party. The next thing we knew, Jake went running past us, back in the direction of the car that we had parked about two blocks away. Not knowing what was happening, but a little concerned, Tingsly and I turned around and started trotting back down the middle of the snow-covered street after him. Within seconds the two of us were flat on our backs in the slushy snow, each with a short-sleeved stranger on top of us about to show us how things could be in Peoria.

Under some of Tingsly's guidance and with lots of practice, I had become pretty good at getting out of situations like this. The guy on top of me had his fist cocked ready to let me have it. But rather than trying to swing back I held my arms in front of my face and pleaded, "Wait, wait a minute, hold it!" He hesitated. When he did I was equally quick to explain that neither Tingsly nor I even lived in Peoria anymore, that we'd just hooked up with Jake that evening, and that we had no idea what was going on between them. Both guys ceased their onslaught, bought the story, and let us back to our feet. We stood under the lights on that snowy Peoria street as they told us about how Jake had shorted them earlier that week on a drug transaction. We told them we understood. Then, we actually chatted about how Peoria had changed and answered their questions about what it was like to live in other places. They asked us if we would bring Jake back to the party if we saw him again that night. Momentarily sacrificing an unspoken allegiance to our friend, we said we'd do that if we ran into him again. Of course, this time we were lying through our teeth.

The next night, New Year's Eve, started where the previous night left off. Tingsly had heard about a party that one of our old high school classmates was having at his new apartment, across from Lou's Drive-in where we used to drink nickel root beers and eat chili dogs as kids. I'd never really known the guy who was throwing the party and I already feared for Jake's well-being if he ran into some of the older guys from high school who always seemed to be after him for one thing or the other. But eventually we all agreed to go and check it out.

Just walking into an apartment full of people from high school after two years of being away in Chicago was an event in itself. Tingsly and I were now outsiders to any sort of Peoria scene and, maybe because our appearance had changed fairly dramatically, it seemed we were taken with more than a little hint of cynicism by some of our prepped up, still obviously very straight friends. We had long hair and well-worn blue jeans. They looked like they all had day jobs at the First National Bank.

All things considered it didn't go too badly reconnecting with our old high school friends until Jake somehow managed to spill his mixed drink all over the host's fancy stereo and records. Knowing Jake as well as I did, I had to wonder if he'd done this on purpose – perhaps as payback for something that had happened years earlier. As he had clearly demonstrated in Chicago, Jake was a master at creating a scene when he decided that one was called for. In a flash, there were about a half a dozen guys in his face threatening him with his life. Tingsly and I were a little hesitant to jump in the middle of the fray, but as we had done so many times over the years, we decided to stick up for Jake again. We eventually talked everyone down and agreed that we would take Jake and leave the party.

As we were in the doorway leaving peacefully and while the host had already started washing his Beach Boys records with soap and water in the sink, Jake shouted back at everyone that he was having a party at his house later that night if anyone wanted to have some *real* fun. Following that remark, more shouting ensued as Tingsly and I physically dragged Jake off to the car.

We didn't know Jake was planning to have a party at his house that night. Neither did he, I suppose, until that moment. He quickly reasoned that since it was New Year's Eve his folks would be out very late and that it would, in fact, be fine if we went to his place for a while. Somewhat reluctantly, we did. When we got there, Jake chased his two little sisters up to their room and told them they had better shut up about what was about to happen at the house. They were obviously pretty used to this kind of thing from their older brother, and scurried off up the stairs.

Within an hour or so, the house it seemed as though I had not visited since I was a kid was teeming with people from the high school party and many others who only Jake seemed to know. Some of them sat around the kitchen table where Jake's parents always sat when they had coffee, lemonade, or sandwiches. Others fiddled with his father's antique pipe stand which sat next to his recliner in the living room. As kids, we never fiddled with that pipe stand, although we had always been fascinated by it. People came in and out of the front door which no one, except Jake's relatives, ever used when they visited Jake's house. A few ransacked the downstairs refrigerator where Jake senior kept his Stag beer.

I bailed out of the party just before midnight, right after I had watched Jake chug a fifth of Vodka on a bet and instantly pass out on his parents' linoleum kitchen floor. His forehead knocked an open cabinet door off its hinges on the way down. Tingsly and I hauled him up the stairs to his bed, cleared everyone from the house, stuck the cabinet door back in place, cleaned up a bit, and told Jake's sisters to watch out for their brother. Tingsly went off with a girl he hadn't seen in a while. I went off alone in the Mustang.

Though I was pretty intoxicated by that time, my last stop on that New Year's Eve was at my old high school girlfriend's house which was just a couple of blocks away across University Avenue toward Glen. Sadie and I met when I was only fourteen and she still lived "below the hill" in one of the rough Peoria neighborhoods. We dated on and off all through high school and got pretty serious after her family moved to their new house which was safely above the hill, only about a mile from where I lived.

As high school relationships often went, I was never quite sure this one had ever actually ended. In fact, Sadie and I had spent some time together even after I'd visited Dekalb and surprised her while she was sleeping with that other guy. We had known each other for so long and had been through so many of these sorts of things, I didn't think it mattered that much anymore. Regardless of her infidelity, I respected her because she'd had it tough growing up and, even if she did enjoy fooling around, she had always treated me well. So, since I had heard that she was home from college too, I thought I would just mosey on over to her house and see what she was up to around midnight on New Year's Eve. It all felt innocent enough to me; although I already suspected I might be in for more trouble.

I rolled into the cul-de-sac and pulled the car into the end of Sadie's driveway. I saw that the same old pale light was on in the front living room where we used to make out while her parents and little sisters sat in the lower family room watching television. I quickly recalled all the times that Sadie's littlest sister must have caught me with my hands in places that I didn't fully understand at the time.

I suspected that Sadie was there on the couch, doing what we used to do with whoever she was with on this snowy New Year's Eve. After all, she had taught me almost everything I knew about sex before many of my high school friends had even started dating. And from our experience since, it appeared she had probably tutored a number of others as well. My head was racing. I guess I just couldn't leave well enough alone.

After sitting in front of her mother's house in the Mustang that I had no doubt she would recognize, I finally decided I would go up and knock on the door. Sadie answered in a long robe covering an older-lady-like night gown she must have borrowed from her mom. She opened the front door just a crack so I wouldn't be able to see inside. I smiled, wished her a "Happy New Year," and asked how she was doing.

She smiled back, thanked me for the holiday wishes, and then quickly asked me to go away. I persisted for a while as I felt a surge of emotion coming on. Of course I knew she wasn't alone, but it didn't matter. I had just started to raise my voice as she pushed the door shut. I stood at the door talking to myself for a while. The next thing I knew, Sadie's grandmother and mother opened the door a crack and began pleading with me to go away or they would have to call the police. They always liked me, but it was clear that they were taking their instructions from the couch.

Partially out of my respect for the elders, I walked back down the concrete doorsteps and into the middle of the deserted circular drive where the house sat. Within a few moments, I found myself on my knees in the wet snow crying like I had not cried in my budding adult life. It felt as though every event that had ever stirred my sadness tried to jam its way into my brain at the same time…everything from all the years past and every crazy thing from the present. Instantly, I felt as though the past was now going to be done for good, yet the future seemed so incredibly blank, empty, and uncertain. I looked at the sky and thought about hollering out to my older sister in Milwaukee who I knew would understand. She had told me before that she would hear me if I looked at the moon when I called. But I didn't. There was no moon and I never really bought into stuff like that anyway.

Instead, I hauled myself back to my feet, brushed the snow from my pants, slowly stepped back into the Mustang, and cried myself to my parent's garage where I sat in the car for an hour or so before going into the house and to my bed.

I had intended to hitchhike back to Chicago later that New Year's Day, but my parents surprised me by announcing that I could take the Mustang back to the city with me. This made sense to them because they now had two other newer Fords and none of the other kids were using the older convertible at the time. It also made sense because they knew I was expecting to come back for another visit in about a month. Although I was pleased with their decision and had not looked forward to hitchhiking after the New Year's Eve I'd had, I never cared that much about having a car in the city.

I don't remember much about the drive back, except for looking at the beautiful old farms I always loved on the Route

29 two lane heading north along the Illinois River out of Peoria. Against the fresh blanket of New Year's snow, these places looked particularly peaceful.

We Gotta Get Out of This Place
(The Animals)

Loyola University was on a Tri-semester system, which meant that we would only have classes during the early weeks of January before we would be let loose again for another break at the end of the month. Thankfully, with end of the semester test taking, the turmoil of my New Year got shrouded a bit and the first part of January rolled by fairly quickly.

Joon had just turned twenty-one. He was a tad older than the rest of us at the apartment and sometimes acted like it. He was a tall, good-looking, heavily-mustached kid with long black frizzy hair like steel wool. For me to have come to Chicago from Peoria was one thing. For Joon to have come from an even smaller place like Bloomington must have been something else.

At times Joon was a total gentleman with a gentle demeanor, wonderful social skills, and excellent manners. However, at other times he was as crazy as anyone I knew. I had seen him break the speed record for shooting six beers in a row with a group of guys cheering him on in the dormitory bathroom. I had joined him and my other roommates for our ceremonial circle dance to "Cripple Creek Ferry" at each of the endless parties at the apartment. I had even seen him rip a pay telephone off the wall in the foyer of one of the neighborhood bars just for fun.

Joon was always around and everyone liked him. However, he rarely went out of his way to be very social. Perhaps the apathy in the air had affected Joon more vividly than others. There were times he didn't act like he cared about much of anything. This became particularly evident the first semester of junior year when Heart and Skip cajoled him into running for some sort of office on the student government at Loyola. Joon's campaign slogan characterized him perfectly.

While running for the position, he took every opportunity to declare that he, "Would work very hard to do as little as possible to accomplish as little as he possibly could," if he were elected. While his slogan might have been a fitting sign of the times and we wondered if he might actually win, he wasn't elected for the job.

Although the rest of us sometimes *felt* twenty-one because we all had fake ID's so we could get into Vic's Star Bar, Joker's, or Hamilton's to buy alcohol, Joon quickly realized that actually *being* twenty-one had other advantages, not the least of which was that he could now qualify to secure a "drive-away" car.

I don't know if the drive-away business continued much past 1971, but back then it was a pretty interesting concept to three twenty-year-old and one twenty-one-year old college students with a little time on their hands. The business plan was pretty simple. A "Responsible Person" would put some money down on deposit with a broker and deliver a car to someone who, for one reason or another, had become separated from their car and needed it brought to them. When the car was delivered, the deposit or some additional agreed-upon amount of money would be provided to the Responsible Person. Our crew now had a Responsible Person who was interested in actualizing the drive-away concept.

Although we only had about nine days before classes were to start again, we decided in a matter of minutes that we wanted a car that needed to be delivered to Los Angeles. There wasn't any special reason for us to pick Los Angeles other than the fact that none of us had been there and we assumed it would be warm on the West Coast. Nobody we knew went to Florida for Spring Breaks in those days.

We guessed that Chicago would have a pretty busy drive-away office and that they would surely have a car that needed to

PHOENIX TO LA

go to another big city like Los Angeles. Joon went off to the drive-away office to get us a car. Of course, he had to go by himself because the rest of us did not yet qualify as Responsible Persons and we weren't sure what the drive-away folks would think if they knew Joon would be accompanied by three not-yet-responsible twenty-year-olds. After our miscalculation at Munchkin's, I guess we'd become a bit more careful about some things we didn't fully understand.

So much for the best of reasonably well made plans. Joon returned from downtown late that morning in a shiny blue, brand-new Chevy Impala with a white vinyl roof. However, he told us that the office had no cars bound for Los Angeles. So, being responsible on his size thirteen feet, he got us a ride that was headed for Phoenix, Arizona. He didn't appear too concerned about getting to Los Angeles because the guy at the Chicago drive-away office told him that when he got to Phoenix, he could go to its drive-away office and pick up another delivery bound for Los Angeles. Of course all of this sounded good enough to the rest of us as well.

Joon plunked down a $150 deposit on the Impala. To our surprise, he told us that he made the deposit with a new personalized credit card that he had gotten over the holidays when he was at home in Bloomington. None of us had much experience with credit cards, but Joon explained that we would be able to pick up the $150 in cash when we delivered the car in Phoenix. Then we would use that money as deposit for the next car that we would secure to the Coast. Once again, it all sounded reasonable to us.

We figured that, if we pooled our resources, it would cost each of us about $40 to make the round trip between Chicago and Los Angeles. Gas was usually around thirty-five cents a gallon at the time. We would only need motel rooms for a couple of nights because we would be driving most of the time

91

and sleeping in the car. Joon, Skip, and I were able to come up with the cash. At the end of January I still had money left from the $50 check that my father handed out to each of his kids on Christmas Day, a family tradition that had always come in incredibly handy for me.

Unfortunately, Cowboy was short on cash after having spent a chunk of his student loan money going back and forth to Pueblo, Colorado for the holidays. As a result, he quickly talked himself out of making the trip with us, even though we offered to come up with a way to cover him. Cowboy was like that. If he couldn't pay his own way, he would find something else to do. I really admired that part of Cowboy and suspected that his pretty girlfriend Jewelie did as well.

But we figured that in order to make the trip economics work, we really needed to have a fourth person in the car. Though we were disappointed that Cowboy wasn't coming along and there weren't many other guys around who didn't already have plans for the break, it didn't take fifteen minutes to find a solution to our problem. We called The Cork who had already gone to his home in South Chicago. He spoke to his mother and then immediately signed on for the trip. It turned out that he had been looking for an excuse to limit his holiday visits and this trip would provide good one. However, we had to promise him that if we got anywhere close to the Grand Canyon we would make a special stop. The Cork and his mother seemed enthralled by the thought of seeing the Grand Canyon.

By noon we had our stuff packed up in the Impala, including Skip's old guitar, and we were ready to leave the freezing north side of Chicago for the sunny desert of Phoenix. For me, it was a refreshing feeling. Cowboy and Rose, a girl I enjoyed being around, were there to wish us a grand bon-voyage. Everyone was excited and hugging each other, even Joon, Skip, and I who would be making the trip together. In the midst of my playful enthusiasm, I gave Rose a big kiss on the lips, which I had not even considered doing until that moment. My exaggerated display of happiness suddenly felt very real. In an instant, Rose became sweeter than Sadie, Nikki, and Sunshine all put together. Given the right combination of things, I had begun to notice that my changes were often taking place just that quickly.

We got on Lakeshore Drive and headed out of the city on Interstate 55 toward The Cork's house in South Chicago. Joon was driving partially because he was our Responsible Person and partially because the drive-away rules prohibited other drivers. I don't know if Joon thought he might actually drive all the way to Phoenix, but it was too early for us to be thinking about details like that. On the way out to The Cork's house, we passed the spot where I had been stopped by the State Trooper when I was hitchhiking. I gave Joon and Skip my expanded version of what had happened. We laughed a lot. We were off to a nice start.

Characteristically, The Cork wasn't quite set to go when we got to his house. He invited us in and we sat down at his kitchen table with his mother while he got his bag together. Although The Cork's mom asked a lot of questions about each of us and our trip plans, fortunately she seemed more intent on showing us some raccoons that the family had befriended from the nearby woods. We were happy to fill the time talking about the raccoons because there weren't a lot of personal details or trip plans that we cared to talk about. We had a drive away car to Phoenix. Any concerns she might have had beyond that would not have been quelled by talking to us.

The Cork was a big Teddy Bear who was not nearly as tall as Joon, but he probably outweighed him by thirty pounds. He was built like a tank. Not surprisingly, he was a primary part of the offensive line on the football team at Loyola. He seemed a tad less worldly than the rest of us and this became clearer as he was saying goodbye to his mother and his pets. With all the hugging, kissing, and warm words being exchanged, it was as if he was headed out of their cozy little nest for the first time in his life. Frankly, I was touched by all the affection and might have wanted to hang out a little longer if the afternoon was not calling for us to get back on the highway.

The Cork hadn't been involved in the hour or so of trip planning we had done back at the apartment, so I am not sure he fully appreciated our expectation that each of us would bring $40 for the trip. Unfortunately, this issue came up within fifteen minutes of getting him in the back seat of the car. As it turned out, The Cork had only been able to borrow $10 from his mother, so he only had thirty bucks in his pocket for the trip.

Although we found a way to make it right by arbitrarily subtracting one of our planned nights in a motel, The Cork's announcement put a damper on the first part of our trip down old Route 66 to St. Louis. I felt pretty badly for him, much like I always seemed to feel bad when things went wrong in other people's lives. Once again I concluded that we had used our momentary exuberance and spontaneity about the trip as a shield from the turmoil and disarray we all knew was going on around us in the world.

For at least a couple hours that afternoon, The Cork's little shortcoming was accompanied by silence. I spent some time watching the telephone poles roll by as I often did while traveling. I worried a bit about Joon because, as gentlemanly as he could be, I also knew he had a notorious history of responding to unwanted surprises more vividly than the rest of us. And, after all, he had to be our Responsible Person. I was less concerned about Skip because I knew he always had a way of smoothing over the rough spots that came his way. Nevertheless, I sensed his need to keep things cool. Skip always wanted to keep things cool. Of course I was worrying about The Cork because I suspected this sort of thing wasn't new to him and I didn't know him well enough to predict if or how he'd react. I have no doubt that each of us wondered, if only for few moments, what we were doing in a brand-new Chevy Impala headed for Phoenix with just $150 between us.

During our silence, I also spent a little time thinking about having kissed Rose like I did. Rose was one of the most gentle girls anyone would ever meet. She had short wispy blonde hair surrounding her fair-skinned, Italian-looking face. She didn't speak a lot. She had a tendency to smile at the silly things that other people did and she would often laugh at what she must have believed were her own shortcomings. Somehow she must have felt that she had a lot of them, but that never made any sense to me. While she was always present at events around campus, she was a bit of a mystery because she stayed to herself and was rarely heard. I didn't know exactly what "demure" meant at the time, but the word sounded good to me and she was exactly that. There was nothing artificial or pretentious about her.

Fortunately, the gloom and silence in the Impala didn't last long. As we approached St. Louis and spotted the Arch, we realized that we were passing through the "Gateway to the West." We joked about it because the West was where we actually wanted to go. It was cause for a little celebration as we crossed the muddy Mississippi River into Missouri. We were out of Illinois and on our way.

After about a hundred miles and an hour and a half of carrying on about St. Louis and the Gateway to the West as if we were stoned, it had turned dark and we decided to stop somewhere around Rolla, Missouri. Already, this place felt like a long way from Chicago, but Los Angeles would be so much farther. We spotted a junky straight-line, drive-up motel with a bar next door that seemed like a fitting place for the four of us to spend the night.

Although none of us actually understood what was meant by "the Deep South," Rolla seemed like it must have contributed to the definition. Almost all of the business signs were hand painted and almost all the vehicles were trucks. Night Crawlers and fishing gear appeared to be big business. Old Airstream campers and trailers constituted neighborhoods. Readily assuming his role as Responsible Person, Joon dropped the rest of us off to kill some time at the neighboring truck stop while he went into the motel office to get us a single room. We were concerned that it would cost too much if the motel people knew that there were going to be four of us sharing a single room and none of us knew what would happen if we got caught, particularly in a place like Rolla, Missouri.

Joon got a single for ten dollars, scored two six-packs of cold Pabst Blue Ribbon from the bar, and pulled the Impala up in front of the room. About ten minutes later we got his "all clear" flash of the room lights, sprinted across a field from the truck stop to the room, and quickly consumed our ration of PBR's to dash our concerns about where we were. Joon and The Cork, the two biggest guys, opted to share the double bed. Skip and I grabbed a couple well-worn extra blankets from the closet, fluffed our coats as pillows, and slept on the floor. Of course I didn't say anything, but I actually preferred to sleep on the floor because the bed didn't look like it had been changed from the night before or maybe even the night before that. I think we all got set to sleep pretty quickly so that we wouldn't have to think about the conditions we were in. If it had been summer, I would have preferred to sleep outside on the ground.

We made it through to the morning even though semi-trucks were rolling in and out of the parking lot and their lights were shining through the stingy curtains of the room all night long. After some very quick cold showers we took off for Phoenix knowing that we were not going to sleep inside again at least until we got there. We figured it would take us about a day and a half to cover the eleven hundred or so miles we still had to go before we got to Phoenix.

Although we had some delays along the way (as when Skip got stopped and warned by two Oklahoma State Troopers for doing 77 mph on the 70 mph stretch of highway past Tulsa) things were going pretty well that Saturday afternoon of January 23, 1971. I remember the date so well because it was my father's birthday. I actually called home collect from a truck stop to wish him a Happy 55th Birthday. He was a little surprised to hear that I was somewhere in Texas at the time, but otherwise he was just happy to hear from me. He was always happy to hear from me, no matter where I was.

Even though I was driving part of the time and paying close attention, there wasn't much to see. We passed by the lonely exit ramps for places like Oklahoma City, Clinton, Amarillo, Tucumcari, and Santa Rosa. None of us really thought there was much to look at until we got into New Mexico. We were approaching Albuquerque at about 4:00 AM on Sunday morning. Joon was driving again and Skip was awake in the front seat keeping him company. The Cork and I had been sleeping off and on in the back seat. It was surprisingly nice sleeping in the back seat of a full-size car, except when he started using me as his pillow.

Suddenly The Cork and I were awakened by Skip shouting one of his characteristic "Holy shits," and Joon twisting the Impala onto the shoulder of the empty highway. We had no idea what all the excitement was about or whether it was good or bad news. Skip's "Holy shits" never provided much of a clue. We jumped out all four doors of the car and gathered in a clump by the side of the road.

There we stood on top of a small wave of a hill about a hundred miles out of Albuquerque looking at what Skip had thought was a flying saucer. It was a happy and sad moment for the four of us. Sad because Skip was so messed up from being tired that he had mistaken a big star for a flying saucer and happy because we were suddenly surrounded by the natural beauty of the New Mexico landscape in the incredible silence of a January morning. We stood there in our little huddle and looked around in awe of the landscape. As if to leave the moment as undisturbed as possible, the Cork whispered that he was pretty sure Skip's flying saucer was actually Venus.

When we got moving down the road again, the sight of Albuquerque in the early morning light was equally inspiring. As I recall, which in this case could have been a bit more fantastic than real, when we drove down the hillside from the east, Albuquerque appeared as if it were an array of flickering rowboat lights dancing on clear black water in a huge valley surrounded by the panorama of the rest of the earth. It might have been the most beautiful sight I had ever seen. By dawn we'd driven through my vision, up the other side of the valley, and into the final three hundred fifty miles of our remaining jaunt to Phoenix.

As we rolled into Arizona, we realized that we had a little time to burn because we were only about seven hours from Phoenix and we didn't have to return the car to its owner until the following morning. For the first time, we slowed down and took some time to savor our journey. We veered off Interstate 40 at Winslow and followed Route 87 through the mountains toward Payson. About thirty miles down that road, we found a bit more of what we must have been looking for.

Strawberry, Arizona was like no place any of us had ever seen before, even on family vacations in our station wagons. At an elevation of over six thousand feet, it rested in some impossibly rugged and silently gorgeous small mountains. The dark blue sky and meandering white clouds seemed to be right in front of our faces. At one point, we were so taken by the mountain views that Joon pulled over at a convenience store, splurged on a six-pack of Coors beer, drove back up the road, and parked the Impala at a picnic table pull-off by a gently rolling stream. He and Skip jumped out of the car and immediately went climbing up the hill next to the stream while The Cork and I soaked in the atmosphere and our ration of the beer from below.

When Joon got to the top of the hill he began hooting as only Joon could hoot. It was great to see him looking so happy. After he got back down from the mountain and had his Coors, he peed in the middle of the two lane road to mark his spot at that special place. The Cork jumped up on the steel railing that bordered a sharp curve and joined him, as if to form some kind of special, animal-like bond. Though we resisted the notion of acting like tourists, Skip took some pictures of our hour and a half near beautiful Strawberry, Arizona with his Kodak Instamatic camera.

Humming a little Glen Campbell, by the time we got to Phoenix that afternoon we had spent $54.32 on gas, oil, and two turnpike fees. We were pleased, especially since we had only spent $10 on the hotel room and possibly another $15 on beer and food. Between us we still had more than $110 in cash for the rest of the trip because Joon had already volunteered to start putting some of the gas on his credit card on our promise that we would pay him back later.

We planned to enter Phoenix from the Tempe side of town. We figured that Arizona State University was there and, if we could find it, we might also find a place where we could spend a night. As it turned out, Arizona State was renting out rooms to visitors in one of the empty women's dorms for $6 per person per night. Of course we had no plans to actually pay for four people. Joon got the dorm room and we decided to wait until after dark to figure out how the rest of us were going to get in.

In the meantime, since we were feeling pretty well-to-do, we decided we would hop back in the Impala and go hunting for something to eat. An amazing thing happened on the way to the Big Boy hamburger place where we decided to treat ourselves. Along the highway we found ourselves driving by a place that looked like a bowling alley called "JD's" with a sign out front announcing, "Opens Tonight – Zephyr." In my unanticipated excitement, I coaxed Joon off the road and up to the building so I could find out if the sign was for real. It was; but I was already wondering what a band as good as Zephyr was doing playing on a Sunday night at a dive like JD's.

Given that we had a little time on our hands to get some food and still make it back to JD's in plenty of time to beat the $3.00 cover, we relaxed at the Big Boy. In addition to our hamburger platters, we ate every cracker on our table, as well as those on the table next to us. Somehow The Cork was graced with an extra salad. Although he was afraid to ask for more dressing to go with it, we finally convinced him to take a chance and go for it. He did and the waitress never blinked an eye. She might have even said, "Sure thing Sweetie," as she gave him some Thousand Island dressing and a little pinch on the cheek to go with it. This seemed like a significant breakthrough for The Cork. We had become increasingly certain that he had not done a dishonest thing in his life.

In those early days of 1971, places like JD's seemed to become homes away from home for a lot of young people. In fact, not just because Zephyr was playing, the inside of the place took on the same flavor for me as the parks in Denver and Berkeley and the farm in Heyworth. It looked like some people actually lived there or at least as if they had moved in for the night. It was big and dark with the pervasive pale purple glow of fluorescent black lights.

At about 8:30, the opening band started their act. They played on a plywood stage raised not more than six inches off the floor. While it was easy to feel connected with the band, it was also clear that there were a lot of other things going on around the building that did not include the four of us from Chicago. When the music started, the smell of pot absolutely filled the main room.

Even with the ambience, the opening band didn't hold our attention very well, so Skip and I began exploring the place. We decided to go into a back hallway to see if we could find Candy Givens, Tommy Bolin and the rest of Zephyr. At one point, we ran into a big guy who looked like he might have been a bouncer for JD's. We automatically stopped when we saw him and he asked us what we were doing in the hallway. Although we weren't sure who the guy was, I told him that I had seen Zephyr at the Denver Pop Festival and that we hoped to get a chance to say hello to them. I told him that we'd come all the way from Chicago and that seeing them again was going to be really special for us. He just shrugged, said "Okay," and let us pass. Afterward, we figured that he probably had nothing to do with the place.

At the end of the hallway, Skip and I came to the open door of a small room off to the left side. Right smack in front of me was crazy-looking Candy Givens somewhere between sitting and lying on the floor in the middle of the room leaned up against her lanky, bass-playing husband, David. The rest of the band was parked along the walls intermingled with their gear. It certainly didn't look like anyone was thinking much about doing music at that moment. I am not sure any one of them could have even moved if they tried. Serious drug paraphernalia was everywhere. To me it felt like I'd just accidentally walked into a room to find my little sister having sex, except that in this case no one seemed to care.

Not knowing exactly what to do, I looked at Candy and said, "I saw you and the band at the Denver Pop Festival and I thought you were fantastic." She looked up at me for a while from her spot on the floor and then called out over her shoulder, "This kid saw us play at Mile High." I was not sure anyone heard her because no one responded. We looked at each other again. I didn't know what else to say, so I didn't say anything. I just stood there surveying the morass of the band. After a few more moments, as if gathering her thoughts to finish a sentence, Candy said, "And he thought we were great!" After this comment the others shuffled around a bit, made a few unintelligible comments, and laughed.

By that time in my life, being around scenes of intoxication was no longer a new thing for me. However, being around this degree of oblivion and passivity was. Weren't any of them concerned about getting busted with heavy drugs? More importantly, I wondered how a band as talented as Zephyr, who had brought down the fences in front of fifty thousand people at Denver and kicked butt on their debut album, could be in this condition. They were carrying their own equipment, for Pete's sake. They appeared to have no one watching out for them. They were playing in a dive like JD's when I had considered them to be one of the best groups on the planet. I didn't get freaked out by much, but this came pretty close.

Skip and I wished them well, made our way back to the front room, and sat down on the floor just as the opening act was winding up their show. We didn't know what to expect from Zephyr when they finally took the stage that night, although I did have a sense of knowing them a whole lot better than before. We stood just to the right front of the stage, very close to the speakers. There was no big fanfare when they arrived on stage. They just walked on, started noodling around with their instruments, and pretty soon they were into their act. "Hard Charging Woman," "Huna Buna," "Sail On," and a half-hour version of "The Creator Has a Masterplan" sounded great, but the show was considerably more mellow and jazzy with longer jams and solos than I had heard from them before. The music was not nearly as inspired as Denver. Though I tried to convince myself and my friends it was still brilliant, it was clear that something had changed. I was troubled by it all, but couldn't pinpoint why. Maybe it was the atmosphere. I also considered that it might have been me. Sometime later I concluded that it was mostly just Zephyr.

The band broke up shortly after that night. Tommy Bolin went his own way through James Gang, Deep Purple, and Moxy before his early and untimely death from poly-drug ingestion. Apparently, he was only twenty-five when he died in Miami just a few hours after finishing an opening set for Led Zeppelin with his drug anthem called "Post Toastie." I understood that Candy and David Givens divorced sometime later, but Candy struggled on with her music until her death from an alcohol and Quaalude overdose. David went off to live somewhere in Hawaii.

We didn't get a chance to talk about Zephyr's show much more that night because we had to put our focus on sneaking into the guest dormitory back at Arizona State. Joon went on in while the rest of us snuck around the side of the building which was protected from people like us by a six-foot high chain-link fence. We saw the room Joon had secured when he blinked the lights on and off several times and pointed toward a side door that he intended to open if we could get over the fence. Skip and I made it fairly easily, but The Cork had a bit of a time getting over. He was concerned that his weight was going to break the fence. So were we, although we didn't say so. We finally made it in the side door and into the little room. Joon and The Cork took the bed. Skip slept on the floor. Due to the tight space, I actually curled up on top of the built-in desk.

I stayed awake that night thinking about how much things had been changing. The best music no longer seemed fun, exhilarating, or enlightening. Eric Satie, Paul Horn, and others made it seem moody and private. To me, it seemed that young people were paying less attention and directing less energy toward doing one's part to change the world. That had apparently become someone else's thing to do. Instead of coming closer together, it seemed to me that people were retreating...more silent and self-indulgent than before. Whatever causes there had been, they seemed strangely in the past. These thoughts reminded me of what Tingsly and I had seen when we got to Haight Ashbury a little too late back in 1969. Packed in a tiny room with at least two of my closest friends, I finally drifted off to sleep.

The next morning we took turns sneaking up and down the hall to the dormitory bathroom to clean up. By that point we weren't too worried about getting caught since we had already gotten some sleep and there was almost no one in the building. Then we cleaned out the Impala to get it set for Joon's rendezvous with the owner at the Phoenix drive-away place. At around 8:30, Joon dropped us at a nearby park where the rest of us planned to wait while his transaction was taking place. We were all having a nice time speculating what kind of car we would wind up with for our ride to Los Angeles.

Joon came lumbering back to the park about an hour later. To our surprise and disappointment, it turned out that we had a couple of problems. First, Joon only got $50 in cash back from his deposit on the Impala. He was told that the rest had to be credited back to his card. Second and even more important at that moment, there were no drive-away cars headed for Los

Angeles. Apparently, the only vehicle headed anywhere that morning was a brand new pickup truck headed for Las Vegas, and someone else had just taken it.

Phoenix to LA

It was a tough way to start on a Monday morning. After the four of us walked around in different directions, which we had a tendency to do when things seemed to be going wrong, we reconvened around an old iron merry-go-round in the park. I knew that there was really only one thing to do. No big deal. Keep smiling. We would just have to hitchhike to Los Angeles.

Although I was the only one of our group who had done much distance hitchhiking at the time, it didn't take long for the others to go along with the idea. I figured it was slightly less than four hundred miles to Los Angeles. If we got on the road quickly, we could probably get there by 8:00 or 9:00 o'clock that night.

But, we had to get moving. Everyone realized fairly quickly that it wasn't going to be practical for the four of us to hitchhike to Los Angeles together, particularly since I anticipated we'd encounter our most difficulty getting started in mid-city Phoenix. I suggested that it would probably be quickest if we each traveled separately. However, this didn't go over too well, particularly for The Cork, who had never done this sort of thing before. So eventually, we agreed that we would go in pairs, Joon traveling with Skip and The Cork coming along with me.

We also had to decide how we were going to link back up once we got to Los Angeles. It was remarkable how simply we thought about things in those days. We considered meeting at the Los Angeles YMCA. This made sense because it was likely that there would be one and, if there was, we might even be able to spend a cheap night there. The Cork, however, talked us out of meeting at the YMCA. He suspected that, if there was one, it would likely be in a rough section of town because that was where all YMCA's tended to be located in those days. Everyone appreciated The Cork's contribution on that one.

Knowing that it was important to get going, we quickly decided we would meet at "the Holiday Inn on Main Street." Of course we didn't know if there actually was a Holiday Inn on Main Street, but we suspected there would have to be one close to downtown. By that time Holiday Inns were beginning to show up everywhere. There were Main Streets everywhere too. But just in case there was no Main Street in Los Angeles, we decided our meeting point would be the Holiday Inn closest to the center of downtown.

The Cork and I hit the road first. We started from somewhere around Papago Park just to the north of the Arizona State campus. If we went west on Route 202 we would either connect with Interstate 10 heading directly through the desert to Los Angeles, or we would wind up going north on Route 60, connect back with good old Interstate 40, and head into the city that way. Sometimes when you were hitchhiking, it didn't matter exactly which road you were on as long as you were moving and headed in the general direction of where you intended to go. In many ways, this sort of logic could have been applied to our lives as well.

It was a good thing that we were thinking flexibly when we were leaving Phoenix because The Cork and I found ourselves heading northwest out of the city, which probably was not the preferred route. Our first ride dropped us off near Sun City at the turnoff for Peoria, Arizona which was just a few miles out on Route 60. I was killing some time along the side of the road telling The Cork about my childhood in Peoria, Illinois about the time a car pulled off the road behind us. We were encouraged because we thought we might have another ride already, but it turned out to be Joon and Skip getting dropped off from their first ride. It looked as though almost everyone going out of Phoenix that morning was headed up to Peoria. Though we were just a little way from where we'd started, our reunion was cause for another small celebration due to the coincidence. It also seemed to be a good thing that both pairs of us found ourselves on the same route, even if it was probably not the best way to go.

Using proper road etiquette, this time The Cork and I invited Joon and Skip to venture out first. They got a ride fairly quickly with a hippie couple in an old pickup that was decked out with a handmade plywood camper on the back. Presumably as an indication of their connection to the rest of the world, the couple had painted "The Hobbits" in bright orange paint on the side of the camper section of the truck. After Joon and Skip rolled off, The Cork and I put our thumbs in the air again and joked about all the wealthy old ladies who probably resided in Sun City. When time started to pass with us still standing by the side of the road, we joked about going door to door to see if we could borrow one of the Cadillacs they'd stored in their garages next to the old snow blowers they'd probably lugged with them from Wisconsin, Minnesota, North Dakota, or some such place.

But about then our trip began in earnest. Just past us, a shiny new Chevy pickup slid to a stop on the gravel shoulder of the highway. In it were two guys in dark sunglasses who might have looked a little shady around the edges. The Cork balked a bit as we started to hop into the open bed of the pickup truck. He glanced at me as if to say, "Are you sure about this?" Particularly because it was a brand new truck, I hadn't thought a thing of it. The driver popped his head through the fancy sliding window on the back of the cab and asked, "Where are you headed?"

The Cork and I responded in unison like choirboys, "Los Angeles."

The driver said that he was headed for Las Vegas, but that he would "…get us up the road a bit."

"Good enough," I said.

We would have a short ride…probably only as far as Wickenberg or Kingman. It didn't matter. We were going to be moving away from the city. We positioned ourselves against the back of the cab to block the wind as the truck spun its tires in the gravel and took off up Route 60.

The Cork and I were happy to get going again, but it turned out that there were only moments to sit still. Every couple of miles or so the truck would screech to a halt along the side of the road and pick up another stray hitchhiker. One by one, a new person would hop in the back of the truck just as we had a few minutes earlier. Each time, the driver would ask where the person was headed and each time the new passenger would reply "Los Angeles." And each time, we would all hear, "Well, I'll get you up the road a bit." By the time we were coming into Wickenberg, there were nine people in the pickup truck…the two in the cab and seven others packed tightly along the steel walls of its bed.

"Up the road a bit" I suspected that everyone had some notion that something would need to happen because Route 60 would split at Wickenberg for either Kingman and Las Vegas to the north or Aguilla, Blythe, the desert, and Los Angeles to the west. The Cork and I were already anticipating what a mess it was going to be if all the hitchhikers in the truck got dropped off at Wickenberg so that they could link back into Interstate 10. We had already decided that, if it looked like that was going to happen, we would stay in the truck to Kingman and then head into Los Angeles on Interstate 40, just to free ourselves of the crowd.

About that time, the truck veered off the road to the left, bounced its human cargo wildly through the potholes of a huge gravel parking lot, and came to rest in front of a liquor store. There was a welcome silence as the engine shut down and heavy limestone dust settled over everyone in the back of the truck. Slowly, people removed themselves and their stuff from the truck and loosely congregated in something like a circle around the driver.

"My name is Don," said the driver. "On this fine Monday, I am headed to Las Vegas in this truck that I have to deliver there on Wednesday." Simultaneously, The Cork and I realized that Don must have been the other person who beat Joon to the drive-away place that morning. He was the lucky one who had gotten the only vehicle leaving Phoenix for anywhere.

"As you can see," said Don, "I'm already having a good time on this trip." Of course, we could see the nearly empty fifth of rum he held in his hand. "And I intend to keep having a good time, at least until Wednesday."

Then Don said, "You all look like fine people…except perhaps for you, Old Man," as he began to chide one seventy-something guy who was dressed in a slightly tattered but perfectly matching suit, tie, and hat. "I really like your hat," Don said. "Can I wear it?" The Old Man shook his head "no" without making eye contact or uttering a word. Everyone else just watched. Don didn't seem to take much offense. He continued.

"I am headed to Las Vegas, but all of you sons-of-bitches are headed toward LA, right?" Don looked around the circle as each of the newly formed group of sons-of-bitches answered his question or nodded affirmatively. Sure, some were going here or there short of the city, but it was clear that everyone wanted to head west out of Wickenberg in that direction. Then Don said, "Well, if all of you are going to LA, then I am going to LA, too," and started laughing…just as Jake would have done.

Looks of relief and exuberance rolled around the circle as if everyone now felt safe and sound knowing that they were going to make it to their destinations sometime on this Monday. Except for the Old Man. And except for The Cork, for whom Don's proclamation didn't land quite so comfortably. He kept looking at me and shifting his weight from one foot to the other, particularly when Don announced, "Then we will need another bottle," and walked off into the liquor store pitching his used fifth into an unlined trash barrel by the front door. Once again The Cork looked at me as if to say "Are we really going to do this?" I didn't give it a second thought. Of course we were.

When Don returned, he reassumed his group-leader-like role and assigned The Cork and I to ride in the cab with him. It turned out that the guy Don had been riding with when he picked us up was a hitchhiker as well, who was now being relegated to the back of the truck. Others took their positions in an orderly fashion in the bed of the truck.

As Don refired the engine, the Old Man had yet to join the others in the back. He just stood there in the parking lot, silently, holding his small, brown-striped, hard-shelled suitcase in his right hand. Nothing changed until Don took notice, stuck his head out the driver's side window and said "Come on Old Man, I won't bite you." With that, some of the others beckoned to the Old Man as well and he eventually put one foot on the bumper, stretched the other over the tailgate, and settled down right in the center of the circle of humanity in the back of the pickup. We were off again.

Headed out of Wickenberg, I was seated in the middle of the cab with The Cork on the right with his window rolled all the way down. The southwestern air was very warm, so the back sliding window between the cab and the bed of the truck was wide open as well. Don had me crack open the new bottle of rum he had purchased at our Wickenburg stop. I handed it to him while leaving it inside the twisted brown bag that came with it. I thought this little touch might give Don the impression that I was not new to drinking hard liquor from a paper bag in the front seat of a pickup truck headed toward a desert.

Don seemed to appreciate it. He held the bottle in his right hand and took two good-sized gulps. Then he twisted to his right and raised the bottle through the back window of the cab offering a drink to the others. I watched as the bottle gradually made its way around the circle of men in the back of the truck. Some took very hardy gulps and others took tiny sips. I enjoyed watching people share the bottle. No one declined a drink except the Old Man.

When the bottle reappeared on the end of someone's arm at the back window, The Cork and I quickly recognized what was coming next. It was our turn to drink from this bottle that had just passed through fourteen hands to seven stranger's mouths. Nevertheless, we took our obligatory swigs, thanked Don for his kindness, and returned the half-empty bottle to him. Don seemed really pleased with himself. I thought The Cork was going to throw up.

Although Don didn't disclose much about himself and we didn't really ask, he wanted to know all about the two of us. Where were we from? What were we doing? Where were we headed? Why? This sort of interrogation was so common while hitchhiking. Outside of a city, it was usually the case that drivers picked up hitchhikers either to have conversation or to get relief from driving for long distances. It was almost as if one of these two things constituted a hitchhiker's dues for taking a ride. On the earlier San Francisco trip, I'd piloted a brand-new garbage truck for two hundred fifty miles through Iowa while the driver attempted to catch a little sleep.

Although I was giving Don short descriptive answers to all his questions without giving away too much of anything, The

Cork seemed to be more interested in conversation than I had expected. I listened for more than half an hour as he went on about having lost our factory jobs in Chicago, getting kicked out of Technical school, trying to avoid the selective service, being down on our luck, sleeping on the subway trains, having nothing to our names, and looking for a fresh start once we made it to the west coast. I realized that The Cork wanted it known that we had nothing with us, especially money, that anyone might have an interest in. He lied masterfully and within a short time I found myself playing right along. The Cork was probably right that we needed to present ourselves in a way that would not make us an easy mark for anyone in this diverse group of people.

Unfortunately however, we did have one thing that Don had noticed: Skip's guitar, which I had agreed to carry since it was my idea to bring it along in the first place. After chatting for as long as we did and after having several more hits on his bottle, Don wanted to hear it. The Cork called through the back window for the guitar to be passed forward from the tail end of the pickup where two of the men had been using it as a backrest.

Strangers' hands hoisted the case as if it contained the Holy Grail through the back of the truck and through the back window into the cab. I struggled slowly and awkwardly to get the guitar out of its case and to get myself situated in the middle of the front seat so I could play it. I really didn't want to play it because I already knew what Don would be after and that wasn't what I played. Sure enough, after tuning and strumming a few G chords, Don said "Play me some fuckin' country."

Of course, I didn't know any country, let alone any fuckin' country, but based on the way the Cork had been talking about us, I felt that I really should have. I feared that Don would become suspicious of us if I didn't. So, I tried to quell him by singing Cat Steven's "Where do the Children Play" with a fuckin' twang in my voice. It was the closest I could come, but not surprisingly, it didn't work. Don interrupted me by reaching over and placing his right hand over the strings of the guitar. He wanted something by Merle Haggard, Conway Twitty, Miss Dolly, or Buck Owens. He had never even heard of Cat Stevens. I tried to soothe him with one of Ry Cooder's railroad songs, but my version of "Mr. Railroad Man" didn't work that well for Don, either.

Although I kept trying, I could sense Don becoming increasingly belligerent as he continued to drink and I fell short of his musical appetite. Finally, I just put the guitar back in its case and passed it back through the window, for its safety as well as my own. The Cork had become pretty quiet by this point. He knew he had put me in that situation. I knew we both suspected that Don would be on to us.

About that time, we were approaching Blythe. Don had finished the second bottle and decided it was time for another stop. We pulled into a lonely gas station to fill up. As Don began filling the tank, everyone else was milling around inside and outside the station. It must have been quite a sight. I am sure anyone else who stopped there would have wondered what in the world our rag-tag group was doing headed into the desert on a Monday afternoon.

As he was placing the nozzle back onto the pump, Don hollered out that he was up for gas donations if anyone wanted to contribute. Not surprisingly, no one immediately stepped forward with anything to offer. At that awkward moment, The Cork and I were standing off to the side recounting our experience to that point. We were both pretty sure that the reason no one was offering anything to Don was not because they didn't appreciate what he was doing. It was because, if they actually had anything, they wouldn't want anyone else to know about it. It was a way for people to keep themselves safe on the road. Didn't Don know that hitchhikers were not expected to pay for their rides? Presumably that is why they were hitchhiking. That was the way it was. The Cork and I decided we had to hold off on giving Don the few bucks he surely deserved.

After Don's bold call for donations, everyone fell silent for a while, including Don. Finally, someone spoke up. One of the men who had been riding in the back said he had something to contribute if Don could use it. The man appeared to be a healthy, dark-skinned, and well-dressed American Indian who had spent a good deal of his time outdoors. He was as big as The Cork and, similarly, seemingly gentle in demeanor.

Slowly the group reassembled around The Indian. He announced to everyone that he was going back to his home in California from New Mexico where he had recently struck gold on a plot in some remote mountains. As he pulled his nicely worn, thigh-length leather jacket to the side, everyone must have noticed the six-inch knife in a beaded sheath that he had hanging from his belt. He tugged a tiny leather drawstring bag out of his pocket and emptied a small amount of dust into his hand. He showed it to Don and offered him a bit of it to help with the gas.

Without taking more than two seconds to think about it, Don just started laughing, apparently concluding that the dust was not actually gold and declaring very loudly that anybody who thought it was must be an idiot. The Indian got a serious and angry look on his face, but didn't do anything. He just said, "You're wrong," as Don walked off into the station. After that, a few of the others approached for a look, but no one wanted to piss off Don or the Indian by taking sides, so no one said much else about it. It was clear that the Indian remained convinced that he was carrying gold and there was little doubt that he was ready to protect it if that became necessary.

Don paid for the gas and used the outhouse-style bathroom around the side of the building. He also paid for another bottle of rum that he had discovered on one of the dusty shelves behind the counter and a paper bag full of cold sodas that he eventually rationed out to the group. He hoisted his bottle in the air as he returned to the truck as if he had just claimed another trophy on behalf of all his new pals.

Don also made some new assignments. Rocky, a short, toothless, middle-aged guy with stubby hair on his head that perfectly matched the hair on his face was assigned to the driver's seat. The Old Man would sit in the middle of the front seat and Don would take the right side passenger seat of the cab. The Cork and I were shuffled to the back along with the guitar which was of no fuckin' use to anyone anyway.

Although the frequent stops had probably become frustrating for some, we only made it a few miles down the road before pulling off again on the shoulder of the highway. There was a commotion in the front seat as Rocky quickly stopped the vehicle. In an instant, Don and the Old Man were out of the cab standing on the side of the road with everyone in the back watching intently. Apparently, Don had begun to tease the Old Man again about letting him wear his hat. Don kept saying how much he liked it and that he "Just wanted to try it on." The Old Man still wasn't saying a word, which seemed to provide more reason for Don to carry on. Don was getting sloppily drunk and had begun to lose any charm that his seeming acts of kindness might have highlighted.

Others jumped in this time to keep things from getting totally out of hand. Gentle pleas like, "Don't worry about it," "Be cool," and "It'll be okay," came from several different mouths in the back of the truck. Even so, Don continued to taunt the Old Man. Then, a much louder voice was heard above the others from the back of the truck. The Indian instructed Don in no uncertain terms to "Leave him alone."

There was a long eerie silence as everyone became very still. I envisioned Don and The Indian knife-fighting on the side of the highway. Then Clint, a lanky forty-something guy who had just finished telling us about being released from an Arizona prison that morning came up with a solution. He volunteered to switch places with the Old Man in the front seat. Somewhat reluctantly, both Don and the Old Man accepted the idea. Evening was beginning to set in and everyone seemed to know that we needed to get moving again if we were going to get through the desert in the dark without freezing. I couldn't help but think that Clint's solution would also spare him from the cold that everyone knew was coming. He leaped over the side of the truck and into the comfy front seat. With some prodding, the Old Man eventually stepped up over the tailgate and reclaimed his place in the back. I found it interesting that he said nothing to The Indian who had come to his rescue.

Past Blythe, after the third bottle had made another round, Don passed out in the front seat and a sense of calm blanketed the back of the truck. I commented to The Cork that, "We were like a group of strangers thrown together on some sort of mission impossible - huddled around a campfire on a cold and windy night in the woods...going sixty-five miles an hour without the woods or the campfire."

With Rocky, Clint, and Don in the front, the two of us were left with the Old Man, Jimmy, Vince and The Indian in the back as we rolled into the desert with the stars just beginning to show up in the California sky. There was also a sense of safety knowing Don was asleep and The Indian appeared ready to make sure everything went smoothly. We seemed so far away from the rest of the world...certainly far away from the college campus and our concerns about the War.

It was about two hundred miles from Blythe to Los Angeles. On this night, most of those miles would wind through the dark and lonely desert. It was getting colder and there was nothing to do but hunker down and feign sleep, sit quietly, or speak to each other over the bone-chilling wind. Everyone except the Old Man began to move a little closer together. I watched him as he sat up very straight with his hand holding his hat on his head to keep it from blowing away in the wind.

Jimmy, a fast-talking kid who said he was from Milwaukee, started up a conversation with the Indian about his gold. Although I figured the Indian had pretty much already said everything he was going to say, Jimmy seemed to be fishing for more information about where the gold had come from, how much there was, and what prospecting was like. The Indian seemed to tolerate the questions, but it was clear to The Cork and I that he wasn't providing any proprietary information. Between his questions, Jimmy carried on about his own escapades and how he was heading to California to work with a friend who had started a strip club with some "really hot dancers" just south of LA. I took Jimmy with a serious helping of salt because it was clear he didn't know much about Milwaukee. He said he had never been to a Braves game, toured the Miller's brewery, or had a Dal's Hot Dog. Nevertheless, listening to him strut his stuff filled up some of the time.

Vince, a pencil-thin guy with pants that were too short for his long legs, turned out to be almost as quiet as the Old Man. His silence made me wonder if he had something to hide. As he had done earlier in the front seat, The Cork held the audience for the longest time, which continued to surprise me. Once again he carried on about our hard times in Chicago, being down on our luck, heading to California for a new start...his story was even more finely tuned than it had been earlier with Don. He didn't miss a beat. Even the Old Man seemed to perk up a bit while the Cork was going on. I wondered if he was seeing right through The Cork's bullshit in the same way I felt I was seeing through Jimmy's. One time when he appeared to smile, I suspected that the Old Man may have actually appreciated it. Due to his appearance and his silence, I assumed he was brighter than the rest.

A little past what we figured was about halfway through the desert, Don came back to life in the front seat of the truck. He poked his head through the sliding glass window and announced that we would be stopping again soon so that he could get a bite to eat.

Under the street lights of Indio, with nine people crammed into an open pickup truck, Rocky took a slow right hand turn into the parking lot of a Sambo's restaurant. I don't think anyone had any idea how this was going to work out. Who would sit with whom? Would someone actually order something? Who would be willing to show everyone else that they actually had money to pay for whatever they wound up ordering? In what seemed like mass indecision, we all walked around aimlessly in the parking lot until Don finally made his move for the entrance.

The Sambo's at Indio was just like every other Sambo's, Denny's, or Big Boy restaurant I had ever visited. It was just off the street with big picture windows along the front of the building and lots of seats with a view of the sidewalk and the street. It had counter stools, booths, open tables with four chairs, and a couple of big round tables where entire families or groups could sit. The waitresses wore faded yellow dresses with white trim and "Hello" name tags introducing themselves as Marjorie, Susan, or Maxine. Mostly, they waited on older men who sat with their black coffee and morning papers all day long.

Don walked in and took a seat at one of the big round tables. I wondered if he thought we were all going to gather around his table as we had in the truck. Rocky, Clint, and Vince joined him. The Indian was the first to venture out toward another table. Jimmy joined him. Not knowing exactly what to do, The Cork and I headed to the bathroom. When we came out, we also struck out on our own and took seats at the counter, two stools away from the Old Man who was sitting there by himself drinking water and a cup of coffee and eating something from his pocket that had been wrapped in wax paper.

Although it had to have been a while since anyone had eaten, Don was the only one who ordered a full meal. He had the super-duper Sambo's Pot Roast and Mashed Potatoes or something like that. A few others ordered plain sandwiches. Everyone had water or coffee. The Cork and I decided we would split a hamburger platter, although we sacrificed our manners to make it look like we were used to eating out of tin cans. I think the Cork devoured his half-burger in a single bite...partially because he had to have been starved and partially because he didn't want anyone to see us eating.

When it came time to pay, one of the waitresses approached Don with a single check for his table of four. He laid down a five dollar bill which would have been enough to cover his meal, got up, and walked into the bathroom. The Cork and I watched as the others at Don's table settled up their business by laying money on top of the check he had received. The Indian and Jimmy did the same with their check. We followed suit, placing three one dollar bills on top of the check on the counter in front of us. We sat while the waitress settled each of the accounts. It was easier than I thought it would be since most of the guys appeared to pay their bills to the penny and no one was expecting any change.

As we were sitting there finishing up our drinks, Don reappeared from the bathroom and walked by the counter behind the Old Man. Without saying a word, he snatched the Old Man's hat, placed it on his head and started to swagger back through the restaurant toward the big round table. Just as quickly, the Old Man sprang from his seat, grabbed the hat off Don's head, and shot out the door. A few people laughed as Don ranted to the whole place about the "Stupid old coot and his precious hat."

Then, the entire restaurant witnessed one of the most fascinating things that I had ever seen. With his little suitcase in hand, which probably held everything he owned in the world, the Old Man positioned himself on the lighted sidewalk right in front of the restaurant. Everyone watched through the picture windows as he neatly set his suitcase on the perfectly-mowed grass by the sidewalk and laid it open. He took off his hat and placed it on the sidewalk. Next he proceeded to remove two long leather whips and two pairs of plastic machinist's goggles from the very top of his suitcase. He laid one whip and one pair of goggles on the sidewalk next to the hat. He pulled the other pair of goggles through his thin pure-white hair and over his eyes. Finally, he stared in Don's direction inside the restaurant and began cracking his whip on the cement next to the hat.

The vision of the Old Man standing in front of Sambo's with his goggles and whips was almost too much for me. I couldn't quite believe that he actually carried these things around with him in his tiny suitcase everywhere he went. On the other hand, somehow it seemed to make perfect sense. As we stared out the windows with our mouths hanging open, I shared a moment of eye contact with The Cork. I knew I would cherish the moment for the rest of my life.

As our group filed out of the restaurant, Don never did make a move toward the Old Man. He faked like he was going to do so a couple of times just to see the Old Man crack his whip again. Everyone walked toward the truck and away from the Old Man. As we pulled away from Sambo's with Don back in the driver's seat, we watched over the tailgate as the image of the Old Man packing up his things on the sidewalk gradually disappeared from our view. Silently, I was sure everyone except Don wished him well.

Back on the road again, Don rediscovered what was left of his third bottle of rum and began to carry on again with Clint and Rocky in the front seat of the truck. The rest of us sat pretty silently in the back. We huddled up against the cold of the desert and the uncertainty of whatever would happen next.

Somewhere between Indio and the Palm Springs exit, skinny Vince suddenly came alive, made his way through the bed of the truck to the sliding window, and began exchanging words with Don. The wind was too strong to hear much of what was being said, but moments later the truck pulled over to the side of the road again. There we said goodbye to Vince out in what seemed like the middle of the desert. None of us in the back were quite sure what this was all about until we came to another stop at a highway checkpoint a few more miles up the road. As government officials of some kind were checking out our truck, it became clear that Vince probably did have something to hide, although no one hazarded any guesses as to what that might have been.

Pretty soon, lights and other signs of civilization began to become more common again. It was now a sure bet that we were going to make it out of the desert and at least somewhere close to Los Angeles that night. And just as we had come together on the stretch of highway back near Phoenix, our group began to disperse. The Indian and Jimmy hopped out together somewhere around the Beaumont exit, suggesting that perhaps they had formed some sort of partnership. Scruffy Rocky said his thanks and goodbyes just before we hit Riverside. These departures left The Cork and I alone again in the back of the pickup, just as we had been earlier in the trip, jammed up against the cab to protect ourselves from the wind.

In the meantime, Don and Clint seemed to have become good buddies up in the front of the truck. This became clearer as the Cork and I noticed the truck pulling off the highway and heading into Riverside. We both knew this could be a mess if we wound up someplace away from the main route into Los Angeles, so I quickly got to my knees, poked my head through the sliding glass window, and asked Don what was up.

Don was sloppy drunk again by this point. At first he didn't even respond to me. He just kept addressing Clint in the seat next to him. After my second or third inquiry, Don finally informed me that he was going to deliver Clint to his doorstep in Riverside. Remarkable. This guy had just gotten out of prison that morning for who knows what, he had already talked himself into the warm front seat of the truck, and now he was getting Don to deliver him to his front door. Pretty darn skillful, I thought.

We had to drive around in Riverside until Clint was finally able to figure out where he was supposed to be going. Apparently, he had never been to this house before because he had some directions written on a crumpled piece of notebook paper he had pulled from his shirt pocket. We eventually got onto the correct street. And finally, with all of us checking out the house numbers together, we found the right place. Clint announced that this was where his wife had been staying since he'd been sent off to prison. We had no idea how long it had been since he'd seen her.

As Clint stepped out of the passenger door, he politely invited the rest of us into a place where he had never been in order to have a welcome-home drink with his "Old Lady." This idea seemed unfathomable to the Cork and I and we were pleased when Don agreed that, "The rest of us need to get on to Los Angeles." This was fine with Clint. However, that being the case, he asked if we would wait just a minute while he ran into the house. This was fine with Don.

Clint was in and out of the house in a flash with a jacket in his hand. We weren't quite sure if he was going to bring Don some sort of present for having given him the ride all the way from Phoenix, but we might have known better. When Clint returned to the truck, he asked Don if he would take him down the street to a bar so he could see some of his old buddies again. The Cork and I wondered silently about his relationship with his "Old Lady."

After saying farewell to Clint at the neighborhood bar, The Cork and I reassumed our positions in the front seat of the truck and sat silently as drunken Don headed back toward the highway. We figured we still had about fifty long miles to go before reaching Los Angeles.

The ride into the city was a bit disconcerting for several reasons. For one, Don was not in good control of the truck and kept inadvertently changing lanes every time he looked in our direction to talk. Several times I thought The Cork was going to push his sneakers through the floorboard as if he could help brake the truck. For another, Don had begun asking us what we were going to do and where we were going to go once we got to Los Angeles. Without speaking, The Cork and I both knew that, even if we had known, we weren't going to be clear about it with Don. So, we just said we were going to head downtown and find a place to sleep in a park or something. It was at that point that Don said, "I think we should stick together once we get into town."

The idea of sticking together with Don was surely the most troubling part of all. He was drunk as a skunk. We had already seen that he had a temper. Once he sobered up he would realize that he was hundreds of miles from where he had originally intended to go and he probably wouldn't be very happy about it. In fact, we suspected that he might turn on us in some way. Even as we got closer into the city, The Cork and I were not at all sure how the situation was going to work out.

Somewhere around Central Avenue, with the lighted exit signs announcing downtown Los Angeles, Don steered the truck off the highway. Just off the exit he pulled right up to a toilet that was located on the side of a busy gas station. He said, "Before we do anything else boys, it's time to take a fuckin' leak."

Don exited clumsily from the truck leaving his door wide open. Just as he stepped inside the john, The Cork took hold of my shoulder and said "Now's the time!" I replied, "Time for what?" The next thing I knew we were grabbing our things from the back of the truck and running up the hillside next to the gas station toward a stand of bushes back by the highway. I had never seen The Cork move so quickly.

We scrunched ourselves into the bushes and turned so that we would be able to see what happened when Don came out of the bathroom. We were above the gas station, about fifty yards away. It was dark except for the bright lights that glowed around the perimeter of the building. Although there was no activity on the side of the building where the bathroom was located, we could see from our perch that it was a very busy place out front as people moved in and out the of the station. It was as if there were huge stage lights on the whole scene.

The door of the bathroom slowly reopened. Don stepped out, took about three uneven paces, and stopped. Both doors of the truck were hanging open. We could see the last bottle of rum in its twisted brown paper bag on the front seat. A couple of empty soda cans had fallen from the open door of the cab and were lying on the ground. Don's nylon duffle bag was the only thing left sitting in the bed of the empty pickup.

Don moved toward the truck and shuffled in a complete circle around it. Then he glanced in several directions, even up the hill toward the bushes where The Cork and I were hiding. He never walked around the front of the building to see if we had gone inside the store. He didn't need to. Even in his condition, he would understand what had happened. He'd been ditched.

After a few moments of standing alone by the side of the truck, Don pushed the passenger-side door closed with his foot and moved back around to the driver's side. He worked his way inside the cab, shut the door, and sat there a while. The Cork and I watched intently and silently until he eventually pulled away and back up to the highway. He headed back in the direction we had come.

As I sat there jammed in the bushes with The Cork, I tried to reconcile what we had just done. Of course it made sense that we were going to have to part with Don, but I was already wondering if it was necessary for us to do it in the way that we did.

The Cork and I laid back for a time in the weeds, cans, and old newspapers under the bushes. Had it not been around 9:30, had we not had to try to meet back up with Joon and Skip, and had we not had the feeling that we needed to get farther away from Don and this situation, we might have slept in those bushes that night. Instead, we picked up our things and headed back down the little hill toward the street.

Central Avenue sounded about as close to "Main Street" as The Cork and I were likely to get. So, we took a guess which way was downtown and started walking. We talked about whether we should have ditched Don as we had. The Cork was absolutely sure we had done the right thing. I was pleased to be free of Don, but I still wasn't comfortable about what we had done. We hadn't even offered him any thanks.

We didn't really have a clue where we were in Los Angeles. While we'd been driving, it seemed like we had been in the city for a long time before we got to Central Avenue. We had seen the signs for downtown but didn't know how far it might be from the highway. It was too early to think about a Holiday Inn, we knew that for sure.

The Cork and I trudged on toward what we guessed was downtown Los Angeles. I think we were both still a little dazed from our journey. We had already walked a mile or so before we realized we were on a bus route. A bus passed us from behind and stopped about a hundred yards up the street. A half-dozen people got off.

We thought about running to catch it, but we were really tired and knew that it was too far up the street for us to get there in time. However, just at that moment we realized that Joon and Skip were two of the people who had just stepped out of the bus. Apparently they had not seen us. Worn out as we were, The Cork and I ran to catch up with them, hooting all the way up the street.

It was another great reunion. We were all relieved to be together again and there were many stories to tell. Joon and Skip said they had been dropped off just to the south and wound up grabbing the bus out of the Watts neighborhood. They said they were thankful they had not gotten mugged. The Cork and I shared small pieces of our experience in the truck. Each of us had so much to say, yet no one was listening. All of the recent memories were overwhelmed by the fact that we had somehow managed to link up again. Like characters on some strange California yellow brick road, the four of us skipped up the street toward downtown Los Angeles.

Homeward Bound
(Simon and Garfunkel)

Our spring visit in Los Angeles turned out to be relatively uneventful. We wound up residing on the flat rooftop of a three-story Co-op Fraternity House at UCLA. Our free roof accommodations were okay except for one night when all of us nearly ran off the side of the building after having been dive-bombed by birds, bats, or something.

Just like we typically did back at Loyola, we wound up checking out UCLA's Student Union during the day looking for things to do. We scored and smoked pot openly in a nearby park while we played a made-up game of "Derby Man Hat Toss" with what was rapidly becoming Skip's trademark head cover. The game consisted of nothing more than earning points for scoring ringers on the toes of another guy's foot, but we discovered we could play for hours if the pot was good. We also played a little guitar and walked along the beach from Santa Monica to Venice, where Skip and I co-wrote a song about its broken-down dock. Despite our best efforts to have a good time, almost as soon as we got to Los Angeles I was sure that each of us had begun to think about how we were going to get back to the Midwest.

Joon made the trek to a drive-away place two days in a row trying to get a car headed back to Chicago. Responsible as he was, he was having no luck at all. Although Joon kept telling us that the drive-away guy kept saying, "Maybe tomorrow," on the third day we all agreed that Joon should go in and take whatever vehicle they had that needed to go east. We figured that everyplace in the United States had to be east of Los Angeles and it was time for us to get moving again.

That morning Joon came back to the park looking depleted. He explained that he had located a car heading east, but it was an older customized Corvair hardtop that needed to be delivered to an Air Force base in…Minot, North Dakota. The rest of us weren't sure what was worse, the ride or the destination.

As if this news wasn't disappointing enough, there was one other problem. Although we would receive $150 in cash from the owner when we got to Minot, we had to put down $50 in cash in order to secure the car. Except for the credit card, fifty dollars would wipe out our bank.

After pacing around in different directions again, we reconvened and decided that we had to go for it. The Cork, Skip, and I scrapped together almost all the cash we had and gave it to Joon to go back to the drive-away place and take the Corvair. While he was away, the rest of us determined that all we had left were two one-dollar bills and some coins totaling just a little more than three bucks. We decided to use the last of our money for a loaf of bread, the biggest jar of peanut butter we could afford, and a pack of cheap cigarettes from a nearby convenience store. Trying to make light of the situation, I told Skip and The Cork that I had heard that a person could survive on peanut butter alone, and cigarettes of course. Neither of them was very enthused about my wit and let me know it. Since he did not smoke, The Cork assumed the role of the person who would ration out the cigarettes to the rest of us. We all knew that this two or three day trip was not going to be easy, particularly if we were in the midst of nicotine withdrawal.

About 3:00 that afternoon, Joon pulled up to the park with our new wheels. It was beige Corvair with a stick shift, customized interior, fancy aluminum wheels, and barely room for two, let alone four. Clearly, the car was someone's pride and joy, but not any of ours. As usual, Joon took on the initial driving duties while The Cork and I crammed into the tiny back seat. We were homeward bound.

Near the beginning of our trek to North Dakota, we passed within about fifty miles of the Grand Canyon at around 2:00 in the morning. Surprisingly, despite our situation, The Cork still wanted to go see it. Since we had no choice but to rely on Joon's credit card for gas, since our gas tank was pretty low at the time, and since it was the middle of the night, we finally convinced The Cork that it was special enough for him to have been "about fifty miles" from the Grand Canyon. We told him that the terrain where we were must have looked something like the terrain around the Grand Canyon. He eventually played along with us, but it was clear to everyone that he was pretty disappointed. What was he going to tell his mother?

After driving almost continuously from Los Angeles into Colorado and low on peanut butter and cigarettes, we were getting desperate. Not knowing what else to do, we pulled off the highway at Pueblo to see if we could find Cowboy's house. Fortunately, it turned out that it wasn't very hard. Late that afternoon, we pried ourselves from the Corvair and walked up to the door. Although our arrival must have been a huge surprise, it turned out that Cowboy's family was very much like Cowboy. His mother immediately welcomed us into the house for dinner and offered us a place to stay for the night. His sister gave Joon $20 in cash on his promise to pay her back at some point in the future. In exchange, I suppose we provided Cowboy's family with many fresh insights about Cowboy. Their hospitality was so welcome.

By the time we hit the Black Hills of South Dakota the next day, the temperature had begun to drop dramatically, it was beginning to snow, and the little Corvair was beginning to struggle. We had zoomed from record heat on the west coast to what had to be near record cold in the mountains. It must have been tough for the poor thing to haul four guys across country into the hills of South Dakota, because now it had begun to lose power. Every twenty miles or so the lights would begin to dim and we would have to slow to a stop, sit for a while, and then push the car to get it restarted.

None of us except The Cork knew much of anything about cars. The Cork suspected that the problem was with the regulator. On his advice, we pulled into Sturgis, found a station that would take Joon's credit card and replaced the regulator for eighteen dollars.

It didn't work. We were only about sixty miles outside of Sturgis when the car started acting up again. It was totally dark by that time and we were driving on a barren two-lane road with our lights and radio off to save the battery. We didn't think this was particularly dangerous because the snow was lighting up the night and we were only moving about thirty miles an hour most of the time anyway.

Pretty soon the car started dying again, just like it had before. This time The Cork suspected that since we had already replaced the regulator, the problem must have been with the alternator. Somewhere in the hills of South Dakota in what already seemed like the middle of the night with heavy snow beginning to fall, we found a station with an alternator and a guy who knew how to replace it. Just as importantly, he was willing to put the thirty bucks on Joon's credit card.

As we were getting set to leave that station at around 1:00 in the morning, the service guy casually suggested that we better get our chains on the car if we were going to be headed north toward Minot. Chains? Somehow, the guy who owned our little west coast hot rod actually had a set of snow chains in the front trunk of the car. Unlike us, perhaps he had been thinking ahead. We managed to get the chains on each of the rear wheels and headed back out on the two-lane. Time and, to some degree, space didn't matter much anymore. It couldn't. We spent most of the remainder of that night in a blizzard with the chains slapping the wheel wells of the car, rumbling from gas station to gas station so that we could go inside and warm ourselves against the rapidly dropping temperatures. We learned that Corvairs were very much like Volkswagen Beetles when it came to delivering horsepower and heat. There wasn't much of either. Very late that night we rolled into another of what seemed like an endless string of rural gas stations after the plastic dashboard in the Corvair began to crack apart in the cold. In between all the stops, we had traveled about four hundred fifty miles that day. All four of us fell asleep in the parking lot with the car running.

It isn't easy to tell the difference between day and night in a car covered with several inches of snow. We were awakened by someone pounding on the front windshield. The intruder was dressed like an Eskimo with a fur-lined hood that made his beet-red face barely visible. He scrapped some of the insulating snow off the glass, looked in with one exposed eyeball, and said something like, "What the hell are you kids doing out here? You are going to kill yourselves with that car running. You damned idiots better wake up!" The rest of us shuffled a bit as Joon casually switched off the ignition without even looking as if he had awakened. We rested for another half-hour or so before pushing on toward Minot. That gas station got none of our business even though the attendant might have saved our lives.

Actually, even though the temperature was now way below zero, moving up the road in the morning sunlight felt pretty good. I think everyone had some sense of optimism that we would be out of the Corvair before too long. Doing forty on ice-packed Route 83 with our new regulator and alternator, and without the noisy chains, we figured we would get to Minot sometime around mid-afternoon.

Once again I don't think any of us had even given a thought as to what we were going to do when we got to Minot. Of course, we would get rid of the car and we would get our delivery money back. However, I don't think anyone had considered how we were going to get from Minot back to Chicago. Surely there was about zero chance that there would be a drive-away office anywhere in North Dakota and hitchhiking was just about unimaginable since we had no serious winter clothes.

Yet, as the upside of our journey would have it, when we pulled into Minot one of the first things we noticed was an Amtrak train station. Without even speaking to each other we all knew at the same time what we were going to do. Joon was going to get the car to its owner, get our $150 delivery money as well as $48 in cash refunds for the repairs we had done, and we would all purchase tickets on the 8:30 PM Empire Builder train back to Chicago. It sounded like a grand plan until Joon tried to contact the owner of the car from the pay phone at the Amtrak station. It turned out that he was gone on field maneuvers at the Air Force base and was not scheduled to return until early the following morning. It was hard for any of us to imagine what maneuvers must have been like in those freezing temperatures, although by that time we weren't feeling particularly sorry for the guy.

This news was discouraging to say the least. All four of us pouted around the train station for hours. I guess we figured we were just going to be stranded there until the following morning when Joon would go on maneuvers himself, if he had to, in order to get our money. However, it got worse when we were informed that the station would close for the night after the 8:30 train departed for Chicago.

After telling him about our plight, the official at the station was kind enough to let us stay inside until he finally locked up the building at 9:30. At that low point, we retreated back into the below-zero weather in the parking lot, warmed up the car as well as we could, and huddled in for what we all thought was going to be a miserable, if not deadly, night.

After about an hour into our effort to brave the cold, Joon was rustling as if he was well on his way to going berserk and the rest of us were just short of it. Perhaps we were all filled with too much carbon monoxide. Perhaps we were so tired it was just time to give up, tear the car to pieces, and break our way back into the warmth of the station. Finally, Joon said, "Fuck this shit," started the car, and pulled up the street to an empty Ramada Inn hotel. He hopped out of the car, ran across the snow-covered parking lot, and into the office. Within two minutes he was back at the car with a key to a single room. Although the rest of us slipped in a side door, no one was too worried about getting caught. We figured that the folks at the Ramada would be happy to have any guests on such a miserable night. Settling down in that room was another time of relief for everyone. We all made a pact that, if we had to, we would spend the rest of our lives paying off Joon's credit card.

The following morning Joon was up and out of the room before any of the rest of us had even moved. The next Empire Builder was leaving Minot sometime around 9:00 AM and he was bound and determined that we were going to be on it. Sure enough, Joon returned to the room just after 8:00 with our cash. Who cared that the guy was wildly happy to see his precious Corvair, broken dashboard and all? We trotted back down the street to the station, laid down cash for our four tickets, wolfed down a dozen McDonald's hamburgers for breakfast, grabbed a bottle of whiskey and a Yahtzee game at the neighboring convenience store, and jumped on the train for Chicago. We hung out in the club car drinking and playing dice all the way home. In an instant, we felt like we were riding in style on the Empire Builder.

After somewhere close to four thousand miles on the road in about nine days, we chugged into Union Station in downtown Chicago at about 5:00 in the afternoon. We didn't even have enough money to ride the subway back out to campus. Nothing mattered much at that point, though. Someone called and someone answered a collect phone call at the dormitory switchboard and someone drove downtown to pick us up. We were drunk again and exhausted, but very pleased to be back home again.

Tell Me Why
(Neil Young)

Classes started the day after we got back to Chicago. After the first one, the start of a new semester typically constituted a time of brief personal renewal for many students. Everyone seemed to know the drill. Students would check the big board for their schedules, determine where their classes were being held, and shuffle off to the Student Center or class depending on what they had scheduled. Within a few hours, it seemed, everything began to look pretty much as it had the semester before.

However, at the beginning of this semester, I didn't have any sense of renewal. I wasn't making little promises to myself about how I was going to get off to a good start, or how I was going to study harder and stay up with my assignments, or how I was going to get something other than low B's, C's, and incompletes this time around. All I cared to do was to see Rose. Saying goodbye to her as we pulled off for Los Angeles had been somewhere in my thoughts almost the entire time I had been gone, which seemed like it had been forever.

Although Rose had lived at the Edgewater Beach, I didn't feel as though I knew her very well. We had seen each other around for more than two years, but had rarely talked for more than a minute at a time. I knew she thought I was funny because she would always smile from a distance whenever I said funny things or acted silly. At the start of this semester I wasn't even sure where she lived. When I didn't see her around on the first day back at class, I began to ask around in a way that didn't make it too obvious that I was dying to see her. Someone said she had moved off campus, but no one seemed to know where. I started to get the impression that maybe no one actually knew Rose very well.

My lack of any sense of renewal at the start of the semester might have offered a clue as to what was going to happen to me next, but it didn't. I watched as everyone else got started again. Student life picked up right where it had left off the semester before. People huddled around their special tables at the Student Center, talked about the classes that they were taking, and started planning the next list of protest activities that would fill up their spring afternoons and evenings. To me, the whole routine suddenly seemed pretty used up.

I recall walking into the Student Center around mid-morning on the second or third day of that new semester. As I stood in the doorway searching for Rose, I looked around the huge room at all the four by ten tables that were full of students. I watched as people shuffled their newspapers, huddled with their fraternity and sorority friends, smoked their cigarettes, and drank their cokes or coffee. I listened as they commented on the latest stories from the War, laughed about how the Cubs were probably going to stink again, and cursed about the impossible schedules they had been assigned for the new semester. As I stood there in the doorway, all of the sudden I imagined that the room became very still and everyone looked in my direction. Someone pointed my way and made a comment to his friends. Someone laughed out loud. Others gestured for me to come on over and join them.

I didn't. I turned, walked out of the Student Center and across campus to the University Administration Offices. I asked the student-worker receptionist if I could see an academic counselor and sat down to wait my turn. The wait was fine by me because I had nothing planned and I didn't really know what I was going to talk about anyway. I had just found myself there…not much different than when I found myself in the back of the pickup headed to LA.

When my name was called, I picked up my little backpack and followed the counselor into his dark leather and wood-clad office. He asked me to sit down, which I did. Then he asked, "How can I help you?" For the longest time I didn't know what to say. I just sat there waiting to see what would happen next. Finally I said, "I haven't been to class yet this semester." My comment didn't seem to strike the counselor as being particularly unusual. He uttered a prolonged, "Yeeeesssss," and waited for whatever I had to say next. Then out of the wild blue I said, "I think I probably need to quit school."

From that point the counselor became very polite. I suspected that he could tell from my long silences that I was struggling a bit. In fact, I felt almost as I had as a child when I had to tell my father that I was feeling sick to my stomach. I knew that he was the person for me to talk to and that he would try to help me, but reporting discontent made me feel vulnerable or scared or something. When I was little, reporting that I was not feeling well was usually accompanied by tears. I certainly didn't intend to cry for the counselor. Finally, he asked me why I felt that it was necessary to quit school.

As usual, whenever somebody asked me a *why* question, I struggled to come up with an answer. Of course, I always had an interest in knowing *why* I felt certain ways, *why* I did certain things, *why* certain things had occurred, or *why* the stars went on shining, but there had already been countless times in my life when I simply did not know the answers. Sometimes I gave up trying to find answers and just watched as things happened around me and I responded to them. But this way of thinking would never do at a time like this. When it came down to it, especially at moments like these, people were expected to know. I was expected to know. People would think that it was my business to know. Who else would know?

I started hypothesizing as to *why* I needed to quit school and shared a few of the possible reasons with the counselor. I explained that I couldn't make up my mind what I was interested in studying at school. I had already changed majors twice with no concomitant change in my interest. Maybe I was bored. After all of the amazing things I had done in the previous two years, it now took a lot to excite me. I had not gotten very good grades up to that time. Bottom line was that I didn't know *why*. For all I knew, maybe space aliens or FBI agents were in command of my behavior. Maybe there was something else that I was supposed to be doing with my life…

Although I felt that I had given the counselor a lot to chew on, after I'd finished he didn't hesitate. He asked, "What is your draft number?" I recall thinking that my draft number wasn't much of his business, but I told him that my birthday was September 24th and my number was one ninety-five. He went to one of his file drawers, pulled out a sheet of paper, and said "That might not be good son." Placing his fingers on his chin, he said that it was only February, just a little over a month since the new draft had started, and they were already calling numbers higher than one hundred for induction. Clearly, the Counselor was attempting to provide me with a reason *why* I should stay in school.

We both sat there silently for awhile. Finally, as much to break the uncomfortable silence as anything else, I told the counselor that I wasn't sure that the draft made any difference with respect to my decision to quit school. My comment seemed to energize him a bit more and he went on about school deferments, the draft, and the importance of staying in school to avoid it. I had already heard all of his scary facts and although I continued to say that I thought I needed to quit school, the counselor pretty much tried to ignore these comments for the rest of our meeting.

As we were finishing up, he finally told me that there was really nothing for me to do if I wished to quit school. Although this sounded easier than I thought it would be, I told him I didn't understand. He explained that, since the bills had not been sent out yet for that semester's enrollment, all I needed to do was continue *not* going to class and to *not* pay the bill when it arrived from the Bursar's office. This was simple enough, although it was also clear that he had not given me an option to make a decision at that moment. As we were parting the counselor said, "If you decide to do this, I want you to know that you are welcome back to Loyola at any time." I thanked him for allowing me the opportunity to have been included in the first place. I was momentarily proud that I had proved them wrong about flunking out during my sophomore year.

I didn't tell any of my friends about my meeting with the counselor or about my inclination to quit school. Since I didn't actually have to do anything, there didn't seem to be any immediate reason for them to know.

The next afternoon as I was sitting by myself smoking a charcoal-filtered Lark cigarette on the front steps of the Student Center, I saw Rose walking up to the building from Sheridan Road. She was covered in her familiar blue pea coat and a long, hand-knitted scarf. Her short blonde hair had been wisped more than usual by the cool but almost spring-like breeze. She looked beautiful as always and, all bundled up, even more demure than ever. Our eye contact made it clear that we had both been waiting for this moment to come.

I stood up on the steps and waved to her. She saw me and waved back. I moved in her direction as she approached. We stood face to face on the sidewalk for a few silent and intense moments. Students were rushing around us to and from the building. Finally, we gave each other a very prolonged hug.

I didn't have anything else to do and there was nothing I would have rather been doing than spending time with Rose. As we sat outside on the steps, she wasn't talking much so I told her all about the trip, especially the part about hitchhiking from Phoenix to LA. I also told her how happy I was to be back in Chicago and to be seeing her again. Eventually, I told her about not having been to class and my thoughts about quitting school.

Rose sat close to me, listened well, and seemed content to have me do all the talking. Considering that she appeared to be showing up on campus just then, several days into the new semester, and considering that she was even more quiet than usual, I began to suspect that something important must have happened in her life. Over the next few days, this became clearer as her silence continued and she seemed to want to be with me as much as possible to walk her to her apartment, to the Jewel Food Store where she worked, and back and forth to campus.

I think others noticed that my relationship with Rose had developed pretty rapidly. Mostly, I thought they noticed because everyone really liked Rose and I imagined that many were not so sure about me anymore. I suppose they suspected I would wind up hurting her the way that they felt I had hurt Sunshine when it was time for that relationship to change. Rose was just not the kind of girl anyone in their right mind would have wanted to hurt.

Although Rose and I were spending almost all our available time together and it was clear that we had come together at an important time in each of our lives, our interaction didn't become sexual other than holding hands or each other for brief moments of time. One night alone at her apartment, about three weeks into our new relationship, I thought this situation might change. We had just finished a wonderful spaghetti dinner that she had prepared for the two of us. We laughed when I complimented her obvious cooking and homemaking skills. After we finished washing the dishes together and started to move from the kitchen to her sitting room, I turned in front of her, thanked her for the wonderful dinner, held her, and started to kiss her.

I was surprised when Rose instantly broke into tears, pulled away from me, and hurried over to a corner chair in the room. Before I had time to wonder about what I might have done wrong, she was apologizing through her tears for not being able to kiss me. I tried to console her by telling her it was okay and that it was not a big deal to me. I just wanted her to share whatever was the matter. She continued to cry as I knelt on the floor next to her chair. Finally, she told me that while I was gone she had been assaulted in the alley behind her apartment by two neighborhood boys. Watching her cry and listening to her describe the unthinkable details of the attack made me cry as well, but I was so happy to have had the opportunity to be there for her when she really needed someone. We held each other for a long time.

Father and Son
(Cat Stevens)

Other than my relationship with Rose, I had done my best to avoid seeing very much of my roommates and other friends since returning from Los Angeles. I had less interest in seeing them because I was afraid they were going to ask me how classes were going and I would have to tell them that they weren't. Then, of course, there would be a million other *why* questions that I wouldn't be able to answer.

However, I did know that I needed to talk face-to-face with my parents. I was concerned that this conversation would need to happen fairly quickly because soon my father would be receiving the bill from the Bursar's Office as he always did and I needed to tell him not to pay it. The following weekend in mid-February, I jump-started the Mustang that had been sitting out on the street for weeks and headed out for Peoria. The timing worked out pretty well because Rose was also planning to go to her family's home that weekend. I drove by the exit where I thought she lived on the way out of the city. That triggered a soft parade of warm thoughts about her that followed me almost all the way home.

My folks were always happy to see me when I arrived home from college late on a Friday night. I always acted years younger than I was whenever I walked in the door to the family home, as if nothing had changed me from the last time I left. My father typically thought I could use something to eat, so he got right to work making up bacon, egg, and Velveeta cheese sandwiches on white bread to which I would add the ketchup. It was his specialty and I ate them partly because I knew how much he liked to make them for me. The three of us sat in the squeaky metal stools at the old kitchen counter as I told them about my trip to Los Angeles. As I shared some of the stories, they shook their heads and smiled a lot, as usual. They seemed mildly shocked but simultaneously proud of my experiences. I also got caught up on the details and photos of dad's birthday which I had missed while traveling through Texas.

The next day I snatched an opportunity to be alone with my father when we went out to the Ben Schwartz Food Store to pick up a few things for the dinner that my mother planned to cook that evening. By the time we made it to the store, I had already broken the news that I had not been going to class and that I was pretty sure I was going to drop out of school. This came as a bit of a surprise to my father, so we sat in the car in the parking lot and talked some more.

My father was a very reasonable man. He rarely got upset in a way that anyone would have noticed. I think he had already been through enough with all my other brothers and sisters to get too upset about much of anything with me. However, he was concerned. One of the first things he asked me was if I understood that he and my mother could no longer help support me if I dropped out of school. This meant that I would no longer receive the one- or two-hundred dollar monthly checks he'd send me while I was enrolled in college. It had always been a rule in my family. If you were in college, you got financial help. If you were not or if you ever got married, the help would stop. I told my father that I understood the rules and respected them.

Then he gave me a little lesson on the reasons for going to college. He said that college was a place to find out what you wanted to do with your life. He also told me that, if I ever expected to have a job that paid any *real* money, I would need to have a college degree. When I told him that I didn't care much about making money and that I didn't need much to get by, he said that he'd felt that way once upon a time in his life, but that he eventually learned differently. He told me that somewhere along the line he discovered that, "Money is freedom."

My father knew I wouldn't like hearing this little mantra, and I didn't, even though I understood his logic. Finally, he asked me, "What are you going to do with your life?" At first I said that I didn't know, which in that moment was very true. I told him that many times it seemed as though I was just along for the ride. But he kept asking, "You have to do something, what are you going to do with your life?" I tried to sidestep the question again, but he didn't give up. He asked again. Then another amazing and completely unanticipated thing happened. I said, "I don't know what I'm going to do with my life...maybe I'll join the Army."

This air-splitting verbalization seemed to surprise both of us and it produced a long silence in the car. My father finally said, "You do know there is a war on don't you?" Of course I knew there was a war on and we both knew how much I disliked it. We had talked about it many times. Then, after another moment of silence, my father said, "Well, maybe joining the Army wouldn't be such a bad idea," and proceeded to reminisce a bit about doing part of his medical residency in Europe during WWII. My father had never talked much about his involvement in WWII, but at this moment he seemed pretty proud of it. I listened. As he finished, he paused and said, "...but this War is different."

Eventually we made it into the store where we picked out thick T-bone steaks, frozen peas, and other things we needed for our special dinner. As we were getting set to leave the store my father met one of his doctor friends by the check-out register. I remember him saying to his friend, "You remember my son Marty...he goes to college at Loyola in Chicago." Apparently, they both thought that was very nice.

I don't think I ever said anything about dropping out of school to my mother. At that moment, I think both my father and I had an understanding that she probably didn't need to know. Perhaps we both suspected that she would not have been very pleased.

After making the trip to the store, the rest of the visit was pretty relaxed and uneventful. I do remember my father coming to the basement on Saturday afternoon as I was playing my guitar and asking me, "Why don't you play any happy songs?" Until he asked, I don't think I had ever thought about it. It was true that I didn't really know any. I told him that I didn't know why; it was just what came out of me.

Not surprisingly, I felt pretty good about having confessed about school to my father. It was something like the good feeling I used to have whenever I got caught doing something terrible back in high school. I typically felt better for having been found out. It was good having moments of honesty with either of my folks. Each time I felt like they got to know me little better. I also knew that in earlier times, even if I got grounded or had my allowance cut in half, any imposed discomfort wouldn't last long. In fact I only stayed grounded for one day after a bunch of us got hauled in by the police for having borrowed one of my friend's uncle's cars before any of us had a driver's license. My parents had a special way of supporting their kids through the good times and the bad times. And I knew what they expected from me even if I couldn't always live up to it. We had a great visit.

Once again I found myself driving the old Mustang up Route 29 along the river away from Peoria. It was such a wonderful drive and once again the old farms on the hillsides next to the river carried me away. They were especially striking in the winter when I could see the pickup trucks on the snow-covered driveways, cows blowing smoke by the barns, and smoke curling up from the chimneys on the white, two-story farmhouses.

I was driving north toward Interstate 80 where I would cut east for the city. It was cold, but the sun was shining very brightly. It was Sunday around noon. The car radio was still tuned to a local Peoria station. When I noticed, it appeared to be the end of the weekend news. For whatever reason, the radio caught my attention. I turned up the volume.

The announcer was reading a list of local casualties from the War in Vietnam. He would state the person's name, say something about whose child they were and where they had lived, and then report the high school that they had attended. I had heard people read lists of the dead all the time at protest events, but I had never heard anything quite this close to home. Suddenly, it was as if I knew there was a reason for me to have been listening. I started to drive very slowly and waited.

It didn't take long. Within the next few listings, I heard the announcer state the name "Randy Jarrell," followed by the names of his parents, his home address, and our high school. I pulled the Mustang to the side of the road as the few cars that had been trailing me whizzed by. I switched off the radio. I noticed that I was breathing heavily. I leaned my forehead into the steering wheel and rested it there for a moment. Then I crumbled into tears.

I'd known of Randy. We all knew of each other in a high school that included less than a thousand students. He was a Holy Family kid, like Tingsly. He had been in most of my classes. He'd always had a girlfriend. He played football and wrestled. He was well liked.

But I'd never really known Randy. We didn't grow up on the same block. We didn't hang out together. We didn't go on double dates or anything like that. In fact, we'd rarely even spoken to each other. I hadn't even known he was in the military.

Nevertheless, there I was on the shoulder of the highway with my forehead bouncing against the steering wheel...crying as if I had just lost my best friend.

At that moment, although it seemed unbelievable even to me, it became clear what I was going to do next.

In Search of the Lost Chord
(An album by the Moody Blues)

The following afternoon, another Monday, I rode the elevated train a few stops south to a neighborhood I didn't know very well. There, just a block or so from the platform, was a military recruiting office. I walked up to the front of the building and stood outside for a few minutes while I finished a cigarette.

When I finally walked into the office, there was no one at the reception desk, so I poked my head into the doorway of the first office on the right side of the hallway. Inside were a couple of big guys in pressed uniforms standing around a desk where an older man in uniform was seated. They turned and looked at me. Without doubt, they noticed my wind-blown, shoulder-length hair, my faded blue jeans, my wet shoes tracking melted snow on their shiny floor, and the spacey look I surely had on my face. The older man at the desk said, "Can we help you young man?"

At that moment I wasn't quite sure if the question matched the answer I was about to give, but I responded, "I am here to find out about joining the Army." There was a long pause and I could tell they probably thought I was fooling around with them. Based on my appearance, they might have suspected I was there to start some kind of trouble. I wasn't sure if they were going to get angry and pitch my scrawny body back out on the sidewalk. Since they were just looking back and forth at each other and me, I restated my interest in a question: "Is this where I find out about joining the Army?" The men shared a few more inquisitive glances and smirks with each other as I stood there in the doorway. Then the older man said, "Son, this is the office for the Marines." "Are you here to join the Marines?"

I really didn't know the difference. I didn't fully understand that Army was one thing, the Marines were another, and the Navy and Air Force were something else again. I just considered them all a part of a big thing called "the military." After all, they all shared the same building to recruit people. Until that moment, I am not sure I had ever thought about their critical distinctions.

Not caring to own up to my ignorance, I finally said, "No, I am here to think about joining the Army."

"Well then," said the older man, "You need to go to the office down at the end of the hall."

I shuffled for a moment, thanked the men for their time, and backpedaled through the doorway into the hall. As I slowly began to move toward the room at the end of the hall I heard laughter from the Marines' office. I figured that they probably wouldn't have wanted me anyway.

When I got to the Army's office I already felt a little better prepared with my new recognition that the military consisted of different branches and that they recruited separately. I tapped on the wall next to the open door of the Army office. Inside at the desk, another older man looked me over and asked, "Can I help you young man?"

This time my response was a little clearer yet. "I am here to consider joining the Army." This uniformed man invited me in to sit down.

I sat in a chair in front of a big metal desk as the Recruiter leaned forward to get a better look at me. He asked me a few questions, including the one that always threw me about *why* I was there. I told him about school. I told him about not having any plans for the next part of my life. And I told him that I didn't understand very much about the War and the military and felt that I needed to learn more about what was actually happening in the world.

We didn't get much accomplished that afternoon, but I did learn a few more things. I remember that the Recruiter asked me, "What would you like to do in the Army?" This seemed like an odd question because, as far as I knew, soldiers were not given a lot of choices. I said, "I don't know, I thought I would be told what to do in the Army." I wondered to myself if that might have been a good thing for me at that point in my life. The Recruiter then explained that a draftee would spend two years in the Army doing whatever the military assigned him to do. This sounded like what I had understood, but it wasn't the whole story.

Acting a bit surprised by my lack of knowledge, the Recruiter then gave me a little smile and said, "If you enlist in the Army for three years, you can choose what you would like to do." Huh? Three years? Whatever I wanted to do?

"What are the choices?"

The Recruiter explained that he couldn't tell me exactly what I would be qualified to do in the Army until after I took an entrance evaluation. He was optimistic though. He was sure that since I had completed two and a half years of college, I would be likely to do well on my entrance examination and I would surely have lots of choices. He asked if I wanted to take the exam to see what I would be qualified to do. I had come this far, so I said, "Sure."

At the end of our conversation, the Recruiter scheduled me for an entrance examination. I went out of the office with a little sheet of paper that contained the date, time, and location of the test.

A few days later I showed up at the building where I was to take the examination. It was just west of the Loop, over near the neighborhood where the Maxwell Street Flea Market was held on Sunday mornings. I had been in this rough part of town several times before, but never realized that the testing station was there too. This was where we had purchased the miniature antique wood-burning stove that wound up at Munchkin's from six guys who were standing around it one cold Sunday morning. We gave them a dollar each, emptied the hot coals onto the snow, and hauled it away not knowing if any of them actually owned it or not.

The building looked like an old warehouse that had been remodeled for the purpose of giving military entrance examinations. I got there early and stood around outside smoking cigarettes. There were a hundred or more other guys hanging around out there doing the same thing, but I didn't speak to anyone.

After standing in a long line to get signed in, the first part of the agenda was the military intelligence test. I was welcomed into the testing room by a man in uniform who instructed me to sit in one of the desks. As I was looking around for an open desk, I heard a call from one of the front seats across the room. It was Cosmo from Loyola. Cosmo was some sort of drama or performance major who was well-known as a freak around campus. Although he was taller and typically wore a Santa Claus-like stocking hat, otherwise we looked pretty much alike. He called me over his way and invited me to sit in the empty desk behind him.

As I was getting seated Cosmo said, "So they called your number too, eh?" I wasn't about to tell Cosmo that I was there without having been told to show up, so I just mumbled something I knew he wouldn't be able to hear. Then we had a little small talk about the circus that was going on around us and Cosmo told me he was going to find a way out of it.

Maybe it was good that there wasn't much time to talk. The Sergeant at the front of the room introduced himself and welcomed everyone to the testing session. He gave incredibly detailed instructions about how to fill in the little circles on the answer sheets with the pencils he was about to hand out. I suspected that the instructions were probably relevant because many of the guys in the room might have never done this sort of thing before. Then the Sergeant walked over in front of Cosmo and said, "Take these pencils and pass them to the rear."

Cosmo hesitated. I wasn't sure what was going to happen next, but it was clear from his shuffling in his seat that something was about to. He didn't reach out to accept the pencils. A little miffed, the Sergeant repeated his instruction for the whole room to hear. "Recruit, take these pencils and pass them to your rear." Instead of reaching out for them, Cosmo looked back at the Sergeant and mimicked his order in a very loud theatric voice. "Sergeant, take those pencils and shove them all the way up your ass." While some in the room cracked up laughing and others just sat in dismay, two other Army guys showed up in the doorway and firmly invited Cosmo to leave the room. As he did, he looked back at me and said that he would see me later.

Although I suspected that the Sergeant had seen me talking to Cosmo and might not have been sure what I was going to do, he took a chance and repeated the instruction to me. I might have hesitated for a split second or so, but went ahead and passed them to the rear. I wondered if some sort of check mark went down next to my name for either having had words with Cosmo or for complying with the first instruction I'd been given from someone in the Army.

I figured that I probably did well on the military intelligence test. I remember being sure I was right on the question about the best way to pour a beer to avoid creating a foam overflow from a glass. After our brains were tested, the group was ushered into another area for the physical exam. Everyone stripped down to their underwear as instructed and placed their clothes in little baskets like those we used to use at the public swimming pool when we were kids. Without my clothes, I weighed in at one hundred thirty-five pounds, five feet eleven inches tall. We proceeded in file from station to station getting our eyes, ears, lungs, gonads, and butts checked out by guys who looked pretty much like us except for the length of their hair and the white coats that they wore over their military clothes. I felt like I was part of a herd of cows being shuttled through a stockyard. In fact, I was so distracted when the examiner grabbed my nuts that I momentarily forgot to cough. I didn't appreciate it when he made some sort of smart remark about how much I probably liked it, but I didn't say anything.

At one point, when we were jammed shoulder to shoulder in a smelly little waiting area for one of the next tests, one young kid passed out cold. None of the recruits were quite sure what do as he sprawled on the floor in his dirty stretched-out underwear. There were no *real* Army guys in the room. We recruits just looked at each other. One guy prodded the fallen kid in the chest with his bare foot. He didn't move. Finally, I knelt down next to him, held his head up off the floor, and asked one of the other guys standing by the exit door to call for some medical help.

Eventually, someone in a white coat meandered in and tended to the kid on the floor. Others just stepped over him when we were called to move to the next area. I was the last to move. I wondered how the recruits would respond if one of their own was wounded since it appeared they wouldn't have given a shit. I finished my entrance examination, got dressed, and walked through Grant Park to Lake Michigan where I sat and watched the boats on the harbor for the rest of the afternoon.

The next day I went back to the Recruiter's office. This time I knew enough to walk past the Marines' office and on to the end of the hallway. I tapped on the wall, poked in my shaggy head, and sat down once I had been invited. I figured that since there were not a lot of others banging on his door and my appearance had not changed, the Recruiter would probably remember me. Sure enough. Before I even sat down he asked, "Did you complete your test?" I told him that I had and he went to search for my results in a stack of papers sitting in his "in" box on a file cabinet.

After he found my results and sat back down at his desk, he was quick to say that I had done very well. I got a one thirty-nine on my military intelligence test and my physical exam was all clear. Then asked me again what I wanted to do in the Army. Once again I said, "What are my choices?" He said, "With these scores and two and a half years of college, you can do just about anything you want as an enlisted man." Finally, he handed me a list.

The list contained about twenty "Advanced Individual Training" options in alphabetical order with number and letter codes next to each entry. To that moment I still had not considered that the choices were that important to me, so I looked at the items one at a time rather than perusing the whole list before asking questions. I passed by "Artillery." I passed by "Infantry." I was confident that I had no interest in hurting anyone, even from a distance. Then I came to a choice labeled "Journalism." In some disbelief, I sought some clarification from the Recruiter. "I could be a journalist in the Army?" After some checking, the Recruiter told me that with two plus years of college and my scores I could be a journalist in the Army. But that was not the way it turned out.

He said, "You want to come into the Army as soon as possible, right?"

Although I had yet to decide, I said, "Yes, I suppose so."

Then he checked some sort of schedule sheet and informed me that the Journalism training option would not match up with my schedule of entry. As it turned out, we needed to find an Advanced Training option that was scheduled to start right around the time that my Basic Training would be scheduled to end. Okay. My choices were going to be limited after all. The Recruiter suggested that I keep looking at the selection list.

While I was a bit disappointed because I thought Journalism would have been a nice match for me, I kept looking down the list. I passed "Machine Maintenance" although I'd liked tinkering around with my brother's go-cart when I was younger. The next thing on the alphabetically-ordered list was "Map Drawing." I immediately asked the Recruiter if I could be a Map Drawer in the Army. I had always liked drawing and my older brother had become an architect. Once again I was greeted with the same response – that option would not match with my schedule of entry. I started to wonder if I was being guided toward a particular selection. Perhaps I was.

The next thing that grabbed my attention on the list of Advanced Training options was "Psychiatric Social Work." This choice seemed unbelievable. I hadn't yet considered that the Army might need guys who had an interest in helping in this way. Could I be a Psychiatric Social Worker in the Army with two and a half years of unrelated college education, marginal grades, and zero experience? After checking, the Recruiter's answer was "Yes."

I would have eight weeks of Basic Training, probably at Fort Lewis in Washington or Fort Leonard Wood in Missouri, followed by ten weeks of Psychiatric Social Work training at Fort Sam Houston in Texas. I signed the papers. The recruiter never said a word about what would happen after Advanced Training and I didn't ask. I was to report for induction into the Army a few weeks later on April, 2, 1971.

After my visits to the recruiting office, I had even less interest in interacting with my friends or anyone other than

Rose back at Loyola. I was especially concerned about seeing Cosmo around campus because I knew he would be curious to know how things had turned out for me at the examination station. Actually, I was equally curious to see what had happened to him.

That weekend I asked Rose if she would make a trip to Peoria with me. I told her that I needed to let my parents know what I had done and drop off the car with them because I wouldn't need it anymore. I really hadn't needed it in the first place.

I was pleased that Rose quickly agreed to make the trip with me. The morning we left she was sporting a gray felt hat and a tight neck scarf which gave her an unusual, but sweet cowgirl kind of look. Until she put on the hat, I hadn't noticed what an Italian nose she had. We spent time laughing about this and a lot of other things all the way to Peoria, although it might have seemed like it should have been a more serious time. I was not yet thinking about the ramifications of my decision.

My mother and father, as well as my little brother and sister, thought Rose was pretty special. She was dressed like a fashion model. She was intelligent and humble. My little sister tried on her cowgirl hat and I suspected that my little brother had quickly fallen in love again. Everyone treated her so nicely. I knew they would.

My news was no surprise to any of them by that time, so we spent very little time talking about it. Rose and I caught the Amtrak at Chillicothe for our ride back to the City after the weekend. It was as good of a time as either of us had experienced in quite a while.

Riders of the Storm
(The Doors)

I should have known what would be waiting for me when I got back to Chicago. A couple nights after my return from Peoria I came back to the apartment after walking Rose home. It was pretty late and it appeared as though a small party was just wrapping up. Heart, reverend Blimpie, The Cork, Cowboy's girlfriend Jewelie, and Sunshine were just coming out the front door as I was coming in. We greeted each other, but no one said anything else. We hadn't been seeing each other much anyway, so it made sense that there wasn't a whole lot to say. I did notice that they looked at me like I might have had some sort of disease and talked under their breath as they moved away up the street.

I walked down the steps and into the front door of the old basement apartment. The place was pretty quiet by that time, but I could tell there was still someone stirring in the kitchen. I had to walk through there to get to my room. I pulled off my coat and scarf as I entered the kitchen. There were my friends Joon, Cowboy, and Skip sitting at the vinyl and chrome table. There were also about twenty empty beer cans littering the table, shelves, and counters.

As casually as I could, but sensing that something was simmering, I greeted the guys and started to move past them toward my room. Joon asked me to put away my coat and join them for a cold one. Sit at the kitchen table and have a beer? We hardly ever just sat at the table and had a beer. "Sure," I said reluctantly. I tossed my coat into my room, grabbed a can of Hamm's from Joon's outstretched hand, and sat down in the open seat at the table.

For a few moments we just sat there awkwardly drinking our beers. It was especially unusual because there was no music playing on any of the three record players we had in the apartment. The uncharacteristic silence was broken only by the sounds of the cans clanking and tapping on the table top. I finished my beer quickly and grabbed a second from the icebox. Then, in an attempt to ease the tension, I asked, "So, what's been going on?" The clanking and tapping continued for a moment and then stopped.

Cowboy looked at me and said that he had seen Cosmo that afternoon. I was playing innocent and said something like, "Oh, that's cool. How are things going with old Cosmo?" Someone said that Cosmo was actually doing really well because he had been designated as "incorrigible" after he showed up for his induction screening. I said something like "Huh, imagine that," and took another big, uncomfortable gulp of beer.

My comment about Cosmo must have triggered something. Skip and Joon started firing vague remarks back and forth at each other almost as if they were arguing. Perhaps they were trying to determine who was going say what from some previously rehearsed script. In the midst of their volley, Joon abruptly turned toward me and said, "We know what's going on with Cosmo, it's you we are here to talk about."

Of course I knew that, but where would I begin? My friends looked upset. I was obviously stumbling for words. Then, in his sensible and pragmatic style, Cowboy said, "I think the boys want to know what's been going on with you lately. You know we haven't seen much of you around here."

I realized that it was time for me to speak as clearly as I could. I grabbed my third beer in about as many minutes and thought about how I was going to explain what was up without becoming critical of any of them or shedding too negatively on myself. I figured that whatever I said, it needed to be about me and no one else. I felt that I had to tell them what I had done and identify reasons that I still didn't fully understand.

I started slowly. I told the guys that I had been troubled since even before we took the trip to Los Angeles. I said that a lot of things had not been making sense to me for a long time. I said that I had lost interest in school and had stopped going to classes. As I spoke, I could feel myself becoming upset so I tried to keep my explanation as simple as I could. I hadn't planned on having to say anything out loud just yet. I hadn't fully considered how it would sound.

In stark contrast to his typically cool demeanor, Skip interrupted. Getting right to the point, he said that he had heard someone say that I was "joining the fucking Army" and that he had told whoever it was that they must be crazy because I hated the War and would never do something like that.

The gig was up. These three guys had been my closest friends for the past two and a half years. We had been through so much together. I owed them an explanation. I had to tell them what was happening whether I was ready or not, whether I understood or not, whether it made any sense or not.

I restarted by reminding them that, like each of them, I had been opposed to the War for as long as I could remember. Everyone knew that, but more than anything I felt I needed to be very clear that those beliefs had not changed. Then I went on to say that I no longer saw much point to the protests we had been attending and that I had not seen any obvious results from those efforts...people were still dying and, if anything, the action in Vietnam appeared to be escalating again.

By this time I couldn't stop myself. I had already stepped in deeper than I had cared to, but I had to keep going. I suppose I inadvertently pointed a finger at my friends when I stated that I didn't think most people who were protesting, including myself, really had any idea what they were talking about because none of us understood hardly anything about the military, the War, or the guys who were being sent to fight it. I asked the guys to consider that maybe all of us just participated in "the movement" because it was something to do, not because we truly gave a shit about what was happening. At the end of my little unrehearsed catharsis, I said that I was tired of it and couldn't handle it anymore: I continued to care a great deal about what was happening...to all the protesters and to all guys who were off participating in the War. Although I tried, I couldn't state my position without sounding as though I was blaming my friends for being part of the problem. If anything I was blaming us all, but beginning to separate myself at the same time.

By that point, Skip seemed to know what was coming and couldn't wait any longer to get to the truth. He started pacing around the kitchen and then shouted, "Fuck the War and fuck all the protests. I'm not talking about those things! Fucking shit, you joined the Army, didn't you?"

But Skip didn't care to hear my answer. Without even allowing me time to respond, he went into an uncharacteristic tirade about one of his friends from high school who had been killed "over there." Then he leaned on the table, looked at me with angry tears in his eyes, and said, "If you do this by your own fucking choice and you get killed, don't expect me to cry for you...and, don't expect me to go get a gun and follow you."

By that time, unfortunately, the conversation had turned into something more like a shouting match. I got up out of my chair, stood eye to eye with Skip and told him that I also knew someone who was killed, that I had no intention of getting killed, and that I wasn't asking for him to cry for me or pick up a gun and follow. I asked him to try to understand that I felt I was living some sort of contradiction and that I somehow felt compelled to go find out more. I said that maybe once I understood the problem a little better I could become part of a more effective protest from within. Although that thought had just crossed my mind, it suddenly showed up as a potential reason *why* I had already made the decision to join the Army. I finished by saying that I had always believed that the best way to solve a problem was to get closer to it, not just go on acting as though it didn't exist.

This little litany didn't fly either. My best friend Skip threw his hands in the air, spun in a circle, and walked out of the room. Joon and Cowboy just sat there looking at me as though I had finally gone over the edge. We were all fighting back tears. I told them I was sorry if I'd offended either of them and that I honestly hadn't intended to. I told them that things had been happening so fast, I didn't completely understand what was going on with me. They were polite, but I could tell they were as confused as I was. Cowboy left the room saying to himself, but loud enough to hear, "This whole thing is fucked up." Joon followed him.

Maybe it was. I sat at the kitchen table by myself thinking about what had just happened. I drank several more beers, but I still didn't sleep much that night. I don't guess any of us did.

On the Threshold of a Dream
(Another album by the Moody Blues)

My last month in Chicago was difficult. I had begun to make a little more sense out of what had been happening in my life, even if I was still very unclear about what was going to happen next. At least, I was more able to put words to the script that I appeared to be acting out. Strange as it may seem, I recognized that I was making up the explanations for my actions after they were already initiated. All I really knew was that I was going to find out what the military was about: to see who was there, what they were doing, what they were thinking, how I could help, and how I might help put a stop to the War.

In an effort to add some substance to my personal anti-war agenda, I made a few phone calls and visits to some Veterans' Affairs offices to see if there was any organized protest movement from within the military. The closest I ever got to an answer was a fold out pamphlet about the Vietnam Veterans Against the War, but no one at the VA seemed to know if there were active-duty members of this group or whether its proceedings were accessible to active-duty personnel. I quickly got the impression that asking a Veteran's office to provide information on anti-war activity might have been viewed as barking up the wrong tree. I quickly stopped making those contacts, but it comforted me to think that I was somehow going to generate protest from within the Army. I reasoned that, just like the student protests that had shut down the school, if no one fought, then there could be no more war.

Regardless of where they stood on the issues, I don't think anyone around Loyola would have viewed joining the Army as a sound decision on my part. Although I wasn't going out of my way to talk about it with anyone, I found it interesting that no one asked me about it either. Most times I just accepted this as being a byproduct of the apathy that seemed to have permeated the campus: maybe no one cared about what I was doing. Other times I figured that a few folks might feel that my action made a little sense, but they wouldn't care to bring it up for fear that I might expect them to come along. Of course I wouldn't have expected that of anyone. Most times though, I got the impression that people who knew me best just chalked up the decision to my temporary insanity. I figured that it wouldn't matter what anyone thought much longer anyway.

By the middle of that March, I had gotten back on reasonable terms with Skip, Joon, and Cowboy even though we avoided talking about my decision in more detail. It was good enough for me that we started getting drunk together again. Under the circumstances I didn't really expect anything more.

On St. Patrick's Day, we had an all-day party that was based out of the apartment. St. Patrick's Day was always one of the biggest days of the year in Chicago. This one was going to be extra special for me because I was fairly Irish and I knew it was going to be my last big blow out before I would be leaving. I was looking forward to a really good time.

Joon, Cowboy, and I were up early. We walked down to the Jewel grocery store at around 9:00 and bought several cases of cheap beer. Sometimes we got cases of beer extra cheap if we purchased stray cans of mixed brands that were left over from broken cases in the backroom. On a day like St. Patrick's it didn't matter what people were drinking, so we loaded up on as much of the cheapest beer we could find. Rose was working that morning and checked us out. Sometimes that resulted in a little extra discount if she marked her purchasing code on the receipt. I remember her looking at me in a way that said "Be careful out there." She said she would see all of us back at the apartment when we returned from the parade. Rose and I rarely talked directly to or about each other when others were around.

It became our way of detracting attention from the fact that we had become very close. Not doing so would have produced too many questions and opinions.

A big group assembled at the apartment to get geared up for the trip downtown to the parade. All the regulars showed up, as well as several other, straighter guys who we rarely saw at our place. By 10:30 that morning, people were hooting and hollering and carrying on inside and outside the apartment. By 11:00 the police had already stopped by to tell us to settle down. This was not a big deal. In fact, given their connection to Mayor Daley and their increased tolerance for revelry on this special day, the police were in particularly good spirits. They even graciously allowed us to take pictures with them by the squad car. For that, we assured them we would settle down. We knew it would be easy to follow through on our promise because we planned to leave for the train just a few minutes later. We stuffed our pockets with every drop of alcohol we could carry as we headed out the door.

It must have been quite a sight for passengers on that train to see twenty or more buzzed college students hopping on with them that morning. Our entire group crowded into one of the cars. Already, guys were unabashed about lifting their bottles and cans, shouting things like "Erin, go braless," and inviting anyone who looked vaguely female to "Kiss me, I'm Irish." Many of the guys were far from it, but it didn't matter in Chicago.

Once downtown, our group became fixated on finding a way to march in the parade. This wasn't as hard as it might have seemed. Heart was one of those guys who could talk his way into or out of just about anything. We watched him canvas the staging area where the groups were getting set to march. He came back in no time. It turned out we could either join a local politician's group if we agreed to carry one of his campaign signs or we could slip in with a group that had something to do with promoting the pickle industry in Illinois. This was a no-brainer. We would fit right in with the pickle promoters.

Marching across the green-dyed Chicago River and into the downtown Loop with the pickle promoters and the rest of the parade was a treat. Thousands of people had lined the streets under the tall buildings and crisp blue sky. Fire engines had their sirens blaring. A high school band was tapping out cadence and marching songs just in front of our crew. Joon, Cowboy, Skip and I danced like high-stepping majorettes around the rest of our loose formation. Everyone seemed to enjoy the show. Joon got more kisses from more pretty girls along the route than any of the rest of us. As usual, Blimpie copped a few feels along with his kisses. He had always been very bold about that sort of thing, but on this day it seemed to come especially easy for him. No one was taking any offense. Everyone was having a good time. We carried on for hours.

By the end of the afternoon, most of our group got scattered in the disarray at the end of the parade route. However, a few of us met back up on one of the bridges spanning the still-green Chicago River. Someone said that Joon, Cowboy, and Heart had gone into a bar at the Marina Towers which we could see from the bridge, but I was still content watching all the people and didn't care to go. At one point, I leaned over the rail of the bridge and stared at the water for a long time trying to locate my reflection among the crowd.

About six of us wound up riding the train back to Rogers Park together. There had been some talk about reconvening at Joker's Pub after the parade because they were supposed to be serving green beer and cheap corned beef sandwiches. By this time, I was almost tired of being drunk, but I wound up there standing by myself in front of the bar. As I was waiting for my green beer, I saw a big guy everyone called Mack start moving in my direction from across the jammed packed room. This was a little odd because Mack was a year or so older than I was, we didn't really know each other well, and I considered him to be some sort of politically-connected and fairly straight fraternity guy. He certainly always looked the part. His sweater vests and slacks suggested that he might have worn out the grooves on his Ray Steven's records. It had always seemed strange to me that, although I didn't recall ever having seen him at an anti-War rally, he wrote most of the editorials about the War for the school newspaper.

As Mack moved toward me, I had the uncomfortable sense that our interaction was not going to be a good thing. It wasn't. He shuffled in next to me and we stood in the midst of the crowd scrunched chest to chest at the bar. Then, without even greeting me, he asked very loudly so others could easily hear, "Hey, what's this I hear about you joining the Army?" At that moment, the bartender delivered my glass of green beer. I thanked him, took a very large drink, and looked back at Mack.

All day long, with so many other people who might have asked, no one had said a word to me about joining the Army. I figured that was because they knew it was a day for having a good time, they didn't care to spoil the fun, they could see I was having fun, and their silence was a way of showing me a bit of respect. I concluded that Mack was insensitive to any of this. In a flash, I determined that he was just too much of a jerk to understand. I continued to stare at him with all sorts of potential scenarios as to what might happen next rushing through what was left of my brain.

But none of them were worth it. I looked back toward the bar, gulped down the rest of my beer, told Mack I'd see him around sometime, and made my way out of the bar toward the apartment. As I did, I could hear Mack's loud mouth in the background. "What did I do? That fool joined the Army. I can't help it if he's an idiot." I just kept walking.

When I got down the street, Rose was sitting on the outside step of the apartment with a few others who were still hanging around after the long day of partying. I nestled up next to her on the front step without saying much. She knew I was terribly drunk. She knew something had happened. She knew that, although I'd made my decision about the Army, it was still confusing to me. She knew that, as the time to leave was approaching; I was getting increasingly apprehensive about what I had done. We sat for awhile before she walked me to my bed where I passed out. I hadn't even considered walking her back to her place that night.

I was not at all sure what was going to happen between Rose and myself in the days to come. She had needed me so much after her trauma and that didn't seem to have changed much. Likewise, she had listened to me through all of my changes. We both knew she never agreed with me and never truly understood what I was doing, but she stuck with me anyway. By this time we knew each other better than anyone else knew either of us. And we both knew we were making it through some incredibly important times in our lives together.

Even by the end of March I still hadn't made love with her. One time during the day we went into Joon's room at the apartment and put John Barry's soundtrack from "The Lion in Winter" on his new stereo. We sat with our legs tangled on the floor facing each other. As we listened to the incredible music, we touched the tips of each of our fingers together and started moving our hands and arms as if we were dancing. We looked deeply into each other's eyes. There were no words, just occasional gentle smiles and deep expressions of our caring for each other. I had never cared for anyone in my life as much as I cared about Rose. And I was very clear that no one had ever cared that much about me.

What's Going On?
(Marvin Gaye)

By April Fool's Day 1971, I had pretty much gotten rid of the few things I still had around the apartment. I had planned to leave anything I wouldn't need and couldn't give away. That was okay with my friends. I didn't even paint over the deep yellow and blue sunset mural I had created on my bedroom wall. Skip agreed to watch out for my cheap stereo, LP records, and guitar although neither of us knew exactly what that would entail.

Finally, knowing I would eventually have to do something about it, I asked Cowboy if he would cut my hair. This was a bit of a switch because I had always been the one who cut hair around the dormitory when we first got to school. The job had become obsolete after everyone stopped cutting their hair.

There weren't many instructions to give Cowboy about how to do it. I just told him to leave me about an inch or so all around. It might have been sad and symbolic, but it was more of a melodramatic way of marking the change that was coming in my life. I sat in a chair in the middle of the kitchen and he went to work. I asked him if he remembered the time that I nicked his ear with my thinning scissors. We laughed when he said that he had kept his hair long so that it wouldn't show the scar. Afterwards, when I looked at my trimmed head in the mirror, I looked like the kid in my high school graduation photo. I guess I had begun to believe that the length of one's hair was correlated with their political beliefs, wisdom, and general level of maturity.

The night before I was to report for induction there were no big goodbyes with anyone at the apartment. I think this might have been the first time I realized that I had never really said goodbye to anyone in my life. Typically I just said things like, "See you later," or "Catch you down the road." I'd always acted as though I expected to see people again even when I was hitchhiking. We four roommates had a beer or two as we stood around in the kitchen. We had already said everything that needed to be said and nothing was any clearer to any of us than it had ever been. I left that evening to go see Rose.

Rose knew I was coming though neither one of us looked forward to the meeting. We visited on the steps outside her apartment. It was an exceptionally quiet night on her block. As if not to disturb anything, we were also very quiet. For the first time, I told Rose that I loved her. It had never seemed to matter that much to actually say it before because we both knew it. We laughed because it seemed so trite. She loved me as well and I appreciated it a great deal.

Although we started and stopped our farewell a few times when we discovered other things to talk about, it was finally time to go. During our last quick minutes, we agreed that we would write to each other often. She would tell me how she was and what was going on around school and I would tell her all about what I was learning in the Army. We shared very soft and warm tears as we hugged each other on the sidewalk out in front of her place. I turned around and waved back in her direction several times as I walked back toward the apartment for the last time, even after I had turned the corner and could no longer see her.

The next morning, April 2nd, I was up early and gone from the apartment before anyone else had awakened. I left my key on the kitchen table and grabbed the small bag in which I had packed some underwear, an extra pair of jeans, and a few papers.

As I was riding the elevated train to the induction station it was beginning to soak in that I was actually leaving Chicago. Once again, it seemed as though my thoughts were just catching up with what I was doing. It felt as though I had been there such a short time, but yet so many amazing things had happened. I watched the backs of the buildings go by just like they always had whenever I rode the train. Considering my apprehension, it seemed fitting that the train ducked underground as we approached the Loop.

When I arrived at the induction station, I checked in and received my first set of typed military orders on a single sheet of paper. I was sent to a holding area where we would wait for our formal induction, be loaded on buses, ride out to O'Hare airport, and catch a flight to Seattle, which was somewhere near Fort Lewis, Washington. As I stood in the holding area smoking a cigarette with everything I needed packed in my little bag, I noticed that it was getting crowded and a few of the guys already seemed to know each other. Perhaps they were on the "buddy plan" that the Recruiter had told me about. I hadn't paid much attention to that part of his presentation because I knew I was not likely to have buddies that would take this kind of trip with me. Before we left the holding area we were instructed to put out our cigarettes. Then we were led into a more formal-looking room, raised our right hands, and got sworn into the Army. I suspected that it was another routine day at the induction station.

I immediately noticed the diversity in the group of guys that got on the bus with me for the airport. There were about as many blacks as there were whites. Most looked like they had just come from high school. Some had surely been in some sort of trouble with the law and were given the choice at court to either go to jail or join the military, a common practice in those days for teens who ran into legal problems. I imagined that a few others must have had experiences and beliefs like mine, but there was no reason to find out about any of that just yet. I watched, listened closely, and kept to myself.

The airplane ride from Chicago to Seattle was my first. I was surprised to see that it was just a regular commercial flight that the thirty or forty guys I was with on the bus found themselves joining. I sat next to a man who I could now view as a "civilian" who was headed home to Seattle after a business trip to Chicago. It surprised me when he asked me where I was going. I would have guessed he already knew. I said I was going to Fort Lewis, Washington. We didn't talk much after that so I spent my time looking out the window of the plane, replaying some recent memories, smoking a few cigarettes, and wondering what Washington State was going to look like. I was approaching the trip as if I had my thumb in the air on the highway.

As we were getting set to exit the plane in Seattle, the man who had been sitting next to me said, "Good luck to you." I think it was the first time anyone outside of family or friends had ever said anything like that to me and I appreciated it. After we got off the plane the recruits that I flew in with joined up with another bunch of guys that was already sitting in the waiting area by the baggage claim. Then, following a short delay, two heavy-looking green buses pulled up to the terminal doors. There were a few commands shouted out inside the terminal, but over all the noise I couldn't hear what was being said. I followed everyone else out of the building and onto the sidewalk next to the buses. Pretty soon, names were being called for people assigned to "Group Alpha." That group was to board the front bus. Everyone else, presumably "Group Bravo," was to load on the bus in the rear. I didn't hear my name. In fact I had yet to hear my name, which made me wonder if anyone knew I was there. I had a fleeting fantasy about hitchhiking over the border into Canada, but hopped on the back bus anyway.

It was dark by the time we arrived at Fort Lewis. The buses pulled up at a reception station and all the recruits spilled out in front of them. We were put in two formations with several lines of guys facing what appeared to be the main building on the base. Within a few seconds, the Army guys who appeared to be in charge started shouting. One of them got in a kid's face who had brought two big bags of stuff with him and said something like, "What do you think, Asshole, you're moving in?" Without having yet received any training, the kid instinctually responded, "No, Sir." The more-seasoned Army guy shouted, "Well you're wrong already, Asshole, you are moving in and for the next eight weeks, you're mine." There was no way that kid could have answered that question correctly.

Interactions like this were taking place all throughout the formations. Guys were being lambasted for their looks, their hair, their weight, their mothers, their girlfriends, and anything else that might or might not have stood out about them. Their bags were being kicked and thrown around in front of the formations. Loud "Yes, Sirs" and "No, Sirs," could be heard everywhere in between the insults. Fortunately, I had yet to get insulted by anyone and the hazing ended when an officer-looking man came strutting out of the building and stood in front of the group. Someone hollered for the group to stand at attention. Only a few knew exactly what that meant. Everyone else just followed the example of guys who looked like they knew what they were doing. There I was, within minutes of my arrival at Fort Lewis, standing at attention because someone said so. I wondered what Cosmo and my friends would have thought of me then.

After a short introduction to the Army and the "Post" at Fort Lewis, we grabbed our bags and got herded off in ragged formations to the barracks that we would be occupying during Basic Training. My group's was a two-story wooden building with lines of steel bunk beds on both sides of each floor and a four- or five-stall bathroom at the end of each floor. There were no walls between the shiny white toilets that were mounted on the walls. Bright red-painted cigarette "butt cans" hung from nails on the support beams throughout the building, but we quickly learned that they were not to be used for anything because they were to be kept absolutely clean at all times. I wondered if the toilets were off-limits at times as well.

I took the first open bunk that presented itself. It turned out to be the top bunk of the one of the beds on the second floor. My bunk-mate was a black guy who called himself "Paris" from Chicago. As I fell asleep that first night I reminded myself that I was in the Army to watch, listen, and learn. And I decided that my primary objective in Basic Training would be to do my best to stay out of trouble. I wasn't sure what that meant exactly, but I figured I would be doing well if I didn't give anyone any reason to shout at me. I suspected I would have a hard time with that and couldn't predict how I might react.

The following morning we were awakened before the sun came up with the command to, "Fall out in five minutes!" To "Fall out" meant to immediately get out of bed, groom with fifteen other guys battling for space, get dressed, and line up in formation outside the building. This particular morning everyone rolled out very quickly, used the toilets, got dressed in whatever they had on the night before, and pretty much skipped the grooming part. There would have been no time for it.

I wondered what was the big hurry. We stood outside the building at "Parade Rest" doing absolutely nothing for about an hour in the damp and chilly Washington air before we were finally marched over to a mess hall for breakfast. Just outside the entrance to the mess hall was a set of about fifteen parallel bars which were raised about ten feet off the ground. There was one additional bar about a foot and a half off the ground on each end that was used as a step to mount the device. We were required to get in a hanging position from the first bar and then, only when instructed, swing cross-armed down and back before we were permitted entry into the mess hall.

It was not a pretty sight watching guys try to make it down and back. Of course, there were a few who attacked the bars and made it with no problem. But some of the larger guys, strong as they might have been, slipped off the steel bars before they were even instructed to begin. The likelihood of slipping off was increased because it was still damp outside and the bars were built so that they would spin in the six-by-six wooden beams that held them.

The rule was that if you didn't make all thirty bars at once, you were sent to the back of the line that was waiting to get into the mess hall for food. Guys who didn't make it not only endured the taunting of those in charge, but also the silent audience of their fellow recruits.

I was worried as I stood in line and waited for my turn. Considering the way I had lived in Chicago, I was not only a skinny one hundred thirty-five pounds; I was also not in any kind of physical shape. In addition, I had not played on monkey bars since I was a kid and I never even liked playing on them then. However, following my newly-devised plan to do whatever was necessary to keep myself out of trouble, I hopped up on the first bar, held on tight to keep it from spinning, waited for the instruction to go, and whipped off thirty bars with hardly any difficulty at all. I got to join the other guys who'd made it inside the mess hall. In our enforced silence inside the little building, we could all hear the shouting and the insults going on outside. I ate every speck of dry French toast and potatoes that were placed on my tray. If this was how it was going to be, I suspected I would need all the energy I could get.

Although I am pretty sure everyone was eventually allowed to eat something, the last guys into the building who

176

had not passed that morning's first test were barely provided two minutes to do so before we were herded back outside the building and put in formation again. Even though the last guys were still chewing their food when we cleared from the mess hall, we wound up waiting some more before we were marched over to the barber shop. Once there, the group received instructions regarding acceptable military haircuts. The instructor pointed to a picture on the wall that showed a guy with an inch of hair on top and sideburns that came down to the little knot at the middle of his ear. He looked okay I suppose and, in fact, the cut that Cowboy gave me was not that much different from his.

However, as it turned out no one got the pictured haircut. Word spread quickly through the waiting line that anyone who actually got that cut would be making a big mistake. I noticed that none of the guys in charge were sporting the longer hairstyle. So, like everyone else, I sat down in the chair and asked the barber to take it all off. I watched in a mirror as he ran the electric trimmer through my hair and the remaining clumps of it rolled off my shoulders and fell to the floor. When he was done I realized that I had never looked like this in my life. I could barely stand to touch my own scalp. There would be no mistaking it now. I was in the Army.

From the barber shop we single-filed through the supply room and picked up the clothing and other gear we would need for Basic Training. I got my duffle bag, fatigues, backpack, fold-up shovel, blanket, green T-shirts, baseball-style hat, and boxer-style underwear. Boxer style underwear? I had never worn boxers in my life and could not imagine what life was going to be like without the support of my jockeys. But that turned out to be one of the least of my worries. I wasn't nearly as concerned about my new boxers as I was about my new tin dog tags, helmet, and M-16 rifle.

During the next three weeks at Basic Training we were kept absolutely engaged, it seemed, almost twenty-four hours a day. We made formations. We marched. We waited. We did calisthenics several times a day. We ran with and without our gear. We waited. We "smoked them if we had them." We policed the grounds. We buffed the already shiny floors of the barracks. We did inspections of our quarters and our equipment. When there were any breaks in the action, we smoked more cigarettes and policed the grounds again.

I watched and listened. I ached for the guys who were having a hard time with the physical tasks, but there was no stopping to help them. No one stopped to help them. I kept my mouth shut. I ate everything in sight. I did everything I was ordered to do. And I started to look and feel healthier than I ever had.

It was difficult to follow my plan when we went out to the rifle range to fire our guns for the first time. Most of the other guys couldn't wait to get there. We had learned how to take apart and clean them. We had learned how to load real bullets into their clips. We had learned how to hold and carry them during different sorts of exercises. Nevertheless, I was not certain how I would respond when I actually had to pull the trigger. I had never fired anything but a cap gun in my life.

I finally convinced myself that I could get through it since I had no intention of ever firing a gun at anyone. I was placed on my belly in a prone position and pointed down range. After my first shot, I was struck by the reality of my decision to join the Army and, for a moment I fought back my tears. However, the pain didn't last as long as I thought it might. Acting more like a student, I became intrigued by the power of the M-16, its machine-gun like capabilities, and the tracer bullets that would leave a red trail as they whizzed through the air. In fact I turned out to be a pretty good shot. I got my Marksman's bar with no difficulty at all.

During the first half of Basic Training, we were kept so busy that no one took much time to talk. At night when that might have seemed more likely, most guys were so tired they immediately went to sleep. Somewhere along the line though, that began to change. I started to talk to Paris from Chicago quite a bit. It was never quite clear to me whether or not he was married, but he had a girlfriend and a child. He was about two years out of high school, but had not been able to find a good-paying job. He had been drafted, but hoped to get trained in Machine Maintenance if at all possible. I learned that draftees usually didn't know what Advanced Training they would actually wind up getting until they got their assignments at the end of Basic.

After Paris and I began talking, other guys from Chicago started gravitating toward us. Solotorzynski, a Polish kid who the Drill Sergeant had always referred to as "Alphabet," had not completed grade school. He was a short guy who was already built like a rock when he arrived at Fort Lewis. Alphabet hoped to be an auto mechanic someday. Smutz was a good-looking city kid who had graduated high school and had plans to start a snack bar on the South Side when he got out of the Army.

Within a short time I had met several guys who admitted to either having had some college education or actually graduating. Having college education before the Army was something like having money when you were hitchhiking. In Basic Training guys were often ridiculed for it as if education made them less of a man. As a result, it was not something that others needed to know. But, as it turned out, there were at least two teachers, one business major, and a master's level psychologist in our platoon of thirty guys. The college guys typically had some ROTC background, but that didn't give them much of an edge in Basic Training either. If anything, ROTC background also tipped off some of the lesser-educated men in charge that you had been to college, which sometimes compounded the problem.

I was still trying to pay attention, learn, and keep myself out of trouble. And in general, I felt like I was doing a pretty good job on all counts. I had already gained about fifteen pounds and I could do the physical tasks about as well as anyone. If I expected to stay out of the way of problems, I didn't see any other choice.

Up until the half way point, training was mostly focused on physical preparation. Nobody ever talked about what we might have been preparing for though. Of course, Vietnam was in the background of everything, but it was the elephant in the room that no one seemed very anxious to talk about. After the halfway point though, things began to change. On the physical side, things became even more intense and violent. Hand-to-hand combat, pugel stick training, gas-mask training, and attack exercises suddenly provided good reasons to become even more physically fit - if not to survive the War, then to survive Basic Training.

At the same time, on the educational side, we began to file into classroom buildings to learn more about the military, our enemies, and the roles we were expected to play as soldiers in the U.S. Army. Although I was very interested to see what these parts of training would be about, most of it was not much of a surprise. I expected to hear conservative views regarding the country in which we lived and the reasons we were at War. I expected that there would be little opportunity for discussion or debate about what we were being taught. I expected that nearly everyone in the room to agree with some of the blasphemy that was being preached and to refrain from saying anything if they didn't.

However, some of what I learned was unexpected. For example, I learned that the title "G.I." stood for "Government Issue" and that, although the military existed to protect our democratic way of life, the military itself did not operate as a democracy. It imposed Martial Law upon its members, meaning that orders were provided according to the hierarchy of rank and they were not subject for any sort of discussion, debate, vote, or second-guessing. Although this made sense, it seemed odd to me that there would be no time for these sorts of things in the heat of protecting democracy. That soldiers needed to sacrifice their freedom in order to protect it for others seemed strange. I also learned that I could face charges in the military if I did any damage to the government-issued property that my increasingly fit body was considered to be, including getting sunburned.

I suppose that, in the hustle of getting in shape, I became distracted from many of the things that had moved me to join the Army in the first place. The military education parts helped bring some of these things back for me. I started to feel some of my anger beginning to return. I realized that any hint of interpersonal coercion or deceit had always had that effect on me. I recall being pleased when I started to feel like myself again even if I was not going to speak a word about it to anyone else.

These feelings reached a high point for me during our "Race Relations Training." Up until that time, I hadn't noticed anyone having any difficulty getting along with guys who were another color. I suppose I might have even anticipated some problems, but they hadn't arisen. Everyone knew that Paris from Chicago and I had become pretty tight. We were even planning to take a weekend furlough together once that was permitted. I spent as much time hanging with the black guys jiving on Marvin Gaye as they did with the white guys singing along with Carole King.

In my view, everything had been going just fine until the white instructor of the Race Relations classes started stirring things up. He had our platoon watch a movie with grossly contrived vignettes showing how black people were often treated poorly by whites. The film seemed way out of date to me, much like the sex education movies we had been forced to watch back in high school. Then, during the "open discussion section" after the film, the instructor asked the black guys to recall times when they had personally experienced similar treatment by whites. Reluctantly, but because it was expected, one or two of the blacks shared a few memories. The rest of us just looked around at each other wondering why in the world we were doing this. Did the military hope to create problems where they didn't exist? After some more prodding by the instructor and more reluctance on the part of guys to recall their stories, I broke my own rule. I raised my hand.

With a familiar nervous crackle in my voice, I explained to the instructor that I believed that no one was saying much because, so far, we all had been getting along really well in Basic Training. I went on to say that we weren't having race-related problems in our platoon and that most of us were already learning how to watch each other's backs. Then I gestured toward Paris from Chicago and said that some of us had already started to become good friends.

My words must have been exactly the kind of response the instructor was looking for. He used my proclamation as an example of how white people often like to believe that problems don't exist when, deep down, black people know that they do…and they are very bitter about it. I couldn't believe what was happening. I looked around the room at Paris, Harper, Lee, and some of the other blacks I had begun to know as if pleading with them to jump in and say it wasn't so. But they didn't. The training continued. In my opinion, everyone acted just like they were instructed to act. For the rest of Basic Training, the blacks and whites gradually separated into two groups.

This was disappointing to me for several reasons. Most importantly, a few days later, Paris from Chicago informed me that he needed to start steering clear of me, that he was going to have to hang with the black guys, and worst of all that he would not be able to join me on any weekend furlough. We remained friends, but we didn't get caught speaking together if we could help it.

Worse yet, guys started calling each other out for fights. In general, I believed that fighting was viewed as being okay in Basic Training. In fact, fights could be sanctioned in one of the nearby low-crawl sand pits if both parties agreed to the fight, a formal request was made, and the Drill Sergeant approved it. Fights were usually scheduled before the evening stop at the mess hall so everyone could watch.

Because of my comments in Race Relations class, I started to live in persistent fear of being called out for a fight by one of the black guys. This was disappointing because I felt I had done such a good job of getting along with everyone before the instructor nailed me. One day I thought my time had arrived. Our platoon was doing a leap-frog exercise on the firing range: one guy would shoot down range while the other guy ran forward, dropped to the ground, and stopped. Then, the guy who stopped would shoot down range while the other guy ran forward, and so on through the course. Before the exercise, we had been instructed that when we reached the end of the course, we were to empty any of the remaining live rounds in our M-16's down range.

I was playing this little game with a black guy named Murphy who'd recently been hanging out with Paris. We leap-frogged through the course in fine style. I had one of those strange moments when I felt like the two of us probably could have taken on just about anybody. When we got to the end of the course, I blasted the half-dozen or so rounds I had left in my gun off into the brush. Suddenly, Murphy got angry and said something like, "What the hell are you doing man?" To my surprise, I found myself in his face shouting, "Doing what I was instructed to do, you asshole!" For a moment, Murphy didn't say anything. He just glared at me and rubbed his nose with his thumb like a boxer. Then he stepped back a few paces and said, "I'll see you back at the barracks."

I was especially concerned about this because just a night or so earlier one of Murphy's other friends, Lee, had called out one of my white friends, Red from Montana, for a late-night unsanctioned fight outside the barracks. Lee was a tall lanky kid who seemed pretty anxious to improve his status in the newly-formed black group. Red was also a tall kid, but he was relatively slow. We all knew that Lee would kick his ass. So did Red.

Several of us cautioned Red not to go outside to fight. He kept saying that he had to – that it was the only way to stop the harassment he had been taking. We pleaded some more, but he didn't listen. That night, he marched outside, got the crap beaten out of him before people stepped in, and returned to the upstairs bathroom bloody after having lost two of his upper front teeth. As the white guys gathered around him at one of the bathroom sinks, he looked up, smiled in the mirror, and said, "Well, at least it's over."

After what happened to Red, I was just waiting to hear Murphy's call for me to come out of the barracks and fight. In fact, I wondered if he would even go the formal route and have the fight sanctioned in the low-crawl pit in front of everybody. I wasn't sure whether I would have responded as Red had done, whether I would have whipped Murphy's butt, or if I would have taken some other course. I waited, but the call never came.

Sometime later, Paris from Chicago let me know that he had asked Murphy to back off. Unlike the Old Man with the Indian back in the pickup truck, I thanked Paris for his intervention. I also joked that perhaps Murphy should be thanking him as well.

Other than speaking out in the Race Relations class and shouting at Murphy, there was only one other time when I thought I might have blown my plan to stay under the radar at Basic Training. That happened during pugel stick training. Pugel sticks were five foot poles with dense rubber pads on each end. Although they were padded, everyone knew you could still hurt another guy with one if you were any good. Training was designed to teach guys how to fight in close quarters using their rifles as weapons in hand-to-hand combat. I suppose it would have messed up too many recruits and rifles to use the actual weapons during training, so we used pugel sticks.

After we learned some of the basic moves, we had several sessions in which guys would fight each other and then receive feedback from the Drill Sergeant regarding technique, strategy, and outcome. It was much like watching fights at the low-crawl pit, except in this case guys wore plastic helmets with face guards and had weapons in hand. I don't recall that there were any rules other than to start and stop when the Drill Sergeant's whistle blew. A fight was to end when he determined that there had been a killing blow.

My first time in the pugel stick ring, it so happened that I came up against one of our platoon's Squad Leaders. He was an older white guy who apparently had been in the Army earlier in his life, but had signed up again and had to retake his Basic Training. He had some sort of rank already and was pretty good at everything, making him well-suited for Squad Leader, but neither blacks nor whites actually hung out with him. I believed that he didn't like me, or anyone else for that matter, and the feeling was generally mutual.

We squared off face-to-face with our sticks in hand like a scene out of Demetrious and the Gladiators and waited for the whistle to signal the start of the fight. Our match seemed to attract more attention than usual, perhaps because it involved the Squad Leader, and I wondered if anyone was taking bets. From my biased perspective, I felt the odds would have been pretty even coming in. The Drill Sergeant blasted the whistle to start. We launched into battle making strategic moves and generally whacking the daylights out of each other. Although it seemed that we fought a long time and several of the Squad Leader's blows were killing me, the ending whistle still had not been blown.

It was a grand duel and after a while people started cheering our moves. Then, at a magical moment, the stage was set for me to make a wide-open sweep move with the right end of my stick. Just as my arms were in motion to deliver the blow, the Drill Sergeant blew the whistle. It would have been no more possible to prevent the blow than to stop a basketball in the air at the sounding of a buzzer. The right end of my stick creamed the Squad Leader on the left side of his head. I was amazed to see his body and helmet floating separately in the air just before they both came crashing to the ground in front of me.

For a long moment there was total silence. Would it be ruled a killing blow? Was it a late hit? Was the Squad Leader okay? Was he going to come up swinging? I was even surprised at what an impressive move it was, but I certainly didn't relish the idea of getting gigged for cheating. I was not sure that the Drill Sergeant knew what to do. So, after another moment, I reached out for the Squad Leader's hand and helped him up from the ground. He stood in front of me shaking the stars from his head. Then he said "Nice move, man." Everyone cheered. It felt strange to be proud of the outcome, but I was, especially when the Squad Leader and I were able to walk back to formation together.

I began to wonder if I was changing in a way that I had not planned to – that is, the way in which the Army expected me to change. I had gotten incredibly healthy and suddenly weighed almost a hundred sixty-five pounds. I felt that I was as fit and capable as anyone. I had whipped a squad leader with my pugel stick. There were strange moments when I felt like I thought I was supposed to feel…as though I was now a trained killer in the U.S. Army.

When I had time to think, the contrast between the person I had been and the person I was being trained to be got me very confused. I imagined that the letters I was writing to Rose were different from the ones I sent her in the beginning. I had started out feeling apprehensive and resolute about my disdain for the military and the War. Yet training had made me physically strong and confident. I felt like I had gone undercover and was in the process of being co-opted into joining the other side. In her letters, Rose started to ask about when I was coming home for a visit. I had become increasingly less concerned about it. I wondered if anyone back there would like what they would see.

I went to see the Chaplain to talk about my confusion. I hadn't been anywhere near a church or a priest in a very long time, but I thought that talking to someone might help me understand what was happening to me. There was no service that day, just open hours when guys could go see the Chaplain if they preferred. I sat outside waiting for him to finish talking to someone else and then got called into an office behind the little all-purpose chapel that no one used.

The Chaplain was dressed in Army fatigues with some sort of scarf hanging around his neck. I guessed this was intended to make it clear that he really was a man of the cloth, but I wondered if he was in training too. As we sat down, he asked,

"How can I help you today, young man?" I got right to it. I tried to explain who I had been, why I had joined the Army, and how I noticed myself changing since I had been at Fort Lewis. He listened intently as I expressed thoughts that I had not shared with anyone but Rose. Then, at a particularly serious moment, he leaned toward me, put his hand on my leg, and slowly started moving it from my knee toward my thigh. Startled, I blocked his hand and asked him what he was doing. He didn't reply. He just sat back in his chair and asked me if there was anything else I wanted to say. I told him that there wasn't and left. After that I decided to go back to my original strategy of keeping things to myself.

Although the platoon lost a few recruits along the way for what we assumed were physical or emotional reasons, everyone else made it through their final physical fitness tests in good shape. We could all run for miles in full gear, low-crawl a couple hundred yards in no time, swing like cartoon monkeys on the parallel bars, shoot like Roy Rogers, and kill with our hands, rifles, or pugel sticks. In addition, by that time no one seemed to miss their families or girlfriends too much anymore. Perhaps all the marching chants about some guy named "Jesse" having made it into each of our lover's pants while we were away soured the troops on the importance of these relationships in our lives.

The last few days of Basic Training were mainly set aside for meetings or celebrations of one kind or another. Some guys from closer by Fort Lewis had their families present for the graduation day ceremony on the parade field in front of the Post Commander's office. Most of us considered it more of a joke, although everyone had a sense of accomplishment for having made it through.

Before I left Fort Lewis I was given a promotion to Private First Class, which didn't happen for everyone. I was also taken aside and invited to consider signing up for a total of six years to go to Officers Training School, which I immediately declined. The hardest offer of all happened when Smutz asked me if I would change my plans regarding Advanced Training in Psychiatric Social Work and join him in the Infantry on the buddy plan. He was a good kid and I was concerned about him having been drafted and then volunteering to join the Infantry before he even knew if he might get some other assignment.

Although lots of guys volunteered to go Airborne or join the Infantry after having been beefed up and brainwashed about their physical prowess in Basic Training, I got a sense that Smutz viewed it as his fate or that he somehow owed it to someone to go fight. Maybe he felt he did, but it didn't seem right to me. I truly appreciated his request that I join him, but I declined. For the first time, I told someone in the military, other than the Chaplain, that I had signed up to help, not to hurt anyone. Smutz understood and we went our ways.

On my last day at Fort Lewis, before I was set to be released on an unanticipated seven-day leave, our platoon was busy riding around the base handing in all of our Basic Training equipment. We went to the arsenal and handed in our weapons. We went to the administration office and completed our paperwork. Just as we were arriving at the supply station to drop off our other gear, I heard my name being called out by the Drill Sergeant. Other than at formations, it was very rare to hear one's name called by the Drill Sergeant unless you had done something wrong. I shouted "Yes, Sir…Here, Sir," out of the back of the truck I had been riding in. He called me over to him and told me to grab my remaining things. I didn't ask any questions. I just did what I was told. Maybe it was good news.

The next thing I knew, we were getting out of his Jeep in front of the Command Headquarters. As we walked into the building, the Drill Sergeant told me that I had received a phone call. I saluted the Post Commander and stood in front of his desk "at ease," although I wasn't. The Commander told me that he had received a call from a person identifying himself as "Colonel Roberts from Oklahoma." Apparently, Colonel Roberts had ordered the Post Commander to have me by the phone when he called back in ten minutes. The Commander asked me if I was aware of anyone named Colonel Roberts, to which I replied, "No, Sir." Then he told me that they had discovered no record of a Colonel Roberts anywhere in Oklahoma.

I was led to a side room off the Commander's office and instructed to answer the phone when it rang again. The Commander and my Drill Sergeant planned to pick up simultaneously in the office. I was to keep the other person on the line long enough for them to determine his identity and, if possible, his location.

By that time I had a pretty good idea what was about to happen, and it did. The phone rang. I was given a hand signal to pick up. I did, saying "Yes Sir, this is Private First Class McMorrow, can I help you, Sir?" All I heard on the other end of the line was wild laughter. Of course, it was Jake. He had a knack for pulling off this kind of thing and he had done it again. Unfortunately, he didn't realize what a bad time this was for him to do it. He just kept laughing, as he said, "This is your old buddy Colonel Roberts from Oklahoma, how are you doing Man?" I didn't know how to reply, so even knowing that I had been instructed to keep him on the line, I said, "I am completing Basic Training today and I really have to report back for duty now." I hung up the phone.

Immediately the Commander and my Drill Sergeant began grilling me about the person claiming to be Colonel Roberts. I held my composure and said, "Wait...please wait and let me explain." This always seemed to work and once again it did. I explained that the person on the other end of the line was an acquaintance who I knew only as Jake, that I had not seen him in a long time, that he might be viewed as a little unstable at times, and that I had no idea where he might have been since he spent much of his time on the road.

I had almost told the truth. They asked I if understood the seriousness of the situation since some civilian was obviously impersonating an Army Officer. I said I did, but quickly reminded them that I had not been the one to make the call and I couldn't be responsible for his actions. Eventually they agreed, put me back in the Jeep, and I caught up with the very end of the line headed through the supply room. I had completed my Basic Training. I was pleased that I had made it through and pleased to find out that I was still something like the guy I used to be.

Wounded Bird
(Graham Nash)

The Recruiter had told me that I was not likely to receive a leave between Basic Training and my Advanced Individual Training as a 91G20, Psychiatric Social Worker. At the time, I thought that was reasonable because I would only have been in the Army for a couple of months and I suspected they might have feared a lot of guys would go "Absent Without Leave" (AWOL) if they were allowed a temporary reprieve from Martial Law at this pivotal time in their service. Although it really didn't matter a great deal to me, I didn't mind finding out that the Recruiter had been wrong.

I took off for Peoria. Because it was expected after Basic Training, I traveled and arrived home in my new dress uniform with my Marksman's insignia and a couple of other tags and patches I had earned. I suppose I looked very different from the last time anyone in the "real world" had seen me. My short hair and the extra thirty pounds I had gained during training probably threw everyone off a bit as well. My parents and brothers and sisters were happy to see me and said that I looked good. Although I was also happy to see them, I didn't stay long. I got to the house, threw off my uniform, found some old jeans and a T-shirt, jumped in the Mustang and headed for Chicago as quickly as I could.

I phoned ahead to the guys at the apartment to let them know I was coming and that I was really looking forward to seeing them again. I arrived there ready for a good time.

As I stepped out of the car in front of the apartment, I could tell that a small party had already been assembled and I was excited about it. As always, if there was music or a party, no one would be required to talk much. That suited me just fine. Cowboy, Joon, Skip and I celebrated my arrival on the familiar steps outside. Except for a few cool stares from others who still didn't understand me at all, it started out just like the many of the earlier, good old days we'd had together. Then I stepped through the screen door into the apartment.

There was Rose, standing by herself, looking as sweet as ever. We laughed at the appearance of my head without hair. When we kissed and held each other, a few people started cheering as if we were two long-lost lovers who had just reunited after years of being apart. It could have been like that, everything that anyone might have imagined that it could be, but it wasn't.

Something had happened. From the moment I held her and realized that everyone now expected us to be together as a couple, I began to pull away. I knew Rose sensed it. After our greeting I slowly moved away from her and down the hallway toward the refrigerator to get a beer. The rest of the night I drank and smoked my way toward oblivion. That part was fine. I felt right at home. Rose stood by and smiled occasionally, but we barely spoke the entire evening.

Around 1:00 in the morning, Rose asked if I would give her a ride back to her apartment. I knew that she was looking for an opportunity to be alone with me away from the commotion of the party. After stalling around as long as I could, I got up and walked with her to the car without saying much of anything.

We sat there for a few moments before I turned the key. Awkwardly, I started rambling on about how crazy it had been to see everyone again. Rose eventually asked me if I was happy to see her as well. Although I was reeling from the effects of too much of everything, I believe I told her that I wasn't sure. I said that, for some reason, it was very strange to see her again and that I wasn't sure how I was supposed to act. She knew she was the only person in the world who had any idea how I was really doing. I had told her everything that had been happening in the letters that I wrote. But suddenly, under these circumstances, as if everyone expected us to be madly in love, being with her again scared the hell out of me.

In her gentle way, Rose tried to assure me that everything would be okay. She said it was probably just the shock of being back in the city after everything I had been through. She said that she thought we would both feel better after we had spent more time together again. I could tell she was almost as confused as I was.

The next thing I knew, I had started the car and found myself racing up the car-lined, single-lane street toward her apartment. It was very uncharacteristic of me to drive like that and Rose was clearly frightened by it. She pleaded with me to "Slow down, please slow down; we're going to get hurt."

We came to a halt in the middle of the street in front of her apartment. I didn't say anything. Rose asked, "Will I see you tomorrow?" I didn't say anything. Then Rose asked, "Marty, why are you doing this to me?" I still didn't say anything. Finally, Rose stepped from the car. Without waiting for her to get to the door of her apartment, which I had always been sure to do, I peeled off up the street and into the night. I never saw or spoke to Rose again.

I spent a couple more days in the City, mostly at the apartment, getting drunk and stoned with the guys. We didn't talk about much of anything either. My friends didn't care to know what I had been doing in the Army and I didn't care to talk about it. I suspect they wondered why I wasn't with Rose, but no one asked about that either.

The afternoon before I was to head back to Peoria and on to Texas, Cowboy asked if I wanted to come with him to the beach, the same little patch of sand that we had used for the

Monkey's funeral. I didn't have anything else to do, so I told him it sounded like a good idea.

When we arrived at the beach I was not surprised to see Jewelie out there sunbathing on the warm June day that it was. She looked as nice as ever and Cowboy told me that they had been seeing each other about as regularly as they ever had. I was curious to see that there was another towel lying next to Jewelie's when we walked up to her. Cowboy, Jewelie, and I shared a little small talk and then I left them alone and went for a stroll.

When she approached, I was walking without my shirt, shoes, or socks along the water. She was in short blue jean cut-offs, a halter-style swimming suit top, and bare feet which made her long legs seem very present. She had a couple of little-girl bobby pins holding back her sun-blonde hair. I stood absolutely still as she walked toward me.

Before she said anything, she bent forward, reached toward her toes, and flicked a little sand on my feet. Then, without standing back up, she looked up at me and said something like, "It's good to see you again...how are you?"

Sunshine and I spent the next several hours intermittently sitting and walking by Lake Michigan. I told her that I was okay, that I had been going through a lot of very rapid changes, that I was learning a lot, that I was healthier than I had ever been, and that I had to be leaving again later that evening. I also told her that it was a really nice surprise to see her again. She told me that she had been living in the city for the summer, that she had remained pretty active in anti-war activities, and that she was doing a little singing in her brother's blues band in the suburbs. She also told me that she had missed me, not just since I had been gone, but ever since we had stopped seeing each other the year before. She said she had never understood why that had happened.

That afternoon on the beach, Sunshine appeared a little older and more beautiful in every way than I had ever seen her before. I told her that I was on my way to San Antonio where I would receive my Army training in Psychiatric Social Work. She asked me what I would do after I complete training. I said I didn't know. She asked if I would be going to Vietnam. I said that I didn't know. I told her that I would surely learn soon enough.

Although I am sure it was barely comprehensible to either of us, something very strange happened on that little beach that afternoon. Cowboy and Jewelie were long gone. The sun was going down behind the buildings to the west. By the time I got back in the car for my return trip to Peoria, I had asked Sunshine if she would marry me. And just as quickly, she had said, "Yes."

Magic Carpet Ride
(Steppenwolf)

I arrived in San Antonio for my ten weeks of Advanced Training around the end of June, 1971. Fort Sam Houston was a far cry from Fort Lewis. I didn't see clusters of Army guys running around the base, standing in formations, or white-washing rocks around the buildings. Fort Sam was more like a college campus. There were medical buildings and classrooms. There were no tiny mess halls or monkey bars. The vending machines in the modern cafeterias held cold cans of beer. The city of San Antonio was just down the street.

There were eighteen guys assigned to the Psychiatric Social Work training in which I would be participating. We lived in a barracks similar in design to those at Fort Lewis, but Fort Sam's were larger and much better built. More importantly, there was almost no oversight or military regimen, which may have facilitated the sense that the eighteen of us were on our own. We had a course schedule that we were to follow much like I had in college, except that the content was considerably easier.

At the time many medical professionals who found themselves in the Army wound up at Fort Sam for their military training. Few of them took protocol very seriously, and that attitude tended to trickle down to the "regular Army" troops at the base. As a result, although some of my new friends worked out and stayed healthy because they chose to, the rest of us looked for any distraction we could find. Classes started late and ended early, and we never had weekend assignments. There was lots of free time and very little direction as to what we were expected to do with it.

I made friends quickly with a guy from Massachusetts we called Pete. I had met him at the airport when I flew into San

Antonio and within minutes we discovered that we were going to be in the same training at Fort Sam. Pete had a little college, like me. He had a fiancée, like me. He was immediately attracted to the openness of the base, like me. Unlike me, he had tightly curled black hair and wore glasses similar to John Lennon's. He had brought along his faded bellbottom jeans and brightly-colored, tank-top T-shirts for which he would become known. And he told me right away that, even though he had joined the Army, he already hated it.

By the very first weekend, drugs had permeated our barracks. A guy we nicknamed "Beaver" ran our makeshift company store. It was as if his inventory just showed up, perhaps left over from the previous occupants of the building. Beaver had almost anything anyone might have wanted in the little foot locker at the end of his bed, but pot and different "flavors" of Mescaline appeared to be the most popular choices. Within a very short time, Pete and I were pooling our cash in one jar and sharing drugs out of another.

When I went to the recruiter's office I was so unenlightened that I didn't even realize that people got paid to be in the military. It was just another one of so many things I had never even considered. I was not sure anyone would have needed to have money in the Army, since the essentials like food and a place to sleep were always on the house. Nevertheless, when the money started to come, it sometimes felt like we had enough for just about anything else we might have wanted.

By the second or third weekend in San Antonio, around the Fourth of July holiday, Pete and I had planned to take a trip to the Gulf Coast. We had heard that it was the place to go on weekends since it was less than a hundred miles southeast of San Antonio and there was an open beach on Padre Island where overnight camping was allowed. There wasn't a lot of planning involved. We checked out at the Post Command Office and set out at about 9:00 on a Friday morning. I was not sure anyone would have missed us if we hadn't checked out.

Hitchhiking to the Gulf Coast was a snap. On this weekend, that may have been because half of the Lone Star State seemed to be headed that way. During our first or second ride, the Texan we were with pulled out a joint as big as a cigar and asked us if we wanted to join him. I started laughing at the size of the thing and joked that it was probably big enough to hang in the back window with his rifle. He said, "You fella's ain't from around here are you." Of course, Pete and I said that we were not. Then he said, "Well, welcome to Texas."

We crossed over to the Island on the ferry at Aransas Pass and set foot on the beach at around 1:00 that afternoon. It was a beautiful wide and flat beach that stretched for miles along the coast. There were a few beach houses sprinkled along the land side of the sand. Most of them appeared wrecked and deserted, apparently the result of a recent hurricane. Although we could see lots of people up and down the beach, it didn't seem crowded at all because there was so much room for everyone to spread out. Vehicles were allowed to drive up and down the beach on a makeshift road between the water, the dunes, and the broken down houses. It was a beautiful sunny day on the Gulf of Mexico and Pete and I were ready to take it all in.

We started exploring. After being told by a stranger to stay clear of the purple-laced Portuguese Man-of-War jellyfish that seemed to be everywhere, we went into the water. It reminded me of the Great Salt Lake which I had visited on my San Francisco trip with Tingsly, but it was more primitive and there were no mosquitoes. After dousing ourselves in the small waves of the Gulf, Pete and I stood knee deep in the water for a while and marveled at the beautiful ocean views. A bit later, we decided that we would begin walking down the beach, but it was so huge, within a few minutes we had our thumbs out hitching a ride on the sand. On this trip, it truly didn't matter where we wound up.

Our first ride was in an old rusted-out pickup truck with a guy who appeared to be a regular on the Island. He was well-tanned, unshaven, and dressed only in a pair of tattered cut-off jeans. From the stash of beer cans on the floor of the truck, as well as the one in his hand, we could tell that he was already enjoying himself. He waved at several different groups of people who had set up little neighborhoods along the dunes. We got along instantly, but then it was clear that he probably had no trouble getting along with anyone. About fifteen minutes later and a just a few hundred yards down the beach at two or three miles per hour, the guy pulled off the sandy highway to greet some folks he seemed to know pretty well. He trotted over to see them, hugged each one, and then came strolling back toward the truck. He said, "I'm going to hang out here a while...you guys go ahead, take the truck, and come on back around when you're done."

I took the wheel of the old pickup and headed down the beach. Pete and I marveled at the fact that we had only been at this place for about an hour and we already had our own set of wheels. We tooled down the sand waving at people like we had seen our mentor doing. After a while we pulled off the beach, drove over to a nearby convenience store, and got some beer, bread, peanut butter, and cigarettes. Everything seemed so new: the place, the people, and my new friend Pete.

One place seemed about as good as the next on the beach, so in a little while Pete and I turned around and putt-putted back toward the place where we'd inherited the truck. On the way, we each popped a beer and shared a Texas-style joint that Pete had rolled for the occasion. When we got back to the little neighborhood where we'd started, the guy who'd lent us the truck was nowhere around. So, we just pulled up to the dunes and joined in with the group that had set up camp there. They were happy to have us.

By the end of the night we had spent hours sitting around the open bonfire that served as the center of this neighborhood. The people were extremely friendly. They weren't exactly hippies, although everyone kind of looked like one after a day in the sun and sand. I wound up spending most of my time with a very thin, spunky young girl named Bonnie, who must have had the longest, frizziest hair in Texas. She was so thin that she barely needed a string bikini to cover her almost non-existing breasts. I appreciated her energy and her appearance. She seemed intrigued by the couple of extra years I had on her, but I don't think either of us had anything in mind other than flirting and sharing a little time together. The beach was a great place to do that sort of thing.

At some point, Bonnie seemed to wake up to the fact that Pete and I were in the military. I guess we thought that it was obvious considering our short hair, the green boxers we used for swimming, and the green blankets we used to pack our things. It suddenly became clear that Bonnie had some sort of experience with Army guys. At one point she asked Pete and I in front all the others, "Are Army guys always horny?" I remember looking at Pete, wondering what was behind Bonnie's question, and struggling for an answer. Finally, I said "Some probably are, but I only get horny when there's a good reason to be." Some of the Bonnie's friends laughed.

Recognizing that I had taken a little offense at her comment and had gently fired back, Bonnie became silent and then walked off alone toward the water. I followed a few paces behind. When she stopped I said, "I'm a bit sensitive about being in the Army." She said, "I understand. My comment was pretty stupid."

Then I asked "Is there some reason why you wanted to know?" She said, "My father is a career officer in the Air Force." I didn't know what to say to that, so I just made some remark about what a beautiful night it was.

When it was time to sleep, Pete and I created a little wall out of an old piece of plywood and rolled up in our army blankets to block the wind that was blowing briskly by that time. During the night we wound up totally wrapped in the blankets trying to keep the sand out of our faces. By the time the sun reappeared, our makeshift wall had blown over and we were both covered with about a half-inch of sand. We leaped up, shook like a couple of dogs, stripped to our boxers, and headed for the water to rinse off. Perhaps Basic Training had served a purpose in that we both seemed fairly immune to the effects of the elements.

Saturday was about the same on the island. Pete and I walked for miles and got to know each other that much better. Clearly, we had a lot in common, particularly our views about the military, the War, and anti-war activities. Somehow we had both enlisted to be on this journey and, as if to justify our actions, we were both determined to get as much out of it as possible. At one point Pete asked if I expected to go to Vietnam. It was the first time I had allowed myself to give it more than a few fleeting thoughts at one time. We talked all around the question for a while, but it turned out that we both expected to be going.

Saturday night Pete and I left the group and decided to inhabit one of the battered houses along the dunes. Bonnie and the girl Pete had befriended decided to stay behind, which was fine. The house we adopted was really nothing more than a set of steps leading to part of a floor resting on some stilts, but it completely served our purpose. It raised us off the beach just enough that the sand didn't bother us. We sat up very late that night sitting out on the edge of the platform, looking at the water, watching the fireworks, listening to the parties, talking about the War, and feeling like we were on top of the world. We had already decided we'd come back to this place as often as we could. For about the first time since we'd arrived in Texas, neither one of us was high on anything other than the experience.

The first full week of training at Fort Sam was about what I'd expected it to be. All the guys I was with had some college, so it seemed that almost everyone had something in common other than getting high. Our group got along really well. The classes on psychopathology, personality disorders, mental hygiene, and common military psychiatric ailments were no more challenging than my Introduction to Psychology class at Loyola. We only attended classes for about four hours per day. The rest of the time remained available for reading, independent study, eating, borrowing a guitar from the Special Services Center or just hanging out. At 5:00 Monday through Thursday and anytime Friday through Sunday, it was okay to go off base, downtown, to the zoo, or anywhere else.

In the evenings, Pete and I spent a lot of time by the little river that cut through downtown San Antonio. There was not much there except a brand new delicatessen where we sometimes stopped in between our hikes up and down the river. Occasionally, a gondola-type boat would float by with some tourists on board. In 1971, floating on that river was like a wilderness tour.

Three or four weeks into training, I began to get moody, much like I had been back in Chicago at the start of my junior year there. Later, I recognized that these feelings had shown up after I had participated in an all-night demonstration on the steps of a government building across from the Alamo in downtown San Antonio. Pete and I had been excited about the rally the whole week before it was scheduled to occur. We both thought it would give us a great opportunity to connect with Army guys from Fort Sam and Air Force guys from Lakeland who were opposed to the War. I was particularly psyched up because I thought it might allow me to begin actualizing my interest in precipitating dissent from within as I had told others at home that I was interested in doing. We skipped a weekend at Port Aransas so we could get involved.

Unfortunately, the event didn't turn out to be what we had expected. It was mostly dominated by folks associated with one of the local junior colleges and none of them had anything new to say. Even at the peak of the event when people were stopping by before their evenings on the town, there were only about a hundred people present and only a few appeared to be Army guys. By 11:00 that night, the formal activity was done and virtually everyone had gone home. Even so, Pete and I sat there among the ceremonial candles with a few of the organizers and a few street people all night long as the advertisements had suggested we should. It was a pitiful display of resistance. At one point I walked across the street and, as a sorry show of my own defiance, I peed on the wall of the Alamo. I remember hoping that Davey Crockett and Daniel Boone, two of my childhood heroes, would forgive me. I spent much of the rest of the night writing a little poem that summed up my thoughts pretty well:

Night Watchman

Here on some steps with friends without names
Here to keep watch on the night in the city

The lights have died on a needle to space
Here as I watch the candles burn slow

Here as I sit talking with friends
Watching the night's enchanting dance
in the city

People gone home from city shops
Here as I feel they went home alone
Here as I wonder talking of things
Watching the night and lonely cries
in the city

Cars pass by on paths of stone
Here as I see a land turned hard
Here as I'm sad talking of trips
Watching the night calling this home
in the city

Voices of people from places unknown
Here as I watch faces with smiles
Here as I laugh talking of truth
Watching the night with listening ears
in the city

People have died friends of mine
Here as I feel torn to bits
And that's why I'm here the candles burn slow
Talking with friends watching the night
in the city.

In between repeated viewings of Love Story and the
Original M*A*S*H movie with Elliott Gould and Donald
Sutherland, Pete and I had the opportunity to see a few concerts
in downtown San Antonio at the City Auditorium. Led Zeppelin

put on a great show there. The Credence Clearwater Revival concert was even better. This may have been because Pete and I were accompanied by some chocolate Mescaline that night. Though we had dropped our hits just before we went through the gate, twenty minutes later neither of us felt much of an effect. Sometimes it was hard to tell if a hallucinogenic drug was slow-acting or if the stuff you had was weak. We might have suspected that our failure to get off had something to do with our lack of interest in Bo Diddley's opening act, but we didn't. We swallowed a second hit. That must have been just a minute or so before the first one kicked in. From there we knew we were going to be off to the races.

As soon as we heard the first notes of "Born on the Bayou" we were out of our seats in the upper deck and making our way through the packed house to the floor of the auditorium. Just finding our way through the auditorium was a trip. We eventually made it right up to the front and wiggled into the crowd between the front seats and the stage. "Keep on Chooglin'," "Lodi," "Green River," and "Suzi Q" exploded one after another. After each song Pete would look at me with a silly grin on his face and tell me how high he was. I couldn't do anything except smile back. After the show, we made our way to a downtown movie theatre and watched "2001- A Space Odyssey" late into the night with other people from the concert as we gradually settled down from our wild ride. We slept through most of the next day.

During Week Seven or Eight of Advanced Training, Sunshine came down to visit me in San Antonio. I helped her pay for an airplane ticket and got her a room at a quaint, but cheap motel just down the block from the base. It was great to see her away from Chicago, but apparently she hadn't traveled much before. She was pretty uncomfortable at the motel until I got there and didn't seem to know what to do with herself during the daytime while I was attending classes. She seemed to enjoy it a bit more when she, Pete, and I got back on the highway to hitchhike back down to Port Aransas together.

Sunshine did pretty well as a hitchhiker. Although I don't think she had ever done it on an open road before, she got right into it when the three of us got a lift from a fiesty old man in a light blue pickup truck. She appeared to be having a great time with all four of us packed in the front seat listening to the old guy share stories about his travels during his younger days. Sunshine was really impressed when he asked me to drive so he could rest before getting back to his home in Corpus Christi. We all thought it was funny at first when the old guy kept begging me to drive faster. By the time I got the truck going as fast as he wanted, we were probably doing about eighty miles an hour. That was a little uncomfortable, so I finally asked him why I had to drive so fast. He said it was because he had read that more than half of all accidents happen when a driver gets hit from behind, so he wanted to avoid those by going faster than everyone else. He was absolutely serious. We appreciated his logic, even if we weren't quite convinced that he had his facts right. I slowed down as soon as he dozed off.

Pete and I had been telling Sunshine wonderful things about the beach at Port Aransas and she must have expected it was going to be a pretty amazing experience when we got there. Except for the fact that there were many fewer people around, Pete and I found it pretty much as it had been around the Fourth of July. However, I wasn't convinced that Sunshine was quite as impressed. She seemed awkward on the beach, as if side-stepping jellyfish and eating peanut butter sandwiches was a little trashy or something. She wasn't even that wild about the Boone's Farm Apple Wine I got for her at the convenience store.

Things got a little worse when Pete and I discovered that our "house" was no longer there. Apparently most of the wrecked houses had been cleared since the first visit we had made to the Island. Sunshine was particularly disappointed about not having a specific place to stay and, although I didn't care for it, I started taking it as my responsibility to see that she was as comfortable as she could be. I was never any good at those things.

After a long walk on the beach, darkness was coming on and we located a spot along the dunes to set up for the night. Pete and I did our best to build a lean-to that would keep the wind and blowing sand at bay. However, once again, our construction job didn't work that well. Sunshine was up half the night asking me if there was anything I could do to stop the sand from blowing in her face. There wasn't. I suggested that she do her best to cover up. Although we laughed about it on the way back to San Antonio and Sunshine probably benefited in some way from the road experience, her reluctance to go with the flow during our weekend at the beach caught my attention.

The rest of our visit went really well. Compared to sleeping on the sand, I guessed that the relative comfort of the motel room started to seem pretty nice to her. We both loosened up and had a great time walking around the zoo and the river downtown. But it was also okay when Sunshine left. I quickly went back to not feeling responsible for anyone but myself.

During the last two weeks of training, guys were being sent out on various practical internships around the base at Fort Sam. Since it was a hub for medical treatment in the Army and had a world-renowned burn rehabilitation center, there were plenty of places for us trainees to begin practicing our new Psychiatric Social Work skills.

I was instructed to report to Chambers Pavilion for the hands-on portion of my training. Though I had never been on an inpatient psychiatric unit, it didn't take me long to catch on. I walked into a small foyer at the entrance of the building and immediately came to a pair of locked swinging doors. There was an intercom next to the door, so I pushed the "talk" button and announced that I was there to report for my training. A couple of tries later, someone finally answered on the other end and told me they would be right down to let me in.

Eventually, three young Specialists in neatly pressed white medical coats greeted me at the entrance door. We introduced, conversed politely, and compared notes regarding our home towns like Army guys often do. They joked about the quality of Psychiatric Social Work training as we walked through one of the units. I wasn't sure how to interpret their comments, but I smiled anyway just to act as though I understood. I was more focused on the new place where I had found myself.

All the patients were wearing blue hospital shirts and pajama pants as if they were in recovery following surgery, but they were all physically well. Most of them were either sitting in the vinyl-padded chairs that lined the hallways or walking around aimlessly. Some were talking to themselves, staring off into space, or both. Several staff sat behind a counter that separated them from a social area. It was a classic picture of what I imagined most people would have envisioned an inpatient psychiatric unit to be.

The Specialists walked me into a room about halfway down one of the hallways, told me to sit down, and left. The room was barren except for a desk, a swivel office chair, and another padded chair like the ones in the hallway. There were no views to the outside, but there was one window that looked like a mirror from inside the office. I recognized that it was a one-way glass so that others could observe what was going on from the room next door without being spotted. If it didn't fool me, I didn't think it was likely to fool anyone. I sat down at the desk and waited. As I did, I shuffled through the drawers, but there was nothing in them but a stack of old comic books, some well-used newspapers, and a few worn-out pencils.

A few restless minutes later, the Specialists came back into the room. One of them was on each side of a disheveled young man holding his arms to his sides. The other walked behind them as if prepared to help if it was needed. They turned, physically-guided their patient down into the padded chair in front of me, and told him to stay seated. Since I might have appeared a little nervous, I thought they might tell me to stay seated as well, but they didn't. They instructed me to do an intake assessment and left for the observation room.

Huh. There I was getting ready to do some Psychiatric Social Work with a guy I knew nothing about and three others I had just met who were ready to critique my performance from behind the one-way glass. I looked at the young man but he didn't look back. He was just a kid like me, maybe even a year or so younger. He was dressed in blue hospital pajamas like all the other patients. He was thin and very unkempt, with a powerful body odor and a gaze that made him seem somewhere far away. I was stuck by the obvious seriousness of his condition and suddenly felt that I needed to grow up quickly. Almost instantly, I began to view the young man as being representative of the impact of war on a young life. I was also very pleased to find myself in a situation where I might be able to help.

I knew that the first thing I needed to do was to establish some sort of therapeutic rapport. I said, "Hi, my name is Marty. What's yours?" There was no response; no words, no motion, not even a glance in my direction. Not knowing what else to do, but thinking that maybe he hadn't heard me; I repeated my greeting a little louder. Once again, there was no response. From there I decided I would try to mix it up a bit to see if I could identify something that would catch his attention or trigger some sort of a reaction on his part. "I'm from Peoria. Where are you from?" No response. "I'm into music. Who is your favorite band?" No response. "I used to like baseball. Do you like the Braves?" No response. Not having experienced any success and thinking that I might be overwhelming the kid, I paused for a moment.

As the two of us sat there together in that sterile room, our silence was broken in a way that I would never forget. I heard laughter from the observation room. At first the laughter sounded as if the Specialists were trying to control themselves, but then it escalated to the point that others could have heard them carrying on all the way down the hall. In a moment, they reentered the room with their beet-red faces, took the patient by his wrists, and raised him from his seat. As they escorted him out of the room, the young kid turned his head and made brief eye contact with me.

I sat in the room for a long time thinking about what had just happened. I flashed back to the induction station when the recruit had passed out during the exam and no one jumped in to help. I relived the times in Basic Training when guys fell off the parallel bars or collapsed during the extended runs. No one was expected to help them and usually no one did. I never understood. Not only did it seem that most people outside the Army didn't care about people in the Army, but a lot of guys who were in the Army didn't seem care about each other. I prepared myself for when the Specialists returned to the room that afternoon, but they never did. I sat there for a while and then left. If anybody wanted to ask why I had decided to leave, I would have been ready to give them an ear full.

Instead of getting carried away by my anger at the Specialists, I went back to the barracks that evening and got out some books. I did some amateur diagnostics and ruled out the possibility that the kid was deaf. Instead I decided that he had probably had some sort of trauma and may have been experiencing catatonic schizophrenia, a disorder characterized by withdrawal, lack of communication, and extreme apathy. I looked in the book for ways to treat this sort of psychosis, but didn't find anything other than a few medications. So, I decided I'd just go back the next day and try out some different things. I didn't know any better. I just wanted to help. Maybe we would just sit together. Maybe we would go for a walk. Maybe we would go outside on the lawn and feel some Texas sunshine. Maybe we would go to Port Aransas for the weekend. I didn't know. Maybe I could just get him to look at me again.

I returned through the secured doors at Chambers Pavilion the following morning a little apprehensive but ready to experiment. I saw two of the Specialists standing together in the hallway, but I ignored them. I walked up to the nurses' station and asked where I could find the patient. At first no one responded to me, as if they were too busy or I had said something wrong. Then I noticed one of the nurses look over toward one of the Specialists. Eventually, she looked back toward me and said, "He is no longer on our unit." I asked where he was and she explained that he was in Intensive Care. Intensive Care? She saw the look of confusion on my face. Then she told me that he had stabbed himself in the stomach that morning with a leather hole-punching tool while working in the craft room. I immediately concluded that the patient's suicide attempt was the result of the Specialists' practical joke.

I seriously considered attacking the closest Specialist I could get my hands on, but I didn't. I didn't even make eye contact with either of them. I spent the rest of the day moving around the unit talking to as many patients as I could. As novel as it was, I quickly discovered that I felt right at home. At one point, I might have had half of the guys on the unit sitting in the dayroom…smiling, talking, and looking alive. I was doing what I had come to do.

No one ever said a thing about that first day I spent at Chambers Pavilion or about any of the other days I spent there either. I suspected they wouldn't because they knew I didn't think their joke was funny and they knew I would attribute the kid's suicide attempt to them. Fact is, I didn't interact with any staff during the six days I spent at Chambers Pavilion, but I learned a great deal from my interactions with the patients.

We got our final grades from Psychiatric Social Worker training sometime around the middle of September. Although I was a little unsure how it was going to turn out, I was given an "A" on my internship. I suspected that the Specialists probably feared that I would spill their beans if they gave me anything less. Partially as a result, I finished in the upper bracket of my class and got another promotion out of Advanced Training for the effort. In light of my experience, I felt it was deserved. I was now an E-4 Specialist in Psychiatric Social Work after a bit more than five months in the Army.

I had approached my time in the Army similar to the way I had always approached hitchhiking. I rarely thought about what was going to happen next, just whatever I was doing at the time. My friends and I hadn't known what we were going to do when we got to Phoenix, Los Angeles, or Minot, North Dakota and somehow it all worked out.

Because of this way of thinking, I wasn't too concerned during the final days at Fort Sam Houston waiting for our orders to wherever we were going to be headed next. Even so, there were all sorts of rumors floating around about what would happen with our class. Since we had spent some of our time learning about drug abuse (and several of us studied more in our off time), some guys speculated that we were actually going to be labeled "Drug Counselors," rather than Psychiatric Social

Workers. Others guessed that we were going to wind up staying at Fort Sam to bolster their capacity to handle the psychiatric side of their services. After my experience at Chambers Pavilion, I knew how badly that was needed.

Pete and I, along with some of the others assumed we were bound for South Vietnam. Of course, we didn't have any idea what we would do there, but we thought there had to be some reason why the military had so many of us training in this odd discipline at the same time. People were getting nervous, particularly the two guys who were already married. One had a baby on the way. Pete and I had a long conversation one night and decided that if we were not on the list to go to Vietnam and one of the married guys was, then we would volunteer to take his seat on the plane. We still had no idea how these things worked.

We found out as a group that all but two of the eighteen guys who had gone through Psychiatric Social Work Training were headed to Vietnam. The married guy with the baby on the way was staying in the States at Walter Reed Army Hospital. One single guy was being sent to Germany. The other married guy and the rest of us were scheduled for a flight out of Fort Lewis, Washington on October 25th. Most of us had only been in the Army for less than six months and we were already on our way to the big time. Pete and I reminded each other that we had never imagined it would turn out any other way. I suppose some of the other guys might have wondered why we didn't seem too upset about it. I had thoroughly convinced myself that there could be a lot to learn by getting closer to the problem that brought me to the Army in the first place.

Teach your Children
(Crosby, Stills, Nash and Young)

Once again I almost wished I hadn't been granted another leave before being shipped out to Vietnam. I knew some of the guys relished the idea, but to me it just provided another opening wherein I might actually have to think about what was happening in my life. For me, thinking about such things had become something of a waste of time. I'd noticed that thinking about things in advance rarely seemed to result in my doing anything differently than I would have done in the first place.

I caught a plane for Peoria to see my family. I broke the news to my parents about my next assignment the night I arrived home. It was probably what everyone expected. Since I didn't know much more than they did about what I would be doing or where I would be going once I got to Vietnam, there really wasn't much to talk about.

Other than my father, as far as I knew no one else in my family had ever participated in a war. My older brother turned out to be too old to have been included in the draft for Vietnam and seemingly too old to have been moved very much by it at all. I had never heard him talk about the War, although he told me once that he was sorry that his age group had missed out on the opportunity to smoke pot. That revelation was a little strange to me because I had never actually told him that I didn't. It was interesting that my brother tended to blend conversation about the War and doing drugs as if they were parts of the same thing.

My family decided to throw me a little going-away party. My older brother graciously offered to have everyone over to his house which was in a tiny town called Rome on the Illinois River. Of course, my folks were there. My younger brother and sister were there. My sister from Milwaukee came down. I was

215

surprised when cousin Smiley's folks showed up. I couldn't resist telling them about my brief rendezvous with Smiley at the Kickapoo Creek Festival. They didn't appear to know much about what their son was up to in those days, but I didn't view it as my responsibility to fill them in much more completely.

Considering the nature of the event, I thought some might have been surprised that I didn't come out in my Army uniform. I suspected a couple of them probably thought that if a young man joined the Army that automatically meant that he must have agreed with its activities and would be proud to tout its colors, as if it were some sort of sports team or statement of political position. I felt that anyone who might have been unclear about my take on things should have gotten clear when I showed up at the party in some beat-up bell bottoms and a T-shirt. If anyone still had any doubt, the peace symbol I was wearing with my dog tags should have cleared it up. By that time, I didn't see any contradiction at all. Thus far, in my six months of experience, I had not met anyone in the Army (other than those who were paid to prepare us) who was actually in favor of the War.

After we ate the wonderful hamburgers and hot dogs my brother cooked on his grill, almost everyone wound up outside on the deck watching a river barge go by. As was usually the case in my family, the younger kids were off playing someplace while the rest of us were sitting around having a drink and finding things to keep smiling about. I had a nice talk with my little sister, who was clearly coming of age and beginning to have some understanding of the issues. She seemed proud to tell me that she was learning how to play Joni Mitchell songs on her guitar. My little brother didn't say much at all. I knew that he had always had a hard time with saying goodbye to someone in the family, although being the youngest of seven he had already had a lot of practice at it.

Later on, as I was small-talking with my aunt and uncle, I heard some loud voices coming from the kitchen, which was just inside the screen door from the deck where the rest of us were sitting. It was my mother and my older brother. While it was not totally unusual to hear my mother raise her voice, especially with my older brother, in this case I could tell something was different. My father and I got up and walked to the door to find out what was going on.

By that time, my mother was crying. My older brother was trying to console her, but apparently it wasn't working. As my father and I watched through the screen, my mother got up from her chair and said, "I don't care what you say. I hate this War. No one agrees with it, yet no one gets very concerned about it until it touches their own life." Then, she started crying harder and rushed out of the kitchen toward the living room. As she walked away, she said, "Don't they know it is killing our children?"

This was one of the first times I'd noticed my mother not sitting up straight and keeping a smile on her face, as she had always encouraged us to do. My older brother, my father, and I traded glances. My older brother started to follow my mother into the living room, but I asked him to let me go in to be with her.

I entered the room gingerly and sat down next to her on the couch. Gently, I put my arm over her shoulder, but didn't say anything. She had her face in her hands, crying uncontrollably into a clump of tissues. After we'd sat there for a few moments she said, "I can't look at you…I can't let you go." I didn't say anything. Another moment later, she turned to me and we held each other for a long time as we cried.

Through the tears I told my mother that I agreed with everything she had said about the War. I assured her that I had no intention of hurting or killing anyone. I told her that my intention was to get a better understanding of what was going on and to help others in any way that I could. I told her that I would be back home safely before she knew it. Finally, her crying stopped and we each said, "I love you," (which was a little unusual for us at the time) and walked back through the kitchen and onto the deck with smiles on our faces. By then my father had tears in his eyes. Characteristically, my little brother and sister started clapping and cheering.

Before the evening was over, I was pleasantly surprised to see that my parents had gotten me a present on behalf of the family that I could use on my trip overseas. My folks had always been very thoughtful in their gift-giving. When we were little and one of the children had a birthday, they always had presents for that kid on top of the coffee table and a little something else for each of the others tucked underneath. I guess they thought that this ritual would keep all of the kids interested in somebody else's celebration. Although there were no presents under my older brother's patio furniture, everyone still seemed interested to see how I would react to my gift.

It was a brand new four-string ukulele. My father quickly taught me how to shape three or four chords and I was strumming "Five Foot Two, Eyes of Blue," in no time.

After a few days in Peoria I made another quick trip to Chicago. While there, I stayed at the apartment that Sunshine had been sharing with Jewelie and another girl. Not very many people knew that Sunshine and I were seeing each other again, let alone that we were now engaged. Sunshine's roommates knew about it, but their silence around me made it clear that they weren't particularly enthused about the idea. Sunshine told me that they thought she was as crazy as I was. For whatever reason, she seemed to like that idea.

While I was in Chicago, Sunshine and I made a quick trip out to the suburbs to meet her family. I was looking forward to the visit primarily because it would give me a chance to meet her younger brother who played in a blues band. Within a half-hour of my arrival, we were holed up in a basement music room playing his Guild guitars and singing Neil Young songs like "When You Dance," "Southern Man," and "Down by the River." I also played a couple of the original songs I had written that he seemed to like a lot.

Sunshine's folks were great, too. Her father worked downtown in some sort of executive job for a big steel company. Her mother worked in the office at a local high school. They both liked all sorts of music and, like my mom, Sunshine's mother smoked cigarettes in the house. This came in handy for me because it meant that I didn't have to hide another one of my bad habits. After a nice dinner, Sunshine, her brother, one of his friends, and I put on a little concert in the living room. Sunshine's mom and dad loved old folk songs and the blues, but my version of the Moody Blues' "Nights in White Satin" was also a big hit.

During our visit, no one ever said a word about Sunshine and I having been engaged or the fact that I was going away to Vietnam. I was confident that her folks predicted that I wasn't going to be in their daughter's life for very long, reasonable enough considering that we had already broken up once before. Still, they were very nice to me.

My Chicago going-away party really wasn't much of a party. I think Sunshine did her best to get everyone to come to her apartment, but there was just no way that many would have expected to have much fun at a party for a guy going off to Vietnam by choice. Once again, no one talked about it. No one talked about Sunshine and I being back together again either. She announced our engagement to the group sometime during the evening, but the response was mostly just silence, surprise, or disbelief. I had no doubt that there were people in that room, many of my old friends, who would soon be doing their best to talk Sunshine out of her relationship with me. However, compared to other things, their lack of reaction didn't matter much to me at the time.

Time has Come Today
(Chambers Brothers)

Going back to Fort Lewis was not something that excited me. The difference between what I had seen at Fort Sam and what I had experienced in Basic Training was almost as dramatic as the difference between being in college at Loyola and being in the Army. I checked into the "Overseas Replacement Station" and waited for some of the others from the Texas group to show up. A guy we called "Kool" was one of the first ones that I saw. He had already been there a few days by the time I arrived.

When I first saw Kool he had a long and frustrated look on his face. It turned out that he hadn't been just hanging around since he had gotten to Fort Lewis. He had been doing calisthenics three times a day and doing duty the rest of his time in a nearby mess hall. As it turned out, that is what we all wound up doing for the ten days we had to wait for our plane ride to Vietnam. Although I tried to take it in stride, it was very discouraging to say the least.

Not only did we begin to feel like we were back in the Army again, but it seemed like a waste of our new Psychiatric Social Work talents to be peeling potatoes. Some of our loss of morale, if anyone ever actually had any, was because we all knew we were headed out soon and nearly everyone wished we could just get on with it. This time the military's "hurry up and wait" reputation became seriously irritating. Of course, I wondered if there was some sort of rationale behind the delay.

Somewhere along the way we were issued the new clothing that we would use overseas. We handed in the stateside clothes we had and got brand-new jungle fatigues, boots, T-shirts, and boxers to pack up in our crisp new duffle bags. The worst part of getting all this new stuff was not that it signaled a

221

new era in our military experience. It was that we already knew that all this fresh clothing would make it clear to everyone that we were "Newbie's" when we arrived in Southeast Asia. Up until that time, I had not really considered the potential significance of this, but it turned out that it was not just a little thing.

Finally, our departure day arrived: October 25, 1971. Everyone I'd trained with at Fort Sam was now present and accounted for, including Pete. We got all fixed up in our new clothes and boots which we were required to shine, and boarded a plane bound for... Anchorage, Alaska? I had no idea that we would go through Alaska to get to Vietnam, but perhaps it eased some of the tension that guys were already beginning to feel. It didn't seem so bad that initially we would be flying from one United State to another. I was already thinking that I could add it to the growing list of states I had visited, even if it was only for a stop at the airport. I arbitrarily decided that it would be okay for that to count.

At Anchorage we boarded what looked like a commercial flight on a carrier called Flying Tiger Airlines. Although none of us knew it then, Flying Tiger Airlines was an outfit formed by several ex-military pilots that contracted with the Army to fly cargo and personnel to various destinations around the world. The Boeing 707 they used to haul us looked pleasant enough and we even had neatly-tailored civilian stewardesses for the first part of the trip. Their participation was nice for us, but it was probably considered hazardous duty for them.

All of us Psychiatric Social Workers packed into seats fairly close together near the back of the plane. As the sight of land faded when we flew out over the Pacific Ocean, no one said anything about what we were actually doing on the plane. Instead, guys talked about their families and shared detailed accounts about what they had done with their girlfriends while they were home on leave. I recall that someone said we would be twenty-six hours en route to Vietnam, with stops in Japan and the Philippines along the way. Twenty-six hours seemed like a long time. So, given that no one seemed too interested in talking about our arrival just yet, I gave in to Kool's prodding and pulled out my new Ukulele. At least with him around I knew I wouldn't be expected to play any country.

"You Are My Sunshine" and "Five Foot Two, Eyes of Blue" got great responses from most of the guys on the plane, and since they were the only songs I knew, I just played them over and over again for a while. Then Kool had the idea that the G, C, and D chords I had been strumming could be used for another song. I practiced quietly by myself for a few minutes and then decided I would try out the new song. The response from the guys on that plane was nothing short of bizarre.

The song was Country Joe McDonald and the Fish's "Vietnam Song," or as it was sometimes called, the "I Feel like I Am Fixin' to Die Rag." Everyone within earshot sang the chorus over and over since no one knew more than one or two of the verses. The words and the scene on that plane stayed in my head for days, maybe months:

> "And it's one, two, three what are we fightin' for?
> Don't ask me, I don't give a damn, next stop is Vietnam.
> And it's five, six, seven open up the pearly gates.
> Well there ain't no time to wonder why,
> Whoopee we're all gonna die!"

While almost everybody sang the song the first two or three times I played it, in a little while participation gradually began to dwindle. It became fairly obvious that what had seemed funny at first was beginning to sink in with more and more of the guys on the plane. The sound of the singing disappeared as if it was swirling down a dirty storm drain on some busy city street. It had started out sounding like the background of a holiday parade and wound up something like the funeral march after John F. Kennedy's death. Guys began to slump in their seats. Everyone sat quietly for hours. Whoopee.

Somewhere along the way from Anchorage to Japan, we lost track of the hour and the day. It was nearly impossible to keep up with the changes in the time zones, so pretty soon everyone stopped trying. No one could change their watches fast enough. We stopped for fueling in Japan.

Flying into Tokyo was almost as amazing as the sight of Albuquerque from the mountains in the early morning darkness. It seemed like we flew over the orange lights of the city for at least thirty minutes before we even got close to the airport. Tokyo looked like no place I had ever seen, even from an airplane. Once again the lights looked as though they were twinkling from the bows of boats floating on water. Strangely, there did not appear to be winding roads with little Japanese cars zipping here and there. There had to be more water than land. In the dark, it was difficult to see any outlines of buildings, bridges, Buddha's or anything else, just an endless landscape filled with the hazy orange lights.

We were permitted off the plane at the airport. Inside the civilian terminal, Pete and I talked about how we felt like we were strangers to ordinary civilization. Maybe Japan wasn't ordinary civilization? Several of us poked around in the shops, but they seemed foreign not just because Japan was different from what we were used to in the States, but because our heads were already someplace else. I might have guessed that guys would have avoided reboarding the plane as long as they possibly could. However, we were all back in our seats well before it was time to buckle up for the last legs of our journey. The Flying Tiger stewardesses went off-duty in Tokyo.

It wasn't long before we stopped again in the Philippines, this time to top off the fuel tanks at a U.S. military base. I don't remember anyone getting off the plane. It was a quick stop and we were off again toward our destination. However, I did put it on my new list of countries visited.

It had been fairly silent on the plane ever since I'd stopped banging out the Vietnam Song on my ukulele, but after leaving the Philippines, the silence was deafening. Some guys spent time organizing the things they had brought with them on the plane. One guy passed around a photo of his lusty girlfriend in her swimming suit throwing him a kiss. Then, without anyone having received any instructions, all the civilian-looking stuff just vanished. Guys tucked in their T-shirts. Guys put on their crisp new baseball-style hats. Guys adjusted the elastic garter bands that held their baggy boonie pants at the tops of their boots. It was contagious. Within a short time, everyone on the plane began to look like they were in the Army, including myself. Somehow, even with all the time zone changes, it was still the middle of the night outside.

None of us had any notion of what it was going to be like when we landed in Vietnam. No one had told us anything about that in Basic or Advanced Training. Would we arrive at a commercial Southeast Asian airport? Why had the stewardesses abandoned us in Japan? Would there be people on the ground to greet us and rush us off to wherever we were going? Would there be any immediate signs of the War? Suddenly, I realized that I had been right all along. I didn't know anything about Vietnam. I didn't even know how big it was. Was it all just a jungle? How would an airplane land in a jungle? How prevalent was the fighting? Did we need to be prepared for anything in particular when we hit the ground? How would a guy tell the difference between Viet Cong and a regular South Vietnamese citizen? Was someone planning to tell us what was going on? It was pitch black out there. When was this Flying Tiger going to land? Most of us sat up in our seats.

By the time the cabin lights were turned off, I swear I could hear the pounding of a hundred and fifty hearts on that airplane. Without being too obvious, guys pulled their seat belts tighter and tried to catch glimpses of the approaching landscape out the windows of the plane. There was nothing to see, just the ocean and the dark outline of land at the water's edge. Then we began our descent.

When it became clear that we were close to landing, an announcement finally came over the intercom for everyone to extinguish their cigarettes and lower the hard plastic shades on the windows of the plane. Lowering the shade was hard for me because I liked to have some idea when the wheels of a plane were about to touch the runway. I didn't look forward to being surprised like I had been when I was sleeping upon arrival at Fort Sam Houston. However, for a moment I wished I had been asleep. Perhaps then I could be awakened from whatever dream I was having by the jolt of the wheels on the runway.

Guys looked around the cabin trying to catch glimpses of each other in the dark. I peeked through a tiny crack I had left at the bottom of my window shade, but there was nothing to see, not even the lights on the wings of the plane. We were getting closer to the water and the pale gray land was a bit more visible than before. Just as I was thinking that there were probably a few more miles to go, the big wheels of the plane skidded on the runway. With the window shades still down and lights out, we taxied for a minute or so and then came to an abrupt stop. We had arrived at Cam Ranh Bay in South Vietnam. There were no cheers, just glances and complete silence.

We sat still in the dark for about five minutes. Then, the door of the plane was cracked open and lowered by someone who had come out of the cockpit. In an instant, a sculpted

Sergeant in neatly tailored, but seriously weathered fatigues trotted up the steps of the plane and addressed us. Although it was difficult to hear him from where we sat in the back, he gave us a brief welcome to the country and then instructions related to getting across the runway to the processing station. It did not soothe anyone's sense of apprehension when he told us that the base was on "Red Alert" and we would need to low-crawl for about a hundred yards before we reached the bunkered area where we would assemble.

Guys began to exit the plane. When I got to the door and peered out there was still almost nothing to see except a hundred or so guys on their bellies wiggling across a desert-like field toward the silhouette of a structure on the other side. As I hit the earth at the end of the steps, I flung the cord of the bag that held my ukulele over my shoulder and recalled some of the Drill Sergeant's words during Basic Training...right then I couldn't see anything but "elbows and assholes" scurrying across that airstrip. And one young kid was toting a bag with a ukulele in it, replaying the words of a stupid song that were still stuck in his head: "Whoopee, we're all gonna die."

There was nothing to do at the processing station except find and grab one's duffle bag from the mound of duffle bags that had been piled there and go find a place to sleep for a few hours until the sun came up. Pete, Kool, and I set out together.

One of the first things I noticed about the base at Cam Ranh Bay was that very few people in the barracks areas seemed to be sleeping. The buildings reminded me of cattle barns with their lines of mosquito-netted sleeping racks in the open air under corrugated tin roofs surrounded by five-foot walls of sandbags. Guys were shuffling around everywhere I looked. Some were whispering in small groups in the dark. It was hard to tell whether people were coming or going, except that most of the guys who were coming were still schlepping their duffle bags looking for a place to crash.

As the three of us wandered through the place looking for three adjoining sleeping racks, it became clear that we were attracting attention. As it turned out, we were being examined from the tops of our covered heads to the tips of our shiny new jungle boots. In contrast, the guys who were checking us out were obviously Veterans. Their clothing was faded and their pants fit tightly on their legs. Many were without shirts and their hair was much longer than the standard issue cuts we had been given. Their boonie hats looked as though they had grown like moss on the tops of their heads. Most of the guys who were awake wore beads and braided armbands on their tanned bodies. Their stuff was strewn here and there as if it didn't matter.

As we were parading like Army fashion models through the stares of those experienced eyes, one of the Veterans said to his buddies, "Look guys, some Newbie's have come to relieve us." There was a wave of gentle laughter through the barracks. It sounded deep and mature, much older than the relative giggles our group had shared on the airplane. I immediately respected it. Pete, Kool, and I shrugged off their comments the best we could though they were a bit intimidating. But it was no more intimidating than the appearance of the well-worn forsaken place that formed one of my first and most lasting memories of Vietnam. We finally found three empty racks and climbed in as quietly as we could for a few hours of sleep. The sounds of shuffling and whispers were present through the rest of the night, as was the all-too-familiar smell of pot, patchouli oil, and cigarette smoke.

When we awoke to the sunlight of our first morning in Vietnam we didn't know what we were supposed to do so we just went hiking toward the smell of food. There were not very many people around. It seemed that most of the guys who had been there the night before had already moved on. We walked into a mess hall, saw some of the other familiar faces we had flown with, got in line for some food, and did our best to fit in like we knew what we were doing.

Sometime after breakfast we discovered a bulletin board with various lists of unit assignments. Newbies packed around the board trying to find their names and figure out where they were supposed to be. Eventually, one of the Psychiatric Social Workers found a list that contained all of our names. We were to report that afternoon en masse with our gear to the Drug Rehabilitation Treatment Center at the Cam Ranh Bay base. I suppose it was somewhat comforting to know that someone had claimed us.

Marrakesh Express
(Crosby, Stills, and Nash)

We spent forty-eight hours or so with a Philippine officer we called Major Takatoka at the Drug Center learning his view of what the Army had to say about drug use and abuse among the troops in Vietnam. We spent the majority of our time just hanging around because the information was pretty scant and to the point. Apparently, in its concerted effort to crack down on rampant marijuana use a couple of years earlier, it appeared that the Army had inadvertently shifted the drug of choice among many soldiers to heroin. In contrast to pot, heroin was easier to hide because it was harder to sniff out. Standard use of military discipline had not been very effective in curbing the use of either drug. Apparently, a soldier in the brig was worth far less than one in the bush.

We quickly learned that the heroin in Vietnam was plentiful, powerful, and cheap. Distribution channels were now well-established through the neighboring countries of Laos and Cambodia, in addition to the local fare that was already available. The heroin (Skag, Horse, or "H") was typically above ninety-five percent pure, whereas the purity of that sold on the street in the States was rarely above twenty-five percent. This purity level was important because the heroin was considered more dangerous than that seen stateside and it meant that soldiers didn't need to inject the drug to get the high. They could smoke, snort, or eat it and still achieve powerful effects. On top of that, a two hundred fifty milligram vial of this remarkably pure and powerful stuff sold on the bases for only $2.00 to $6.00 a pop depending on where you were in the country, significantly less than the $125.00 the same vial might have fetched in the States at the time.

Apparently, the bottom line in all of this was that the Army now had a new problem on its hands, one that was far more serious and possibly more prevalent than the relatively innocent one it had attempted to eradicate. Guys were becoming rapidly addicted to heroin, which was not only affecting their performance and morale in country, but perhaps as importantly, people in the States were complaining that their loved ones were returning home strung out on narcotics. I'd already reckoned that a battle wound might be viewed as one thing, whereas coming back home as a heroin addict would have been viewed as something else, even if both represented the effects of participating in the War. However, it was difficult to determine which mattered more to Major Takatoka, the performance and well-being of the troops in Vietnam or the public outcry that was taking place back home.

In contrast to emerging notions regarding treatment of heroin addiction in the States, the military sprang into action on the assumption that narcotics addiction was something that could be addressed, if not cured, in a one-shot rehabilitation experience. I wondered what else the Army could do considering that it would have been terribly inconvenient to either allow guys to go home for extended care or to receive an on-site substitute like methadone. I imagined that if they took one of those courses there might have been no one left to fight their War. In any case, by the time we arrived the Army had already established its plan.

In July of 1971, just after President Nixon declared his "War on Drugs" in the States and just three months before our arrival in country, the Army had christened its new Drug Amnesty Program. This program initially had been designed to screen and treat soldiers who were about to finish their tours of duty in Vietnam to help ensure that they were less likely to attract more negative attention to the War when they got back home. However, while this plan might have helped to address image problems at home, it did not address problems that were showing up among guys who still had lots of time left in country. Something else needed to be done.

As a result, the program was quickly expanded to allow soldiers to self-report their drug use without disciplinary consequences and check into one of the new Drug Treatment or Amnesty Centers that were being pieced together across the country. When the Amnesty Programs first started, guys were permitted to stay for seven days. Within two months, the length of expected stay at most Centers was extended to fourteen days. According to Major Takatoka, a lot of guys were now taking advantage of the military's offer. It suddenly occurred to me that perhaps the Recruiter back in Chicago actually had been directing me toward Psychiatric Social Work knowing that this new initiative was about to be launched in Vietnam. I was about to become a Drug Counselor in the Army, presumably part of the $105,000,000 special project ordered by President Nixon.

At the end of our brief orientation to drugs and the Drug Amnesty Program, we were shown a crude map of South Vietnam, which was divided into four regions and marked with the bases where programs were to be located. Within a few minutes the sixteen of us were divided up among seven bases including Camp Eagle, Phu Bai, Da Nang, Cam Ranh Bay, Bien Hoa, Long Binh, and Saigon. No one was sent to Pleiku, Tuy Hoa, Nha Trang, Plantation, or Can Tho, although the map indicated that there were Rehab Centers there. It turned out that Kool was being sent to the far north to join the 101st Airborne Division at Camp Eagle. A group of three was headed to Da Nang. Pairs were sent to Phu Bai, Cam Ranh Bay, Long Binh, and Saigon. Pete, myself, and Harry, a devoted member of the Latter Day Saints, were assigned to the 1st Cavalry Division at Bien Hoa.

Kool was not at all enthused about his trip up north. I quickly began to see that he was the kind of guy who never seemed to have much luck. Whether or not it was consistently true, guys believed that fighting was more intense closer to North Vietnam. We wondered why they were going to Camp Eagle anyway since the map did not show any Rehab Center there. Perhaps the 101st didn't care to advertise its problems? We also wondered why it was going to take three of us at Da Nang and Bien Hoa. Even so, there was some comfort in knowing that no one was going anywhere alone.

The next morning our group said its goodbyes to each other and loaded in "deuce and a half" diesel Army trucks to be taken off in different directions with all the other Newbies. None of us knew much about where we were, what direction we were really headed, or what we were going to do when we got where we were going. I reasoned that it wasn't all that different from heading out on the road during college, except that in this case there was a war going on nearby. Even so, I had some sense of security knowing that I was not bound for the far north and I was with Pete and the Mormon. It turned out that we were the only three guys headed to Bien Hoa that morning. Strangely, I had a fleeting thought that I really should have been sitting next to Kool.

A deuce and a half was a two and a half-ton truck that usually had an open back end like a huge pickup with wooden bench seats lining its walls. Sometimes there was a canvas cover over the back like a covered wagon. The diesel engine would throw off giant plumes of black smoke, most of which seemed to wind up in the back of the truck with the passengers as the driver ran through the gears. Since they were made of steel, had little suspension and rock-hard tires, traveling even a few miles an hour on rough roads had a tendency to throw guys all over the back. We learned quickly to hold on to our seats as we got our first glimpses of the countryside.

One of the early and most lasting impressions I had of the country was the sight of the South Vietnamese people as we traveled from Cam Ranh Bay to Bien Hoa. Of course, I had never seen a rice paddy before, but my view of the people tending the fields seemed a bit surprising, natural, and refreshing. In addition, I had never seen village streets so crammed with pedestrians, motorbikes, and three-wheeled taxis. Like industrious ants, everyone seemed to be carrying something that was bigger than they were.

I also did not expect to hear people shouting at us as we drove down the roads in our Army truck. It made me feel as though I had been mistaken for someone on the "pro-war side" during one of our protests back home. Although some of the shouts suggested that we should, the thought of "going home" was pretty far from my mind given that I had just arrived, not that I wouldn't have been pleased to grant these folks their wish.

While the rolling green countryside between Cam Ranh Bay and Bien Hoa was really beautiful in some places, my views were tainted by the remnants of years of war that permeated the more populated areas. I was not only enlightened to see the presence of American products like Shell and Texaco gasoline, but also the leftovers of American military occupation that were visible almost everywhere I looked. I suppose it would have been inaccurate to label it American trash because the Vietnamese people were putting it to good use. An old truck bed made a pretty good produce stand. Rusted fuel tanks still worked well enough to store water and barrels of used motor oil kept down the dust on busy village streets. Sheets of corrugated tin were used for just about everything. I noticed that people in the countryside did not appear to have much use for the leftovers and, partially because of my immediate attraction to them; I considered that the people in the villages would have been better off without this junk as well.

Sometime that afternoon we chugged a few miles past an Air Force Base and through the main vehicle entrance to the 1st Cavalry Division Army Base at Bien Hoa. After driving around inside for a bit, we hopped out of the truck at the 215th Medevac Company of the 15th Combat Support Battalion of the 3rd Brigade (Airmobile), although I didn't have a clue what most of those labels meant. The Medevac Company Headquarters was located among scores of wooden pole buildings that looked much like the ones we had seen at Cam Ranh Bay.

When we arrived at the Headquarters it was clear that no one had expected us. We announced to at least a half-dozen people who were standing around the makeshift office that we were 91G20 Psychiatric Social Workers who had been instructed by Major Takatoka to report to the Drug Amnesty Center at Bien Hoa. No one seemed to know what we were talking about, but by then at least ten people had assembled around the Company Clerk's desk to try to figure it out. Finally, a Captain joined our little cubby around the desk. Acting as the leader he was expected to be, he had apparently noticed the confusion and stepped in to resolve the problem.

As if giving an impromptu presentation that he would have rather kept a secret, the Captain explained to all of those present that the Army had just initiated a Drug Amnesty Program and that the 1st Cavalry was now participating. He went on to say that troops who admitted to having a drug problem could avoid military prosecution and punishment if they volunteered to participate in the fourteen-day rehabilitation program that was being started at the Base. From the looks on their faces, it was clear that the guys in the office were hearing all this stuff for the first time.

I noticed that the Captain's news drew different reactions from the guys who were hanging out around the Clerk's desk. In his presence, it seemed like no one was quite sure how to express themselves. Guys fired off one question after another. "What kind of drugs? Who gets to go? Where is the Amnesty Center? What happens during the fourteen days? What happens when you're done with rehab? What do you mean there is no punishment for admitting to drug use? Really? Why should one of *those* guys get a fucking break?" We were as interested as anyone in the Captain's answers, but he didn't take the time to give them. He just said, "Gentlemen, we will all learn more about this as the Program gets going." Then he instructed Pete, the Mormon, and I to report to Captain Thomas Kasser, oriented the Clerk as to where the Program was located, and told him to get us a ride out there.

Although no one but the brass seemed to know it, the Amnesty Center was located less than a half-mile away from the Medevac Company Headquarters. There was no Jeep available, so we volunteered to walk. We hoisted our duffle bags over our shoulders and headed out. The directions were not too complicated. It was a straight shot up the oil-soaked dirt road.

Virtually all of the buildings on the base looked alike...wooden structures, tin roofs, some screened windows, and each with sand bags stacked five feet high around the perimeter. Sets of buildings were packed together in tight clusters for each of the individual units that were based there. As we walked up the road, we noticed different Company insignias on the entrances of some buildings. We also noticed a lot of guys who appeared to be just hanging around like the others down at the Headquarters. Of particular interest was a small building that housed a Non-Commissioned Officers Club.

It had a side window where guys appeared to be lined up for carry-out food of some kind.

When we came to the end of the clusters of barracks, we had been told to look directly across a crossroad to the west. There we saw several things. About two hundred yards to the left was a small attachment of an Artillery Company. Straight ahead, in the middle of an open field, was an odd-looking, pale white mobile-home trailer next to a cluster of three small wood and tin buildings. Two small metal hanger-like structures sat inside a ragged fence down a small hill below. About a hundred yards beyond these round-roofed buildings was a line of rolled barbed wire on the top of a levee-like dirt mound. This mound marked the perimeter separating the Base from the South Vietnamese countryside. We quickly realized why the Army might think this was a fitting place for guys who were going to admit their drug abuse and volunteer for fourteen days of rehab in the Army: It was isolated, fenced, and it would be the first to go if anyone ever came over the top of the perimeter.

We walked up the entrance driveway to the first little building. It had a sign on it which read, "Mental Hygiene Consultation Service (N.P. Clinic)." Apparently the place had operated as some sort of psychiatric clinic prior to being transformed into a Drug Amnesty Center. I guessed that very little transformation had taken place. Little as I knew, I already suspected the Army brass would have viewed mental illness and substance abuse as being roughly the same things.

The front door of the building was latched wide open and there was a desk and file cabinet inside, but there was no one to be found. We left our bags out front and explored some more. We poked our heads inside the other two small wooden buildings which appeared to be lived in, but they were empty as well. We looked down the hill toward the round-roof buildings, but there was no sign of life there either. Finally, we went around the back of the white trailer.

There, on a cement pad about the size of a small basketball court, were about twenty guys. A few were dressed in Army fatigues and the rest wore those familiar sky blue, two-piece hospital pajamas. We were surprised to see that there was a cookout going on. As we walked toward the gathering, a short man in baggy jungle fatigues noticed us and called out something like, "Look, they made it!" as he scooted in our direction. He welcomed us to the 1st Cavalry's Drug Amnesty Center and introduced himself with a mock Army-like salute as, "Captain Thomas Kasser, U.S. Army Doctor, Sir." He might have already had a beer or two, but he was obviously very happy to see us.

Over the course of the next hour or so, we were introduced to the staff and patients, had burgers off the barrel-shaped barbeque cooker, and Pete and I had several beers out of a huge plastic cooler that was placed in the center of the gathering for everyone to share. In contrast to everything else we had seen that day, it was as if these guys were having a picnic at the park.

After the cookout broke up Pete, the Mormon, and I retrieved our bags and claimed our "hootches." At the Amnesty Center, hootches were closest-like quarters sectioned off inside two of the small wooden buildings. Pete found a nice one for himself. The Mormon and I claimed a double-occupancy room next door. After dropping off our bags, Captain Kasser oriented us to the Mama-sans who would do our laundry, the shower house, the outhouse, and the Papa-sans who would collect and burn our shit.

Near the end of our first night at the Center, Pete and I accepted an invitation from two Specialists who already worked at the place to stop by their hootch for an "official" welcome to Vietnam. As would become his way of steering clear of potential trouble, the Mormon opted to go unpack his things and bypass the invitation. By the time we got there the Specialists and the Unit Clerk were drunk, stoned, and absolutely thrilled to see us. We smoked our first Vietnamese pot, drank a couple more beers from a tiny refrigerator one of them had "commandeered off the black market," and listened to their stories about their first couple months at the Center.

The two Specialists were both Medics who had been assigned to the Center probably because of their first-hand experience with drugs. They were so happy to see us not just because they were stoned silly, but because our arrival meant that they would soon be going home. They were good enough guys for sure, but after an hour or so of imbibing in the local fare Pete and I were already wondering what we had stepped into.

Toward the end of the evening we were each gifted with a used boonie-type hat to replace the baseball-style hats that we had been issued back in the States. We each tried on one of the round, canvas-constructed hats that had circular soft bills with bullet-hoop bands around the forehead. In a symbolic sort of way, I suppose the hats would help define who we would become, although we didn't know it at the time.

Working in the Coal Mine
(Allen Toussaint song made famous by Lee Dorsey)

Although we had learned a bit about heroin, the heroin problem, and the Drug Amnesty program, we hadn't been taught anything at San Antonio or Cam Ranh Bay about helping guys through withdrawal or actually providing rehabilitation. It appeared that the Army may not have known enough about either of these things to provide much instruction. Major Takatoka had told us that, until there was a better understanding of what worked, the physicians in charge at each of the individual centers would dictate the practices that were employed there. Presumably, once one or more of the centers experienced some success, they would share that information with the others. Of course, this reinforced our sense of the isolated and experimental nature of the Drug Amnesty Program, as well as the general lack of organization that seemed to characterize the Army in Vietnam. We were on our own.

Captain Kasser, our doctor in charge, turned out to be a pediatrician from the East Coast. He was a gentle man, about as short as Pete, with a patch of dark brown hair combed over his large tanned forehead and prematurely receding hair line. During our initial meeting with him he was the first to admit that he knew virtually nothing about drug use or abuse, let alone heroin, and that he was still trying to figure out why the Army had assigned him to this job. As if to recant for his ignorance, he told us he had only been in country for about a month. "Doc," as he preferred to be called, also told us how happy he was that we had been assigned there with him and that together we were going to have to figure this thing out so that we would have something to offer these guys other than fourteen days away from whatever they had been doing.

It was obvious that Doc cared a great deal about what he had been assigned to do and, although he took a casual approach, he wanted to do the best he could do in his leadership role. After he spent time talking about what he didn't know, he asked about our backgrounds and how we thought we could contribute to the Program. Pete explained that he probably knew less about drug abuse than Doc, but that he'd had some personal experience with drugs that might help guys be able to relate to him. He also said he would be excited to get the opportunity to do some counseling. I thought it was great that Doc was inquiring about our interests. Up to this point in the military, no one had ever asked these sorts of questions.

The Mormon explained that, although he obviously had no first-hand experience with drugs, he did have some relevant psychology background from college and hoped that he might be able to put his spiritual and missionary experience to some use for the Program. When he spoke it was clear that he was very bright and I was curious to learn more about his beliefs. However, I couldn't help wondering how some of the tough guys I expected to see in drug rehab would take to him.

I explained that I had taken an introductory psychology class during my first year at college, that I had grown up with a pediatrician in the house, that I had a little personal experience with some non-narcotic drugs, and that I had joined the Army for the purpose of better understanding the War and finding a way to help, rather than hurting other people. I didn't need to say that even though I had joined the military, I didn't care for it or the War. I was rapidly beginning to understand that almost everyone felt that way.

Although I'm not sure that any of us learned much about each other that was particularly relevant, our meeting with Doc helped establish a sense of mission and camaraderie that guided and fueled our initial efforts at the Center. And at first, we took that mission very seriously. Since there were no standard operating procedures for the Drug Rehab Center, we made some up. We requisitioned every book we could find on drug abuse from the Special Services Library at Long Binh. We created a simple assessment protocol that we could use when guys checked in and out of the Program to try to determine if we were doing any good. We expanded the Clerk's handwritten ledger book so we could record basic information we gathered from our intake and discharge interviews, rather than just count the number of admissions and discharges which he was required to report each week. We created a schedule of individual and group counseling activities. We cleared a space across the entrance driveway for a softball field and set up a horseshoe pit right in front of one of the round-roofed ward buildings. We opened up the gate on the fence that had been placed around the two wards in order to discourage guys from thinking that they were in prison and encourage more informal and spontaneous interaction between the staff and patients.

After the two Specialists left, we succeeded at getting a skilled Medic assigned to the Center who appeared interested in doing drug rehab. We held onto the Friday night cookouts. And we decided that the place needed a name other than, "The Drug Rehab Center." We christened it "High Hopes, 1st Cav. Drug Rehab" and requisitioned round, blue sew-on uniform patches with "High Hopes, 1st Cav. Drug Rehab," scribed within the bright yellow lines of a peace symbol and flanked on one side by an orange rising sun. Without seeking anyone's approval, we donned them proudly on our fatigue shirts right next to the official yellow 1st Cavalry patches that we were sometimes required to wear. Within a few weeks, the place had a mission, a name, an agenda, and a bit of an attitude.

News of the Drug Amnesty Programs appeared to spread around the country pretty quickly after our group of Psychiatric

Social Workers arrived. In fact, we were seeing between five and seven admissions and discharges per week at Bien Hoa, with an average of about fourteen guys in house at any given time, sometimes more, sometimes a little less. Typically, guys came into the program reporting that they were shooting, smoking, snorting, eating, or subcutaneously inserting between two and seven vials per day prior to admission.

About fifteen to twenty percent of the admissions used needles that they had typically heisted from their company Medics. Some admitted themselves close to their estimated time of departure from the country, whereas others came in within a month of their arrival. There was about an equal number of guys who came from field bases as there were from the bigger Division units that supported them. Of particular interest to me was that the Infantry guys or "grunts" who came from the field had a tendency to separate themselves from the guys who provided them with support, and blacks and whites still generally kept to themselves. There were times when I wondered if they'd had the same Basic Training that I did.

After a while it became easy to tell who was actually using and who wasn't, as well as who had a legitimate interest in kicking the habit and who didn't. We could see it in their eyes and hear it in their social backgrounds. Of course, we could also see and hear who was going through withdrawal, or the "Joneses," and who wasn't. At some point, urine screens for heroin were introduced to help us detect who was self-reporting accurately about their habits. To us, this truth mattered most as guys' time in country was getting short because we knew nobody would get to go home if their final urine screen tested positive for heroin.

By late November everyone seemed confident that we had things pretty well together at High Hopes. We had gotten good at assisting guys through the sweats, chills, shakes, diarrhea, and endless vomit of the Joneses with over-the-counter relief like Kaopectate, Benadryl, and aspirin. Although we tried not to advertise it, when extra medicinal help was needed, a benzodiazepine like Valium or Librium would usually do the trick. And although we never knew if it actually did any good, we were pleased that guys were coming to their groups and individual sessions to talk about what they were going through, why they had started using heroin, and what would be different for them after they completed rehab. There were softball games almost every evening and it was nice to see guys having a good time even though we knew it was temporary and they often had to hold up their pajama bottoms as they ran the bases. In general, guys came into High Hopes pretty messed up and left after ten or fourteen days looking pretty clean. Considering the snapshots of existence we saw in front of us, we felt like we were making a difference in a lot of lives.

The Needle and the Damage Done
(Neil Young)

Around Christmas our sense of mission and therapeutic accomplishment began to change. It was hard to determine exactly how or why. Maybe it was all the talk about being away from home at the holidays or the charade of attempting to celebrate Christmas in what was truly hell for a lot of the young people who were there. Maybe it was the seeming absurdity of the widely-advertised ceasefire that was to take place for twenty-four hours on Christmas Day of 1971. Who knows? Maybe Pete and I actually resented the Mormon's emergency leave to go home for a couple weeks to be with his wife.

Or maybe it was the increasingly prevalent talk about an upcoming spring offensive and the subtle changes that began taking place around the Center that appeared to be related to it. Although none of us who were present in late 1971 knew much about the TET Offensive of 1968, other than that it was big, we began to listen more intently as rumors of a new offensive starting after the New Year began to circulate around the Division.

Was it a good thing that the Center was located next to the Artillery group? With the enemy's improved weaponry, wouldn't it become even more of a target than it had been in the past? Furthermore, High Hopes was just inside the perimeter where Viet Cong snipers had already shown up many times in the past to pop mortars at the Air Force Base and the Medevac helicopters down by Headquarters. Episodes like these had often triggered Red Alert conditions on the base which were accompanied by the eerie sirens, lights out, and take cover. We had seen the Cobra Gunship helicopters work out in the countryside just beyond the perimeter amid the dancing light of parachute flares launched by our guys on the ground, but up to then we had rarely felt any imminent danger.

Would it be different now? We never had any weapons at the Center and, most of the time nobody thought a thing about it. In fact I often thought that maybe the Army wouldn't have minded if all their "junkies" turned up missing in action. But if there was going to be a new enemy offensive; we didn't care to be overlooked.

Without a doubt the biggest sign that something was brewing showed up in the form of a regular army First Sergeant and a West Point Captain who were assigned to take over leadership at the Amnesty Center. Essentially, a First Sergeant was someone who already had endured the military for a long time, was cautiously and informally referred to as a "Lifer," and emphasized Army basics like fitness and safety. A West Point Captain, on the other hand, was someone who had been trained and educated by the military, was formally referred to as "Sir," and paid attention to higher-level issues like strategy and execution. We couldn't imagine how these guys planned to shape up their newly assigned staffers at High Hopes, particularly when, in our opinion, the Doc had been doing just fine and there were usually no more than ten of us.

Although it took longer to get Sergeant Cluster to loosen up, we got to Captain Brinkman quickly, mostly due to Doc's good work of emphasizing the need for certain program components and the fact that the two of them had to share living space in the white trailer. The Captain didn't know anything about drug abuse and we convinced him that our loose atmosphere was part of our treatment intervention that benefited the guys. As a result, he began to view it as his responsibility to be the first man out in the evenings for the softball games. Similarly, he would also sit with the Doc and the rest of us at night listening to music and drinking beer as if these things were part of his job.

Sergeant Cluster appeared to have a more definitive mission. Apparently, he was assigned to keep us combat-ready and fortify the compound in the event that the offensive occurred. Large and remarkably unfit as he was, he actually tried to implement early morning calisthenics until we convinced him that we could intermittently build them into an exercise program for the patients. More importantly, he set us about the task of building a new bunker and burning off the weed fields that surrounded the Center. I guessed it might have been important to be able to see the enemy coming. Using hand-held fire extinguishers to pump kerosene on the burning fields might have been one of the most dangerous things I did in Vietnam. Spending time in the bunker listening to artillery exchanges was somewhere among the most frightening. More than anyone, the patients knew that we were sitting ducks.

Within a few weeks though First Sergeant Cluster was stopping by the softball field to watch and some of us began stopping by his hootch for evening conversations over a cold one or two. We never touched on anyone's politics. We suspected those would differ dramatically. Interacting with Sergeant Cluster had everything to do with trying to make our lives as painless as possible. Pete and I quipped privately that being with him was a little like fraternizing with the enemy.

With all the new stuff going on, it seemed like a good time to make some changes of my own. So, while the Mormon was gone on his leave, I packed up my stuff and moved to another hootch in the vacant wooden building next door. I expanded the size of the one I selected by erecting a sleeping shelf about five feet off the ground and placing a small plywood desk underneath it. Although my bunk was now above the wall of sandbags that protected the building and closer to the tin roof during the rainy season, the welcome tradeoff was that there was a lot more ventilation.

I began to spend a lot of my down time in the hootch. I wired up an old six-inch speaker I had found to an inherited Sanyo tape deck and played the only four cassettes I had almost continuously. I wrote more letters to Sunshine and started to anticipate my "Rest and Recovery" week with her in Hawaii as the sounds of America's "Horse with No Name," Neil Young's "Harvest," Jethro Tull's "Aqualung," and Graham Nash's "Songs for Beginners" filled my tiny space. During all of my time in Vietnam I had totally ignored anything else that may have been happening in the world at the time. I rarely saw the Army's *Stars and Stripes* newspaper and, even when I did; it failed to hold my attention. I assumed it represented the Army's view of things which I didn't care to hear.

Perhaps all the time and energy it took to set up and operate High Hopes had distracted my attention from my anti-war stances in the same way that getting healthy in Basic Training had done. However, in our after-holiday doldrums this was all Pete and I talked about.

Before too long almost everyone who worked at High Hopes began to interpret drug abuse, whether it was real or exaggerated, as a way for guys to deal with the pain of their participation in the War. While this probably always had been the case, I suppose we'd been glossing over the issue in the name of our mission to get guys clean. Without a doubt, the vast majority the guys who showed up for rehab had heroin problems, but as importantly we realized that they also had problems with loneliness, anger, and fear that was easily attributable to the conditions they were in.

After we started viewing heroin use this way, it got to the point that we had a hard time telling one guy from another because their situations all seemed the same. Furthermore, virtually everyone we saw disliked the War mostly because they saw no point to it and, of course, because it put them at risk. Particularly for Pete and I, it was like we had gone looking for the root of the problem and we found it. Drug abuse gradually became a secondary problem. We began to view it as a way for guys to deal with their pain and to express their dissention toward the War. As a result, Pete and I sometimes got very confused. Of course we wanted to help guys get clean, but it often began to feel as though we were contradicting our own values in the process.

Perhaps the Army had viewed drug use this way all along. It would have been safe to conclude that most regular Army higher-ups had little empathy for guys who did drugs or resisted doing their War duties in any way. Before the Amnesty Program, drug use was generally either ignored or punished with time at the stockade or a less-than-honorable discharge back home. I felt that the punishment approach to coercing abstinence seemed pretty consistent with the American way that I distrusted and, whether the approach changed anything or not, that seemed to be what guys were supposed to be fighting to maintain. Contradictions seemed to be showing up everywhere.

Clearly, many of the brass didn't like the idea of offering "Amnesty" for drug abusers. In fact, many of them openly viewed it as an unscheduled vacation for their slackers, malcontents, sickos, and junkies. This became especially evident when we would receive notices from First Sergeants or Captains at the various units we served that "Private So and So's ass was needed back in the field immediately." With the Doc's support, it became common for us to ignore these notices as long as we possibly could regardless of how we viewed the primary problem. While it was sometimes a dilemma, we generally considered that the principle of Amnesty took priority.

Even before the holiday doldrums set in it had become easy to spot the differences between the "Heads," (aka. drug users) and the "Juicers," (aka. drinkers). Except for a few guys like the Mormon who refrained from everything except family, hard work, witnessing, and prayer, it seemed that almost everyone who wasn't a Head could have been classified as a Juicer or vice versa. I never noticed any other choices.

To me, it always appeared that the military catered to the Juicers, as if it had concluded that drinking constituted a socially acceptable release from the local pressures. As an example, the beer for the Friday night cookouts had always been part of our regular supply to keep the Drug Amnesty Program running. Perhaps this too seemed more consistent with the American way. If a guy actually had to purchase it, alcohol was readily available and incredibly cheap at the base clubs or PX stores.

I suspected that once heroin arrived on the scene, disparities between the Heads and the Juicers became even more obvious. Guys who did heroin were generally less likely to drink. Guys who drank were less likely to do heroin. Guys who smoked pot usually drank too, but generally were still considered Heads. Unlike alcohol use, heroin or pot use and the dissention that often accompanied it typically represented something to hide. I became convinced that guys who did heroin or pot were not only experiencing desired effects of the drugs, they were expressing their political beliefs as well. Many openly displayed the symbols of their opposition - the boonie hats, beads, peace symbols, and wrist bands - as proudly as my friends and I had carried our protest signs back in the city. Yet, except for at the Amnesty Programs, no one I noticed got together to talk about it.

Although our distaste for the War would have clearly placed us among the Heads, Pete and I probably straddled the fence between the Heads and the Juicers. Perhaps we had less choice. After the piss tests were introduced for heroin, we had to stay clean to keep our jobs. Nevertheless, although neither of us ever knowingly touched heroin, we always had an ample supply of pot that we confiscated during admissions or ward searches. We also had a ready supply of beer that we made sure got left over each week from the Friday night cookouts.

Although we didn't hold the appropriate rank, Pete and I discovered that we could even infiltrate the NCO Club at the Air Force base and fit right in with the Juicers as the dancing girls stripped to their g-strings and pasties. In fact, I was at the club the first time I ever heard Don McLean's "American Pie." It was being performed by a Vietnamese rock band that could not have understood the English words they were singing. On the other hand, we could relate to almost any of the Heads around the base and often did "dap" handshakes with some of the black guys who we had met earlier in rehab. Many viewed these greetings as a sort of secret code of defiance against the military, although this wasn't always the case.

Eventually, Pete and I started to pride ourselves on being able to fit in with just about anybody. In some ways it seemed like it was required in order to do what we were expected to do at High Hopes. Yet I suppose we had identity issues just like everyone else.

As if we had been blinded by our enthusiasm in putting the program together and churning out guys who were dried out and ready for action, we had rarely considered the longer-term outcomes of our efforts at High Hopes. However, as our sense of mission, morale, or enthusiasm began to erode, we must have begun to see things differently. Maybe the contradictions could no longer be ignored. Although we agreed on virtually everything, listening to each other talk about it over and over again did not appear to be helping either one of us. There seemed to be nothing we could do about it. I started smoking and drinking with our new Jeep Driver, Lowery, sometimes without Pete, because by that time our incessant complaining had begun to irritate us both. Perhaps time was beginning to take its toll on all of us who had to maintain our enthusiasm to keep doing what we were expected to do day after day: get guys "better" so they could keep on fighting the War.

One of the stated reasons for the implementation of the Drug Amnesty Program in Vietnam was that guys were coming home to the States with their habits and bringing heroin along with them to places that had never seen it before. This appeared to be exacerbating heroin and crime problems back home and creating yet another reason for the public to view American involvement in the War negatively. Yet, while this may have been a legitimate reason to initiate such an ambitious effort during the War, we came face to face with other reasons that, for some, would have been much more relevant.

For the first several months, we never thought much about how many guys were actually using heroin in Vietnam. Like the Clerk we just counted the faces in front of us at High Hopes - about seven new guys per week or roughly fourteen in house at any given time. However, we knew there were at least six, and probably more like twelve, other Drug Rehab Centers operating throughout the country. Assuming that our counterparts were seeing about the same number of guys that we were, this meant that somewhere between forty-nine and ninety-one guys per week were checking into the Drug Rehab Programs in Vietnam in late 1971 and early 1972.

However, at the time that the Drug Amnesty Program was implemented in Vietnam, there were still around a hundred fifty thousand troops in the country and, according to Major Takatoka, Nixon's report had suggested that between seventeen and forty-two percent of them had either tried or were regularly using heroin. In 1971, that could have represented between twenty-five and sixty-three thousand guys. Eventually, we figured that even if all the Amnesty Programs saw a hundred guys a week for the entire year it would have represented far less than a quarter of the lowest estimate of those who may have been using heroin in Vietnam at the time.

After the first of the year, it shocked and disappointed us to consider that so few of those who may have been using heroin were voluntarily seeking assistance from the Amnesty Programs, even when it meant free time away from whatever else they might have been doing. This became a huge concern for us because we suspected that deaths had to be resulting either from performance errors due to heroin use, or heroin overdoses. We knew that the drug was so pure, that the effect was so enticing, and that the addiction was so rapid for so many guys. We also suspected that dissention had become even more commonplace among the troops.

Yet, we never knew how many overdose deaths actually occurred, in part because we didn't see these guys, "heroin use" was rarely if ever mentioned in death reports, and the words "heroin overdose" were never used as an official cause of death in Vietnam. Casualty reports were more likely to indicate something like "non-hostile ground casualty, suffocation, or drowning," presumably as a result of slowed breathing produced by the drug and bodily fluid filling the lungs. Many times we wondered how much the Army knew about the problem it had inadvertently helped to create and how little impact its Drug Amnesty Program might have been having. Mission oriented as they were, Sergeant Cluster and Captain Brigham typically sat out on these conversations.

Concern about potential mistakes or overdoses among thousands of guys who were not coming into rehab was one thing. Consideration of potential overdoses among guys who had come in for help was definitely something else. Around mid-January, this reality smacked us in the face.

Jack was somewhat unusual in that he was tall and blonde, had exceptional manners, and didn't seem very much like a kid who would be strung out on four vials of heroin per day. But he was. The Mormon had gotten to know him pretty well, in part because he had been assigned as his one-to-one counselor at High Hopes and in part because I believe he was in the process of attempting to save his soul.

As it turned out, Jack had only been using a short time, but long enough to experience intense withdrawal symptoms whenever he attempted to stop. Mostly with the Mormon's help Jack seemed to do really well in rehab. He made it through his withdrawal and was active in all of his individual and group sessions. He played softball with the best of them. In general, he seemed like a really easy-going kid who had just taken a different path for a brief period of time during his tour. He "graduated" from the program after his fourteen days and everyone gave him a very good chance of remaining clean once he returned down the road to his support unit. The Mormon was really enthused that Jack was going to be close by and had even planned to keep seeing him for follow-up sessions, which we almost never had the opportunity to provide.

About a week after Jack was discharged, the Mormon returned to the Center after having walked down to the unit to check on him. Pete, the Doc, Lowery, the Clerk and I were all sitting around the office when the Mormon put one of his dusty boots on the step to the front door. He was silent. He just stood there with an empty look on his face leaning on his knee. Finally somebody asked him what was the matter. After a couple deep breaths, he asked the clerk if he had a copy of the base casualty report from the day before. The clerk found it under a stack of papers and passed it to the Mormon without looking at it. The Mormon glanced through the names on the report, stopped, and said, "It's true." We knew the news was not good.

The Mormon told us that when he went down to the unit, neither Jack, nor his stuff was there. When he asked around about where he had gone, one of the guys in the barracks said that Jack had OD'ed. Then, after another pause, the Mormon said that the guy told him, "Yeah...we were all surprised because he didn't do any more than he usually did."

It was like a shockwave ran through the plywood floors of the Amnesty office. For a long moment, everyone was just frozen. Eventually, we began to talk about it. Not only did everyone feel really badly about the loss of this innocent kid and the Mormon's loss of a new friend, we realized that our work may have inadvertently contributed to the death. Not everyone got it at first. Then the Doc explained that if a guy returned to a "normal" high dose of heroin after having been dried out for fourteen days, it could easily produce an overdose. By way of example, he asked us to consider what would happen to a non-user who ingested a couple hundred milligrams of ninety-five percent pure heroin in a single dose. His point was well taken.

Doc left the office in a hurry as he had a tendency to do whenever he was getting emotional. The Mormon left as well. The rest of us just sat there wondering what we might have done and what, if anything, we could do differently to keep this from ever happening again in the future. We had no way of knowing how many other guys who we had tried to help could have died in the same way.

In the midst of our doldrums and second-guessing about the benefit of the work we had been doing, maybe it was a good thing that our attention continued to be grabbed by increased anticipation of an enemy offensive. By February of 1972 we had completed the new bunker and continued sandbagging everything else in sight. One night Pete, Lowery, and I got so drunk with Sergeant Cluster that we sandbagged another new Jeep driver's hootch door shut while he was sleeping. The next day he didn't think it was much of a joke. In fact, after he calmed down he told us that while he was with another unit he had witnessed some grunts do the same thing to one of their First Lieutenants and then toss a live grenade inside. He told us that "fraggings" such as this were relatively common in the bush when guys disliked those in charge, particularly during and after the TET Offensive of 1968. In the midst of our heightened concern about our own security, his little story was a bit sobering...at least until we got high again.

As it turned out, the depleted People's Army of Vietnam (PAVN) and the National Front for Liberation of South Vietnam (Viet Cong) did mount the most significant offensive since the 1968 TET invasion between March and October of 1972. However, we were told that it was much different in that there were many fewer troops involved, the U.S.-backed Army of the Republic of Vietnam (ARVN) did much more of the fighting, and the battles looked different because there was more artillery and U.S. airpower employed. We might have guessed the latter because we heard more outgoing shells from the Artillery unit next door, we heard more Phantom attack jets coming and going from the Air Base, and we spent several nights crammed inside the new bunker after being startled by the sirens that signaled incoming or awakened by the sound of mud clods that would splatter on our tin roofs.

Lady of the Island
(Crosby, Stills, and Nash)

Sometime around the start of April of 1972, I got the opportunity to take an R & R, or the Army's version of a brief vacation from the War. Although there were times when I thought the concept of rest and relaxation from war was almost as ridiculous as a Christmas cease-fire, the more time I spent in country the more I was attracted to the idea. Of course, there was no going home. Guys had the option to select from relatively nearby places like Hawaii, Thailand, Australia, or Hong Kong. In general, those who were not in relationships back home chose to go to Bangkok because of the ready supply of drugs and women that were said to be available there. Guys who were in relationships almost invariably selected Hawaii so that they could hook up with their wives or lovers on the beaches at Waikiki.

Sunshine and I had been planning our rendezvous in Hawaii for some time. Words that described visions of how nice it was going to be filled the pages of the letters that we had been exchanging for the past several months. Although I got the impression that her parents may not have been particularly excited about the idea of her traveling so far to see a sexually-deprived Army guy like me, apparently they'd relented somewhere along the way – probably after I found a way to wire the cost of Sunshine's round-trip airplane ticket. I didn't mind the extra expense. I considered myself fairly wealthy because I had been receiving extra pay for serving in a combat zone, I was sending all but a few bucks of my earnings to a bank account held by my folks in Peoria, and I had little reason to purchase anything while I was in Vietnam. I was never interested in the cameras, stereo systems, or other Japanese electronic stuff that a lot of military guys spent their money on at the PX.

We saw each other for the first time in more than six months at the reception station at Fort DeRussy, Hawaii. It was a little awkward meeting Sunshine again among all the wives that were there to greet their husbands who had flown in with me. She stood there among the older women in a short white top that was banded just under her breasts so that her bare midriff showed off nicely above her hip-hugger, light-blue corduroy jeans. As I got off the bus and walked across the open-air greeting area, she clasped her hands under her chin, rubbed her knees together, and put on her little-girl smile in a way that made her look like she might have been sixteen. Perhaps the impression was influenced by my own sense of feeling older and terribly out of place among all the others in such a pretty place.

Although it would have been cheaper, I had opted not to stay at the military-operated hotel at Fort DeRussy. Instead, our hotel was a few blocks away, just across the landscaped boulevard from Waikiki Beach. We snatched up the little bit of stuff we had, got out of the welcoming center as quickly as we could, and headed for the hotel. On the way, I could not resist stopping at a McDonald's to taste some familiar American food.

I had mailed ahead for a reservation at the high-rise style hotel, but I had never actually checked into a hotel with a woman before. I thought we might need to pretend like we were married, so we did. Recognizing that Sunshine was so incredibly cute and that I was there on leave, the male hotel clerk was extremely nice to us. He welcomed me back to the United States and spent even more time welcoming Sunshine to the beautiful island of Oahu.

We made our way into the room on one of the upper floors overlooking the ocean, dropped our bags, and immediately began making love partly, I thought, because that is what we would have been expected to do. It felt strange to be enjoying the tenderness and passion of being together again, of being with a woman. I suppose I was a little slow in some ways and a little quick in others but, when I got over the sense of expectation, it felt like a brand new experience to me. It certainly had been a long time. It was also clearer than ever before that if all went according to plan I would soon be marrying the naked young lady who was lying with me on that bed. Nice as it was, after only about thirty minutes neither of us could resist the urge to get over to the beach.

Over the course of the next several days, we did just about nothing except go back and forth from the hotel room to the beach across the street. With her fair white skin, chiseled body, and long curly blonde hair highlighting the skimpy two-piece swimming suit I had encouraged her to bring, Sunshine looked as beautiful as anyone on the beach. Each time we would prance back into the lobby in our bare feet the clerk would smile and ask us if there was anything we needed to make our stay more pleasurable. It quickly became routine for us to smile back and tell him there wasn't.

A day or so before I was to check back in at Fort DeRussy for my jaunt back to Vietnam, I began to act a little erratically. By this point, the beach no longer seemed so inviting. The hotel bars with their "Don Ho-" like shows seemed trite. Sunshine's news from home sounded trivial. The park-like setting honoring the WWII dead at Pearl Harbor was downright depressing.

During our last night together when we were walking on the strip between the beach and the hotels, I became convinced I was experiencing a hallucinogenic flash back of some kind. Faces of couples walking on the street seemed to be glaring at me. The sounds of voices, laughter, music, and passing cars became deafening. The neon lights above the bars and restaurants appeared to have swirling tails. My distaste for this sort of experience had led me to stop doing psychedelics a couple of times in the past and I had not touched any of the manufactured stuff that was available in Vietnam.

I told Sunshine what was happening and she rushed me back to the hotel as quickly as she could. We passed the clerk without saying anything, went up the elevator into the room, and sat on the end of the bed. After a few moments I began to cry. Although we hadn't talked about it much while enjoying our rest and relaxation on the island, I told Sunshine again about how much I hated the Army and the War, and that I had an uncomfortable feeling about going back. Of course, she already knew all of these things, but she did a nice job of listening as I let it loose all over again. The fear and discontent I experienced was like a reoccurring nightmare that I usually tried to keep hidden from my friends and family back home. I always thought that if I talked about it too much they would remind me that I brought it on myself by enlisting. It would have taken me too long to explain that I didn't feel totally responsible for that. Sunshine understood. She held me for a long time before we opened the windows, let in some fresh island air, turned down the lights, and slept.

In spite of my momentary discomfort, after my six or seven days away, I was ready to hop the bus for the airplane ride back to Vietnam. I guess I felt an obligation to get back and do the work that I was there to do, just as I'd felt obligated to be there in the first place. My flight was scheduled to depart before Sunshine's so we said "I love you," "I love you too," and "See you later" at the reception center. I rode away on the Army bus thinking that our visit had been a very special slice of my life.

No Man Can Find the War
(Tim Buckley)

Perhaps the Army's notion of R & R was a good thing because I arrived back at High Hopes somewhat reenergized. There was nothing else to do except continue to help guys dry out and stay as safe as possible during the time they had left to spend in the country. Given our concern about guys inadvertently overdosing if they returned to their normal habit after drying out, we began to stress the point during rehab. This was tricky because we never wanted them to think that anyone ever used again after leaving the High Hopes program. It was also hard because none of us wanted to deal with the potential reality that sometimes, perhaps even more often than not, our program did not produce any lasting beneficial outcomes.

Throughout the life of the program, we continued to struggle with the relation between heroin use and other problems that the guys were experiencing during their tours in Vietnam. Sometimes these other problems were vivid at the admission door. In fact, sometimes it seemed that the units would send guys to the Amnesty Program who they just didn't care to have around. We surmised that this is what had happened with Lowery. He showed up at High Hopes after being ordered to do so by his Company Commander. When he arrived, he appeared healthy and reported that he "smoked a little pot sometimes." Of course, we didn't consider smoking pot to be a problem. However, Lowery wound up staying at the Program permanently because the Doc arranged it that way.

Apparently, in addition to smoking a little pot, Lowery was reported to have experienced some difficulties with somnambulism. Although sleepwalking clearly would not have gone over very well at the bush unit where he had been stationed, I'm not sure any of us ever even saw Lowery turn over in his sleep while he was at the Center. He was just a good kid and the Doc seemed to want to take care of him. Perhaps his Commanding Officer did too. After starting out as a Jeep Driver, which was often where Doc temporarily reassigned guys he wanted to protect, Lowery became something of an all-purpose staff member at High Hopes. It was fine with us and Lowery quickly became a very good friend of mine.

Despite my momentary reengagement with our mission, I continued to get confused as a result of my tendency to equate resistance to the War with heroin use. I believed that heroin use often started with disillusionment about the War and then continued because of the addicting impact of the drug. After several months in country I had noticed that the guys who showed up for rehab tended to look and act the part of the drug abuser more and more, as if to demonstrate the magnitude of their discontent. To me, their appearance often screamed "I want out of the War and (oh, by the way) I am strung out on heroin." One guy even showed up at our door with a string of empty green, white, and pink heroin vials threaded to a bootlace that he wore around his neck. After I saw his creation, I constructed one for myself from the bucket of empty vials I had collected from the ditches around the base, but I was never bold enough to wear it out in public. Instead, I attached it to the strap on my ukulele. To me, it carried as much symbolism as the peace sign I continued to wear around my neck.

About a third of the guys who voluntarily admitted themselves into the Amnesty Program also voluntarily discharged themselves before the completion of their fourteen days. In some cases guys who were truly addicted asked to be discharged because they couldn't tolerate the onset of withdrawal. There was nothing we could do to stop them from leaving, although we spent a lot of our time trying. In the other cases, it appeared to me that guys who were more obviously avoiding the War by coming to Rehab asked to be discharged early because their temporary resistance was rapidly overcome by their sense of responsibility to their buddies who were still out there. Either way, it seemed that guys were characteristically drawn back to the War. Either way, their screams for help often got to me because they reminded me of my own sense of being torn between hating the War and caring a great deal for those who had to fight it.

One Monday afternoon when we were admitting new patients, a deuce and a half unloaded nine guys who were all coming in for rehab at the same time from the same field Infantry unit. Among them was a bright red-haired kid named Caine. Caine certainly looked the part of a grunt. However, his faded fatigues, beads, and boonie hat didn't hide his relative silence and isolation from the other guys who checked in with him. I guessed right off the bat that he wasn't actually doing any heroin, but I was concerned because I knew he was there for a reason and I knew we would only have a little time to find out what that was. By that time, all the guys were getting urine screens upon admission and each day that they remained in the program. Guys who screened negative at admission usually had to leave the next day, unless the Doc came to their rescue.

Being concerned, curious, and knowing that we had to work fast; I volunteered to add Caine to my caseload even though I knew his quick discharge would result in my having to do some extra work. During the admission interview, I listened to him confabulate about his drug history and his current habit. I acted as if I bought everything he told me, purposefully rushed through the assessment, instructed him through his urine test, handed him his pajamas, and sent him down to the ward. As we were parting he asked me if there was anything else I needed to know, but I just said, "Nope, that's it, see you around."

A few minutes later I walked down to the ward and called for Caine to come out to the back of the building. Of course he didn't know it, but we often conducted individual meetings while we sat on the sandbags looking out on the lush countryside. It was a great place to be left alone. I chased away some lizards, grabbed a seat up on the sandbags, and watched as Caine approached. I could tell that he was surprised to see me again so soon. I hadn't even given him time to claim a cot. I asked him to take a seat, which he did. Then, in my most compassionate, sincere, and caring way, I asked "Okay, now what the fuck is really going on with you?"

Caine was momentarily baffled, which I had hoped would be the case. Then he said, "I'm not sure what you mean." I said, "I think you do know what I mean. You're not doing any heroin. That means we don't have much time, and neither one of us is leaving this spot until you let me know what the hell is going on with you." We sat and looked at each other for a few silent moments.

Over the course of the next several hours, until well after dark, Caine gradually let me in. He described his failing romance back home, his inability to deal with the fact that he was a grunt in the Army, and his intense fear that he was about to die in the War. He said that he had expected his life would be so much more meaningful at some point in the future, but right then it seemed like it was an incredible waste. He described his sense of loneliness, despair, and not belonging with the other guys in his unit. There were moments when he would get a little emotional, but mostly he was just to the point, remarkably clear, and coherent. He restated his belief that, if things continued going as they were, he was going to die fighting with someone. All I could do was listen. As I did, I heard the echo of a thousand other guys, including myself, who all confronted similar feelings from time to time, but that didn't minimize the relevance of Caine's plight.

We eventually reached a point where I had no idea what to do next. We certainly hadn't learned anything about dealing with this kind of situation in our training. So, I told Caine that I would go get us some water buffalo cheeseburgers from the window over at the NCO club and see him back in the same place in thirty minutes.

When I came back around the side of the building with the cheeseburgers, Caine was up on the sandbags sitting almost exactly where I had been sitting before. As I jumped back up where he had been sitting, he smiled broadly and said, "So, what the fuck is going on with you?" We shared a good laugh.

After we enjoyed the cheeseburgers and briefly discussed the wonders of well-cooked, ground water buffalo, I told Caine it was great that he had such a good grasp on what he was feeling, but that something was going to have to give. His piss test result was going to come back the next morning and we both knew it was going to be clean. He would be expected to leave. It was not good enough to comfort myself with the fact that I had been successful in getting Caine to vent his feelings. What good was that? I felt compelled to help him figure out what he was going to do next.

There didn't appear to be any good choices, but we considered them anyway. There was no way Doc could come to the rescue on this one. If he did, I envisioned that High Hopes would become a sanctuary for half of the troops in Vietnam. On the other hand, Caine could discount his thoughts, buck up, return to his unit, and possibly die as he feared. Or he could refuse to get on the truck that would take him back to his firebase and wind up in the stockade at Long Binh for desertion. Or perhaps he could share his thoughts with his Unit Commander or Chaplain when so many others didn't, couldn't, or wouldn't and take his chances. Of course, he could also take a big-time dose of heroin and possibly avoid the whole thing by killing himself. They were all possible courses of action, but unfortunately none of them seemed like a good solution.

Caine and I never actually reached a decision that night as to what he was going to do. We just agreed that he was a special and honest person and that when the time came; he would just have to take whatever action presented itself. We both knew he wouldn't do anything that might hurt someone else. We also decided that no matter what he did when the moment came, it would be the right action to take. Actually, while this might not have seemed like much of a conclusion to our interaction, it was really quite powerful for both of us. Caine was going to find out what the best course of action was by simply observing whatever it was that he wound up doing when the time came. His life experience to that moment would have to be his guide. No matter what, we agreed again, it would be the right thing.

Strangely, my conversation with Caine may have changed my life. It suddenly became very clear to me that this was the way I had been making my own decisions for years; to hitchhike to LA, to leave college, to join the Army, to leave Rose, to reunite with Sunshine, all of it.

Dawn came around pretty quickly. About mid-morning, people from Caine's unit had already heard that his urine test was clean and one of the big trucks was already there to pick him up. I was standing out in front of the office with the Doc, Pete, the Mormon, the Captain, and Lowery as we always tried to do whenever someone was getting ready to leave High Hopes. Everyone had some idea about what was going on and most knew that Caine and I had been up most of the night. I saw him walk up the drive from the ward and silently collect his gear from the Clerk. We made brief eye contact, almost as if we were concealing a special secret from everyone else.

Nevertheless, in that moment I had a very strong sense that I had not helped. I was certainly not comforted by the thought that perhaps I had done my military duty by getting this young soldier back to his unit.

I don't think anyone said a word as the truck pulled off with Caine sitting by himself on one of the wooden benches in back. I looked at Pete and Lowery, who I guessed would have a pretty good idea what was going on without even talking about it.

For the next several days, my friends around the Amnesty Center shared my apprehension and fear. Since the death of the Mormon's friend we had gotten into the routine of looking at the daily casualty reports with the hope that none of the guys we knew would be listed. However, after Caine left, everyone seemed to be avoiding the casualty reports. I kept telling myself that he was going to do the right thing no matter how that looked to anyone else. And then it happened.

Just as we were when Caine left the Center, most of us just happened to be standing out in front of the office when he returned. A cloud of dust whirled around a truck that slid to a stop near the gate. We watched Caine jump from the back, grab his M-16 rifle and field pack, and run through the dust in our direction. He was smiling from ear to ear and looking toward the hot blue sky as he ran. He came right up to me and we stood for a moment face to face. Then he dropped all his stuff and bear-hugged me for what seemed like an eternity. Everyone laughed and shouted and carried on as we shared one of our most special moments together in Vietnam. This feeling did not change even when we learned that Caine had abandoned his unit the previous afternoon. After all, as he kept saying over and over through his smile, "I'm alive."

No one felt obliged to report our stowaway immediately. In fact, Caine's action was cause for a night of hard celebrating.

Even though it wasn't a Friday, we pulled out the Friday night beer cooler, I grabbed my ukulele and cheap Vietnamese guitar, and we sat on top of the new bunker late into another night. I played a new song I had just written that combined my thoughts about the Mormon's friend and Caine called "Thoughts for the Dead Man." It was characteristic for us to mix our craziness and fun with moments that were much more serious for all of us. That part of me had gone unchanged since college.

Thoughts for the Dead Man

I met him at a home for all those who have trouble seeing.
And our words crossed paths as we sat on the back by a field.
He spoke to me once of a problem he had with his speaking.
That doesn't seem to matter now, I noticed a crack in his shield.

And all we have left is a thought on our minds
And a song in our hearts for the dead man.

We sat in the stench by fire in the summertime seeking.
But our words seemed to echo in the helpless air of the night.
Listen to the morning, can you hear what the sunshine is saying?
Oh how can we show you the warmth of a day full of light?

And all we have left is a thought on our minds
And a song in our hearts for the dead man.

He left us by daybreak, new day and the way we were thinking.
Went back to the transient world he lived with before.
And sitting with friends who were like him they all went on sinking.
But he shot himself down leaving thoughts for so many more.

He shot himself down leaving thoughts for so many more.

And all we have left is a thought on our minds
And a song in our hearts for the dead man.

Caine left us again the next morning. No one came to pick him up. He just grabbed his gear and walked off down the road. I assumed that he figured he would eventually get discovered and taken into custody by the Military Police. After that he probably would either be placed in the stockade or sent home with a Dishonorable Discharge. It was difficult not knowing what would happen to Caine, but considering his sense of clarity and happiness about what he had done, I felt any consequences would have been better than playing out his death scenario. I considered him to be a very brave young man.

Paint it Black
(The Rolling Stones)

By late April there was increasing talk about demilitarization and Vietnamization around the base at Bien Hoa. We heard the first of rumors that, as the ARVN soldiers got better trained and assumed more of the responsibility for fighting what had now somewhat arbitrarily become *their* War; the 1st Cavalry would be gradually pulling out of the country. Of course, that meant that High Hopes would be shutting down along with it. Perhaps as an effect of these rumors, fewer guys were showing up for rehab. Suddenly, there was a lot of sitting around going on.

Since there wasn't much to do and we had not been instructed to do anything else, several of us had the idea to take an "in-country R&R" over a long weekend. Our fourth refugee Jeep driver, Ollie, said he had heard that the 1st Cavalry could utilize a place on the ocean near the village of Vung Tau. In fact, he actually got official approval from the Doc to use the Center's Jeep to transport Pete, Lowery, and myself down there for our spontaneous getaway.

Vung Tau was about eighty-five miles southeast of Saigon, which was about twenty-five miles southwest of Bien Hoa. Ollie said he had received an okay to bypass Saigon and head on a more direct route to the coast which we figured would be somewhere around a hundred miles. The rest of us trusted that Ollie knew where he was going, though it was pretty strange riding around South Vietnam with four guys out on a weekend in an Army Jeep. The farthest I had been in the country since my arrival at Cam Ranh Bay were quick trips to Saigon, Long Binh, and the Air Force Base.

Some of the countryside in the southeast part of the Vietnam was beautiful and as before, my attention was captured by the sights of people working the fields in the rural areas. Even so, we got a little uncomfortable when Ollie began making jokes about the possible presence of Viet Cong around the more populated villages we passed along the way. After all, regardless of the local politics everyone dressed pretty much alike. I had never understood the attraction to black clothing in such a tropical climate.

When we reached the "resort" at Vung Tau, it turned out that there were no other guests there. In fact, it was deserted but for one ARVN Special Services guy who appeared to be in charge the place. He pointed us toward one of several non-sandbagged, open air buildings with cots where we could sleep. He also gave us a few simple instructions about what we could and could not do around the resort and the village that was just a short stroll back up the road. There wasn't much said about what we shouldn't do, although Ollie seemed particularly interested in these parts and was definitely in a hurry to get it all in before Monday morning.

The four of us dropped off our things, left the Jeep, and immediately headed into the village on foot. The place was heavily overgrown by tall trees, hanging foliage, and beautiful flowering bushes so that it was impossible to see the ocean which was just a few steps away. Like almost everywhere else I had seen, most of the dwellings were very small and partially built from War leftovers. However, others were much statelier with stucco exterior walls, evidence of old landscaping, courtyards where various sorts of commerce might be conducted, and multi-story living quarters off the back. Ollie led our little squad into one of the first such structures we came upon. We sat down at a brightly-painted metal table in the courtyard.

Before we knew it, members of the family who apparently lived and worked at the place were catering to our every desire.

Apparently, we attracted all of their attention because we were the only customers there. Of course we would have an ice-cold bottled beer as we basked in the soft ocean air. Of course we would have a tray of freshly prepared South Vietnamese snacks. Of course we would have one of the women who had begun to parade seductively around our table. Really? We were being swept away with the hospitality.

Before long I found myself sitting at the table in the hot sun finishing my beer alone. Ollie, Pete, and Lowery had each been snatched up by one of the women and taken away through one of the many doorways that emptied onto the courtyard. Finally, I allowed myself to be gathered up by a young girl dressed in a loose floral smock and black pants. She took my hand and guided me through one of the entranceways, down a short corridor, up some steps, around a corner, and into a small room that was obviously her home. As we entered the door to the room she gestured for two young children to go away. I was fascinated by the kids. It had been a long time since I had seen any.

Once we got inside the room, I asked for the girl's name and she mumbled something, but I didn't understand what she said. Apparently, she didn't care to ask my name. She just called me, "G.I." As Ms. X puttered around the room picking things up, she asked, "What G.I. want?" At that moment I pictured each of my friends off in their little rooms with their girls carrying on in all sorts of barely imaginable ways that most might think were characteristic of horny G.I.'s out on a weekend. Even so, I couldn't muster any interest in my girl with no name. She was not only very young; she had kids hanging around right outside her door. I was sure she thought it strange when I informed her that I didn't want anything from her.

I was still standing in the doorway. After my first refusal, she attempted to entice me by showing me her tiny breasts and playfully grabbing at my crotch. I waved my hands in front of her face and said, "No, no thank you, I no want sex." Then she started to undo my pants, and asked, "G.I. want blow job?" Again I let her know that I didn't care for one. After my third or fourth refusal from her sexual menu, she began to appear a little sad, bewildered, or possibly insulted by my lack of interest in her. She sat down on the bed looking disappointed. I thought for a moment that maybe she thought I was cute or that it was somehow important to her to be able to comfort a tired soldier fighting for a cause that she may have believed in. Then I came to my senses.

She didn't care about what kind of sex we had or whether we actually had any sex at all. She cared about dollars and cents. She and the rest of her family were hard at work making a living the best they could and perhaps the only way they knew how. This was just another day for her. She knew that she needed some of my money and I finally realized I needed to find a way for her to have some. Otherwise, I began to think that the situation might actually turn ugly. I was cut off from communicating with my friends. She was already looking a little upset with me. It crossed my mind that some of the men might barge into the room and rob me. So, I decided to quell the situation by making a few requests for which I could pay.

I asked for another cold beer. As if the cash register had just been plugged back in, the girl immediately jumped up, rushed to the door, and sent one of the kids to retrieve it. When it came, I gave her twice what the beer was worth and said, "Thank you, I sit." But our transaction was not complete. She said, "What else G.I. want, you like pot?" Although I really didn't need any because it was always available for free at High Hopes, this offer sounded reasonable, so I said, "Yes, I want pot." Once again, she scooted to the door and instructed one of the kids to run off and get me some pot. The little guy returned to the room with a plastic bag of pot that was as big around as the fat end of a baseball bat. I thought I was about to get skinned out of a lot of money. Then, looking quite proud of herself for pleasing me, the girl placed the bag in my hands. I said, "How much?" She said, "Ten dolla," even though we both knew that meant ten piastres, which were worth less than American dollars. While I might still have overpaid, it was the biggest bag of pot I had ever had and well worth my ticket out of the situation I had found myself in.

After our pot transaction, the girl must have decided that she wasn't going to get much more money from me because she stopped asking me what I wanted. We returned to the courtyard, hand in hand, having completed our business together. I was sure she was pleased because she had produced some income and we were both able to have smiles on our faces as if we had enjoyed a wonderful time together. On top of all this, I now had a huge lump in my pants.

Before long, everyone had returned to the courtyard from their little escapades. As we sat at our table, I found it interesting that no one talked about what they had just done at that time, or at any other time for that matter. Maybe that was because each of us was supposed to have been committed to a relationship back home, but I wondered if it was also because their experiences had been similar to mine. I was particularly sure it had probably turned out that way for Pete, though I didn't notice any potentially intoxicating protrusions in his boonie pants.

Perhaps there was some value to having added the experience of congregating with the Vietnamese people in this way, but for me it was mostly just depressing. I viewed it as one more lousy outcome of American involvement in South Vietnam. At least part of a generation of young Vietnamese people grew up serving our troops as hootch maids, shit burners, or prostitutes. I found myself wishing that they could have found something else to do.

Over the next forty-eight hours, we shuffled back and forth between the relaxation center and the courtyard. To my knowledge, there were no more secret visits with the girls, and for the most part the family seemed satisfied with having us spend our money on beers, snacks, and generous tips. In between those visits, we slept a lot. The fresh ocean air and the isolation of the place made me feel far away from everything in both good and bad ways. Although I was apprehensive about being so disconnected from the military in a place that could have easily left us prey to anyone who would have wanted to harm us, it was also nice to consider what that place could have been like in peacetime. I know I would have enjoyed it much more.

The last night at the Vung Tau R & R Center I went down to sleep in one of the pole buildings closest to the water where I could hear the ocean and get a better breeze. Without telling anyone I took my things and moved about fifty yards from where the others had set up camp. I didn't think my move was any big deal until early the next morning when I strolled back up to the building where the guys had been and discovered that they were already packed up and gone.

I went into the main building to see the Special Services person who was in charge of the place. He informed me that my friends had been in there about a half-hour earlier looking for me, but figured I must have come up with another way back to Bien Hoa and left. Another way back to Bien Hoa? What other way back to Bien Hoa? According to the clerk the only other way back to Bien Hoa would be to walk into the village and see if I could hitch a ride in some other Army vehicle headed that way. Really? I was going to go hitchhiking in Vietnam in the middle of the so-called Easter Offensive?

As it turned out, hitchhiking really was the only way I was going to get back to Bien Hoa. Yet, as I discovered when I got to the center of the village, there were virtually no military vehicles on the road that morning. All I saw were mopeds, three-wheelers, and bicycles. Vung Tau was at the end of a road by the Ocean. I assumed that very few Army guys would have any sanctioned business there on a Monday morning. And on top of that I suspected that I looked very much the part of someone who had been left behind after a long weekend at the beach. There I was, considering my appearance again on a dirt road hitchhiking out of a small Southeast Asian village in a War zone.

There was nothing else to do. I just sat there by the road pretending like I knew what I was doing...waiting for a ride. Finally, I spotted a solo driver in a small blue Air Force truck coming in my direction from the village. I didn't actually hold out my thumb. I stepped into the road and waved him down. Fortunately, he stopped. Looking in the passenger side window, I explained my situation to the driver and didn't give him much room to turn me down. I needed to get moving.

The good news was that he was willing to give me a ride. But unfortunately, he explained that he could only get me as far as Phu My because that was his official destination. Actually thinking ahead, I asked what it would be like hitching a ride out of Phu My. He told me that it would be, "A hell of a lot better than your chances sitting here." I hopped in the front seat of the Air Force truck for Phu My.

The Air Force guy seemed as surprised to find me hitchhiking in Vietnam as I was. Although his reaction heightened my concern, I still didn't see any other way to get myself back to Bien Hoa. I had to rely on my military counterparts to get me up the road. I couldn't envision hopping a moped with one of the Vietnamese civilians who always seemed to be packed up and headed somewhere.

We got to Phu My more quickly than I'd thought we would. This village was a bit larger than Vung Tau and I immediately spotted several military vehicles rumbling up and down the paved road, some going toward my destination. I thanked the driver, jumped out of his truck at a busy intersection, and quickly thumbed down the next faded green truck headed northwest. The Army driver of this truck told me he was making a supply run to the stockade at Long Binh. This was especially good news because I had been to Long Binh. It had a large Army base, it was just a few miles from Bien Hoa, and I had heard that my old buddy, Kool, had ended up there after his stint with the 101st Airborne up north. I figured I could drop in on him when I got there and maybe he could help me find a ride back to High Hopes. Things were looking up.

I rode in the back of a deuce and a half from Phu My to Long Binh. This one was covered with a canvas top which was strangely comforting. For the moment at least, I had seen enough of the Vietnamese countryside and I figured the cover would spare others from having to wonder about what I was doing out there on my own.

I never expected that it could feel so good to get dropped off at the front door of a military stockade. I had certainly imagined winding up in a place like that, but more likely as a result of military noncompliance than from hitchhiking. When the driver stopped and said, "Here we are," I happily leaped out of the back of the truck, thanked him several times, and headed for the main entrance of the prison.

I walked inside to a reception window and asked where I could locate Private First Class Kool. The Military Policeman behind the desk asked what my purpose was and I just said I was there to visit, if he was available. He used an intercom to contact Kool and I heard him say from the other end, "He's good, send him in." To that moment, I had not anticipated that Kool's station would be inside the secure entrance to the stockade. So, when the MP came from behind the window and began to escort me to clearance area, I nearly panicked. I still had the huge sack of pot in the side flap pocket of my fatigue pants.

But there was no turning back. I thought that if I excused myself or said, "Oh, never mind," the MP would have suspected me of something. And I wasn't sure what was actually going to happen at the clearance area. Perhaps since Kool had cleared me, they would just walk me through. I had to act naturally.

I was led through a set of solid glass doors into a small, empty holding area with another set of glass doors leading out the other side. The MP told me to wait as he exited the room the way we had come. I stood there alone in a glass cubicle like a maraschino cherry in a clear pitcher of lime Kool-Aid. Two other MPs entered the room a few moments later. They appeared to be engaged in a hot discussion about something that had happened that morning and seemed a little distracted by it. They barely greeted me. They asked who I was there to see and I told them. I stood spread eagle style as instructed. Then one of them tapped me down: arms, chest, belt line, and...just my left leg! He completely skipped my right leg where the bag of pot was jammed in the side pocket. A person could have seen it just by looking at my leg, but apparently neither one of these guys did.

After getting partially frisked, I signed in on the Visitor's Log, passed through the second set of glass doors, and got a police escort down a couple of long hallways to Kool's station. After the MP's left, I told him what had just happened and what was still in my pocket. Kool nearly crapped in his pants from laughing so hard. He found it especially funny how I'd wound up with it when I didn't even need it in the first place. That was easy for him to say. Supporting the local economy had almost put me in his care.

Horse with No Name
(America)

Around Mid-May of 1972, the rumors we had been hearing about closing up shop began to look like a reality. The 1st Cavalry and its tag-along Drug Amnesty Program were going to be headed home. The Doc was the first to go since he had been in country longer than any of the rest of us. The Captain was pulled down the road to the Medevac Headquarters to help out there. I think The Mormon came up with another emergency medical leave to return home early to be with his family. Ollie and Sergeant Cluster were reassigned somewhere else. When all the shuffling around was done, Pete, Lowery, and I were left behind with loose instructions to sort and pack up any pieces of equipment that could be salvaged from Drug Rehab Center.

For almost two weeks the three of us basically stayed out of sight from the Army, much as we had always done, in the abandoned buildings at High Hopes. We thought that the longer we stalled around there, the less likely it would be that we would get reassigned somewhere else to finish the few months we had remaining on our one-year tours and the more likely it would be that we would be sent home when the rest of the 1st Cavalry cleared out of country. Although Pete stayed put in his original hootch, Lowery and I moved into the Officer's trailer. Either the Doc or Captain Brinkman had left a cache of Playboy magazines behind, which filled some of the time. There was also a full-size refrigerator in the trailer to keep our beer cold.

The three of us spent many days and nights sitting around the living room of the trailer among all the centerfolds, notices from Headquarters, and trash that we could have been cleaning up. While we voted to discontinue the Friday night cookouts because there were only the three of us, we continued to carry on our nighttime traditions of listening to Pete's cassette player, smoking endless cigarettes and pot, and drinking as much beer as we could stomach. Although we would rather have filled our time attempting to help someone, for still being in Vietnam, we considered ourselves incredibly fortunate, but occasionally isolated and a little guilty for the way we were carrying on.

One afternoon when we were doing our best to kill time, a Jeep came bouncing into the entrance at the Center. It was Captain Brinkman driving himself. We were all really happy to see each other again and he and I did a handshake routine in lieu of the hug that probably would have been more fitting. Captain Brinkman knew that we had been up to next to nothing and we didn't even attempt to hide it from him. In fact, we invited him into his old trailer for a beer in the middle of the afternoon. He seemed entertained by our interior design, unkempt appearance, and cavalier approach to military duty. It was as if he understood that we were disheartened by the memories of what we had tried to do at High Hopes and angered by the Army's lack of organization even when it came to pulling out of the country. The image of us sitting with a West Point Captain among all the magazines in the trashed living room of a broken-down trailer with its torn screen door hanging from one hinge has stuck with me for a long time.

Soon enough Captain Brinkman got around to his reason for stopping by. He explained that we needed to finish up whatever we were doing and take up residence down at the Medevac unit because it was very likely we would be getting our new assignments within the next few weeks. That could involve going home. Captain Brinkman also said that the Unit Commander had become aware that we were still hanging around at the Amnesty Center and that he had been sent to check out our progress on getting the equipment ready to be returned to Supply.

It was terribly obvious we had done almost nothing with respect to our assignment. Captain Brinkman asked us how long it would take to get things in order. We were a little torn. We looked forward to the possibility of being sent home, but we also knew that this could be just another false alarm. So, we split the difference and told him that we could have everything in order within five days, knowing that it wouldn't take us longer than a half a day to do what we needed to do. He agreed. We shared another beer, joked with him about reclaiming some of his old Playboys, and told him we would check in at the Unit in six days – one day more than we had seemingly just agreed to.

Captain Brinkman's visit didn't have any noticeable affect on us until several days later. In some ways the idea of packing up just added to our sense of failure and anger regarding High Hopes, the military, and all the guys whose lives had been influenced negatively by having to participate in the War. It certainly did not appear that our work had mattered to anyone in charge. In fact, other than our instruction to have the equipment ready to go to Supply, we received no debriefing or acknowledgement regarding any the work we had tried to do.

On Day Four, we took our anger out on the place and started tearing up anything that wasn't nailed down and dragging it to a burn pile out behind the outhouses where the Papa-son used to burn shit. We stacked all the salvageable equipment in the middle of the softball field that was now overgrown again in weeds. I was convinced that none of the stuff we deemed salvageable was actually going anywhere except to the Vietnamese villagers who would gladly claim it when we were gone. On the morning of Day Five we added the officers' refrigerator and the left-over supply of medications to the pile of junk on the old softball field.

As we were preparing to leave the Center during the last minutes of the last afternoon on Day Six, I walked into the wooden building where the admission office had been and sat down on the frame of an old steel chair. I took a few deep breaths and looked around the space where we had gathered so many memories. I was ready to say some silent goodbyes to my friends, the place, and an important piece of my life.

There, on the makeshift plywood shelf where it had always rested when it wasn't in someone's hands was the hand written ledger we'd expanded to record information on the guys who had volunteered for the Amnesty Program at High Hopes. Much like I would if I had been handling a Bible, I carefully picked the book off the shelf, swiped the dust from its cover, and began thumbing through the hundreds of names that were listed on its dog-eared pages.

Eighteen-year-old Private Burden had come into the Program smoking three vials per day and went out clean after ten days with no follow-up. Twenty-year-old Private First Class Ward came in snorting four and went out clean after fourteen with no follow-up. Twenty-two-year-old Private Samuels came in shooting five and left against medical advice after day two with no follow-up. Private First Class Caine came in doing nothing and was discharged after one day with no follow-up. The Mormon's friend came in doing four, went out clean after fourteen, and was known dead from an overdose. And so on and on.

For me each name constituted a memory and a salient piece of my experience in Vietnam. I couldn't help thinking again about each person who had entered the Program and then about all the other people who we had not reached. Who would know what happened to them? How many American soldiers died of heroin overdoses in South Vietnam? How many of those were accidental? How many of those were suicides? How many of those were resisting participation in the War? How many went home strung out on heroin and how many of those never recovered? Had I helped anyone or had I inadvertently contributed to the military's destruction of young lives much like my own? Angry and unanswered questions about all the guys whirled in my head.

Then it occurred to me that the ledger was still just sitting there on the shelf. No one had touched it or placed a mark in it for more than a month. Although it was not any sort of official military document, it surprised me that no one in charge had taken it or placed it in a file box for safe keeping, future research, or executive summary. To my knowledge, there was no other information kept regarding the guys, the problem, our work, or our findings.

I wondered if information from the other Amnesty Centers was being abandoned in the same way. If so, I figured it would have been an awfully convenient way for the Army to sweep more of its dirt under the rug. If anyone ever asked, the higher-ups could report that nothing had been kept or perhaps that, due to the rush of standing down, such information had to be abandoned. No one would ever have to know. And maybe no one really cared to know about this ugly side of the War. Maybe everyone anticipated that memories of heroin use in Vietnam would just fade away like all the other crumby outcomes.

I couldn't just leave our notes sitting there on the shelf. Back then it was not out of my respect for secrecy or confidentiality. From what I could tell, there wasn't any concern about those things at the time. I couldn't leave it because I felt it was my duty to keep the information protected and to keep my respect for all the guys alive.

Without telling Pete, Lowery, or anyone else, I ripped all of the pages that had writing on them from the ledger, rolled them up as tightly as I could, and tucked them deep down into my duffle bag next to my faded High Hopes patch and the bootlace necklace of empty green, pink, and white heroin vials that I planned to take back to the States. Then I hoisted the duffle over my shoulder, met my friends out by the front gate, and walked down the oil-soaked road to the Medevac Headquarters, just as we had when we arrived.

I'm Going Home
(Ten Years After Version)

Down at the Unit, we had to act a little like we were back in the Army again. We slept in one of several open barracks with thirty or forty other guys. Because it seemed difficult and unnecessary to integrate with all the guys we didn't know, Pete, Lowery, and I found a corner that allowed us to keep our unique camaraderie alive.

Being back in the Army meant falling out for roll call early every morning. On our first day back, we had already fallen out and were getting set to fall into formation for the morning check. Guys were milling around smoking cigarettes when Captain Brinkman came out of the door of the Headquarters office. Before he had a chance to call the group to attention, I walked over to greet him and let him know that we had lived up to our agreement to rejoin the unit.

It was special to see Captain Brinkman in a position of authority over the Medevac Company. And as always, we were both really happy to see each other. Without even thinking about those who might have been watching, we did an abbreviated version of our handshake right in front of all the guys who were waiting for roll call. We might have even introduced a few new moves just to show off our proficiency as two white guys pulling off the customarily black greeting. When we were done, it was as if we both suddenly came to our senses.

Later that morning, Captain Brinkman caught up with me in the Headquarters Office and told me that we couldn't greet each other like that ever again. It was as if he was reminding himself as much as he was telling me. His awkward explanation reminded me of when my father told me that I no longer needed to give him a goodnight kiss on the forehead when I turned seven, even though there were lots of times when I still might have wanted to.

As it turned out, there was nothing much for two Psychiatric Social Workers and an all-purpose Drug Amnesty staffer to do at the Medevac Unit. This was a group of Warrant Officers who flew the Huey helicopters, Maintenance guys who kept the choppers running, Medics and the door gunners who accompanied them on their rescue missions, and support staff who kept the Unit in order for everybody else. Most of the guys seemed to be in reasonable mental health and, at the time, it did not appear that there were many hard drugs floating around. Flying Medevac assignments was serious business.

Without people for us to assist, Pete and I wound up doing busywork around the Clerk's office at the Headquarters while Lowery reassumed a role as a Jeep Driver. Once again, we had lots of down time during the day that we would use sitting around in the barracks listening to music and waiting for something to happen. Some days that meant going over to the Air Force Base with Captain Brinkman to play basketball on their covered cement courts. Other days it meant sneaking back up the road to the Amnesty Center where we could hide out some more. It seemed clear that we were now stuck in a holding pattern, just waiting for the Army to send us home.

The base at Bien Hoa was beginning to look deserted since so many others had already hopped the "freedom bird" back to the world. But after about two weeks of this, all the waiting had left us pretty numb. Each day we watched other guys get their orders to go home. We were happy for them, but wondered what was taking the Army so long to pull its Drug Counselors out of the country. After all, we felt that as far as they were concerned, whatever problem there was had now become irrelevant. Perhaps we were irrelevant too.

Finally, Pete, Lowery, and I got our call. A messenger came down to the barracks to inform us that our orders were in and we could pick them up from the Clerk at the office. We dropped whatever it was we weren't doing and tried to act nonchalant, though we almost ran through the Unit's central area to see the Clerk. Sure enough, there was my name listed on a sheet that contained the names of about twenty other guys. Pete and Lowery's names were there as well. We all stood there looking at the sheet for a long time just to let the good news sink in. I was scheduled to head back to the States with Pete and Lowery on June 21, 1972.

In general, guys who received orders to clear out of country didn't do a lot of last minute celebrating. Although most of the 1st Cavalry had already left, this was primarily out of respect for the other guys who still had to stay. As a result, we continued to lay low for the forty-eight hours or so until we were to catch our ride to the replacement station at the Tan Son Nhut airport near Saigon.

When I arrived at Tan Son Nhut, I was filled with memories of our arrival in Cam Ranh Bay. This time however, there were no Newbies coming into the airport from the other direction. This time, it was the middle of the day. This time, the buildings were all made of cement. This time I was a "Veteran," among all the other Veterans who were about to return to the world.

Even so, I had mixed feelings about it. I was a troubled because it was very clear to everyone that this stand-down was not the result of any "mission accomplished." Not only was it clear that we were pulling out of Vietnam because of what most already considered an impending military disaster, but we also knew that we were unlikely to be welcomed home with any sort of fanfare. Not that I was particularly going to miss that part, but when all was said and done we were still going to be Army guys - Army guys who had participated in the most unpopular War in U.S. history.

After we were checked in at Tan Son Nhut, we were given a brief reorientation about what to expect when our boots were back on the ground in the States. Similar to getting prepped for confession back in grade school, we were advised to be alert for changes in ourselves and among our families and friends, although no one said exactly what kind of changes we might expect. We were warned that we might be greeted, particularly at the civilian airports, by people who did not understand the War and were more opposed to U.S. involvement than ever. As if to make us angry or proud, we were informed of instances where guys in uniform had been verbally lambasted and physically attacked by "hippies and other anti-war protesters" in some of the bigger cities. It was strange to consider that going home might be roughly similar to our arrival in Vietnam when some of the locals had shouted at us. The good news, however, was that I was pretty sure I would not need to be prepared to low-crawl across the runway when we reached San Francisco.

The final in-country urine screen for drugs had been a key part of checking out of Vietnam since the Amnesty Program had started. Of course, we were very much aware of this and had seen guys at the Amnesty Center who had been detained in country due to having turned up dirty screens. As a result we had often used the threat of being detained as an extra motivator for guys to get clean before they headed through Tan Son Nhut for home. Just to be sure neither Pete, Lowery, nor I puffed on anything other than cigarettes for several days before our arrival at the replacement center.

We were surprised to see that the folks at Tan Son Nhut took the urine screening procedures more seriously than we ever had at High Hopes. Guys received their labeled sample containers in small groups from one of several clerks behind a

289

secure window, got escorted to a long stainless steel urinal, and were observed while they filled them to the brim and returned to the window. Pete and Lowery easily loaded their containers and left the bathroom. However, apparently all the hype and publicity in the bathroom did not sit well with my bladder. I got my cup, stood in front of the trough and tried hard, but I couldn't urinate. After dancing around, envisioning raindrops, and otherwise playing with myself for a while, my observer informed me that it was okay to drink some water from the cooler back by the clerk's window. I did.

When I came back into the bathroom, I realized that I was the last guy in my group who had not peed and I was told that I only had two minutes before I would have to leave the secure area so that the next group could enter. I had no idea what would happen if I could not complete the test, but the observer's warning did nothing to improve my urinary performance. I just couldn't get it done, not even a drop.

Finally, I was told to return my empty container to the clerks. As I did, I saw Pete and Lowery through a floor-to-ceiling chain-link fence. They had apparently cleared their test and were headed to the terminal area to wait on the plane. I shouted that I would see them later, but as it turned out, I didn't.

After failing to piss I was escorted to another secure area where I was instructed to stay until I could. I asked when I would get my next opportunity. I was informed that since it was late in the day I would have to wait until the following morning. Although Pete and Lowery didn't know it yet, they would be on their way without me. I would be spending an extra night in Vietnam because I couldn't take a piss.

The rest of that afternoon and night were almost as miserable as any I'd had in Vietnam. I had never spent much time being locked up anywhere and I was the only guy in the secure area who was there because he could not produce any urine. The few others who were there had gotten the opportunity because they had produced and received positive results for heroin. I felt that I knew these guys well enough, but I wasn't thrilled about being with them under these circumstances. Although I tried to sleep on the upper bunk of one of the beds that night, I'm not sure I wound up sleeping at all. Most of the others were into withdrawal. I was up most of the night drinking water and trying to help them out.

After drinking copious amounts of water and not having peed in way more than twelve hours, I was first in line when the screening station opened the next morning. I grabbed my plastic container and filled it to the brim. I could have easily filled fifteen or twenty of them. When I was done I proudly handed my sample over to the clerk, got cleared, and finally got my ticket through the chain link fence to the terminal.

I rode a huge Pan American 747 back to the United States with a couple hundred other guys in faded jungle fatigues who I didn't know. Although there were momentary sparks of celebration at various points along the way, it was not surprising to me that there was mostly just peace and quiet on the plane. I compared it to the Flying Tiger flight that had brought us to South Vietnam. I was pretty sure that the unknown, the anticipation, and a different sort of apprehension consumed most of us as we zoomed toward the San Francisco-Oakland airport. Between trips to the toilet to continue unloading all the fluids I had stocked up from the night before, I slept through most of the trip back to the world.

When we arrived at the terminal, guys grabbed their duffles from the baggage claim as quickly as they could. I was surprised to see how many of us headed immediately for the bathroom. In fact, the place was jammed with soldiers washing up, brushing their teeth, and hustling to change out of their uniforms into civilian clothing. I dug down to the bottom of my bag and I vividly recall the sensation of my hand touching my old blue jeans that had been tucked in there since I'd left Fort Lewis. I pulled them through the wads of other stuff in the bag and held them in both of my hands. I raised them to my face so I could smell them. Then I put them on with a white T-shirt, rustled my hair so it would look as long as it possibly could, and went back into the terminal for my flight to Chicago.

It was either June 23rd or 24th, 1972. Due to the time changes, I didn't know for sure. I was walking through the San Francisco-Oakland airport for my connecting flight home. I was hoping nobody would give me a hard time. I recalled that I had been in San Francisco almost exactly three years earlier in late June of 1969. At that time I was an eighteen-year-old kid riding my thumb, looking for adventure, and wondering what would happen next. Now, I was a twenty-one-year-old Vietnam Veteran in the same old jeans and a t-shirt. For me, the 1960's were over.

Carry On – An Epilogue
(Crosby, Stills, Nash, and Young)

I completed my stint in the Army at Fort Carson, Colorado. Sunshine and I were married shortly after I got home from Vietnam and stayed together for six years before we finally drove each other away. After our wedding I didn't maintain contact with anyone from Loyola until just recently when I reconnected with Skip and Joon. Similarly, I never kept in contact with anyone from the military until recently when I reestablished some contact with Pete and the Mormon. I would really like to find Cowboy and Lowery. After leaving Loyola and after getting out of the Army, I must have been ready to set aside these aspects of my youth for a while.

Following my abrupt exposure to Psychiatric Social Work in the military, I went back to school and completed an undergraduate degree in Psychology at Northern Illinois University in Dekalb and a graduate degree in Applied Behavior Analysis and Therapy at Southern Illinois University in Carbondale. Southern Illinois is where I met and have stayed with Deb, my current wife of twenty-nine years. She continues to be a huge part of my energy for living. We have a fine son, who is a twenty-seven-year-old musician and graphic designer in Chicago.

I have spent most of my last thirty-eight years trying to contribute something to the lives of persons who are considered to be mentally ill, intellectually disabled, or brain-injured, as well as those who attempt to assist them. This work has provided an ongoing context that has fueled my fascination for exploring the reasons why people do the things they do. However, as pleased as I have been with my profession, I find it interesting to think that if the Recruiter had signed me up for

Map Drawing when I joined the Army; it seems very possible that I might still be drawing maps today.

Looking back, it seems barely believable to think that I was among almost three million young men and women who served in Vietnam, yet until now I have hardly ever talked about my experiences with anyone. Fact is I only have one Veteran acquaintance besides Pete and the Mormon who, if I happen to bump into him on a November 11th, will wish me well for Veteran's Day. Several years back I was seriously moved when I visited the Memorial Wall in DC (where memories seem to be vividly alive and well), but I only had silent eye-contact with the others who were there. Similarly, about six years ago I spent a whole afternoon at the Vietnam Veterans Art Museum in Chicago but my wife, son, an inexperienced curator, and I were the only ones around. Just the other day I drove to see a display of the traveling Wall in a grocery store parking lot and had fully intended to use it as an opportunity to swap some stories with someone. But I didn't. In many ways, up until now I have dealt with my Vietnam memories, as well as those from the late 1960's, as a kind of black hole in my life. I suppose it has been easier to remain quiet than to hypothesize regarding the true causes for my own behavior.

Lately however, I've tried to identify some of the reasons for my silence and I now realize there have been many. Certainly, I've feared the old "why did you do it" questions regarding my enlistment, which I would still be unable to answer very easily. Although I have yet to feel proud of it, over the years I have found some solace in knowing that I wasn't the only one who volunteered for the military knowing that I was likely to go to Vietnam. I find it remarkable and oddly comforting to consider that although it was such a distasteful War, some claim that almost two-thirds of those who went to

Vietnam were volunteers. Back then, I would never have had that impression.

Perhaps some of those who volunteered actually believed in whatever the U.S. was fighting for, but I don't think I've ever met one of them. Others probably never thought about the government's purpose and just hoped that serving would eventually lead them to a better life. So many others, like me, apparently just went for the experience and passively resisted the War their entire time in the service. Whatever the case, it seems clear that for the great majority, going to Vietnam was not motivated by an interest in maintaining our freedom or demonstrating patriotism toward the country. I think most of us wound up doing what we were expected to do because we feared negative consequences if we didn't and because when it came down to it, we couldn't let each other down.

Besides my "don't tell and they won't ask" approach, I think there are several other pretty good reasons why I've stayed quiet about my Vietnam experience until now. Perhaps the primary one is that I didn't find myself in a situation where I might have had to kill someone. Crazy as that may sound; I'm still very sensitive to the fact that there were hundreds of thousands of young people who did. I've noticed that I have an unrelenting sense of acquiescence when it comes to thinking about myself with respect to guys who were in a situation where they had to take lives. I suspect I will always think it is primarily their right to represent what life was *really* like in Vietnam, but I hope they won't mind me opening up about it as well.

Furthermore, I didn't die. As of today, it is being reported that more than fifty-eight thousand one hundred seventy-five Americans are known to have been killed in the War. There are still times when I experience a sense of guilt that I wasn't one of them. I am pretty sure many people who served in Vietnam or other wars experience this odd sense of guilt. Similarly, there are still times when I wonder if I should have gone with Smutz to the Infantry or with Kool to the 101st up north.

Finally, I think I have remained quiet about my Vietnam experiences because until very recently I didn't think I had any effect on making either the killings or the deaths less likely. I've frequently wondered if I could have saved a few lives by protesting more actively or effectively when I was back on the streets in Chicago. Similarly, I've wondered if I could have done a better job of generating dissent once I was on the inside, rather than just pissing and moaning with my friends about our continued involvement, just like I had done in college. I suspect there are many others who opposed the War that feel the same way. Perhaps more importantly, I've continued to have questions about the impact of the help I attempted to provide when I worked with the Amnesty Program in Vietnam. I have had lingering doubts about whether our efforts actually did anyone any good.

Although I've not worn it on my sleeve to this point in my life and don't expect to in my future, at least I can finally say out loud that I actively protested the War, volunteered for the Army, *and* served in Vietnam without feeling more than a momentary tinge of contradiction, shame, or embarrassment. I have long stopped wondering if these feelings are ever going to change. Interestingly, I've noticed that others who might have served, but didn't, don't talk very loudly or proudly about their actions either. I find it strange that same-age guys who didn't serve generally don't suspect that I did, and even if they know, they don't question me about it. With the exception of some brotherhoods, it seems like most everybody remains strangely silent on the matter.

From my view, remaining quiet about serving in Vietnam is similar to the more general reluctance that many people who lived in the 1960's seem to have about sharing their experiences. I've noticed that many from this generation don't volunteer and sometimes resist providing information about their drug use, their politics, their sexual escapades, their risk-taking, their law-breaking, and so on. There are probably lots of good reasons for this silence as well, not the least of which is that they must still be fearful about what their families, children, neighbors, and employers might think.

Yet, maybe it is time for more of us to think about our experiences a little differently. We "Boomers" moved from a decade of precious innocence and predictability in the 1950's to a decade of seeming chaos, novelty, rebellion, revolution, and change in the 1960's. Since we hadn't experienced situations like this before, we wound up doing a lot of things without having a clue how they would turn out. Although the novel situations moved many of us to do things that subsequently we may not have been proud of, few would argue that they were not remarkable things. Over the last forty years I have gradually come to view my 1960's experiences as true and critical parts of an incredibly interesting and robust time in my life...a time when I was *fortunate* to have been in a position to be influenced by all the incredible things that were happening in the world around me. And as I continue to age, it seems that I discover more good reasons to talk about it all the time.

Thankfully, by the beginning of 1973 most of our troops had come home from the War and had begun to move on with their lives. While this may have been viewed as long-overdue good news for many, I have been haunted over the years by my concern that life probably didn't progress so smoothly for Vietnam Veterans who became involved with heroin while overseas. When this drug arrived on the scene its use seems to have spread like a virus among the eighteen-, nineteen-, and twenty-year-old American troops who were there. I've frequently asked myself some of the same questions I wondered about then. Who really knows how many young guys became addicted to heroin before the Amnesty Programs were initiated in 1971? And after the Programs started, who knows how many guys actually took advantage of them and, of those, how many benefited? I've been disappointed that the answers still seem very unclear.

In 1971, it was being reported that a soldier a day was dying in Vietnam due to heroin overdoses. Subsequently, another dusty report indicated that as many six hundred thousand guys may have used or abused heroin during their tours in Vietnam. Who knows if these were accurate estimations of the problem? Who knows how many of the guys continued their habits and died from heroin addiction after they got back to the States? And short of winding up dead, who knows the social impact of heroin addiction, at least partially attributable to participation in or resistance to the War?

Part of the reason we don't know very much about these things is because it appears nobody took the time to collect, save, study, interpret, or share information that was available. Apparently, in the decades since the War few have been particularly concerned.

Yet, in 2009 as I was writing this book, I recalled that I had protected the notes that had been left behind at the High Hopes Drug Amnesty Center in Bien Hoa. Since it had been almost 40 years, and since I've had a tendency to accumulate so much paper in my life, I wasn't sure that I still had the pages I had torn from the ledger book. After searching for days through old files in my office and boxes in my garage with no luck, I began to think that maybe they never existed in the first place, or that maybe I'd inadvertently lost them somewhere along the way. I even wondered if maybe the whole incident was part of some fragmented dream and that I'd never really protected them in the first place. I hadn't considered what I would do if and when I did find them, other than stir up a few troubling memories.

After a long search, I finally found the pages along with my course materials and notes from the Psychiatric Social Work training that we received at Fort Sam Houston. They were in an old water-warped cardboard storage box in the upstairs of my garage. Seeing them again triggered a full range of emotion from happiness to sadness and disgust. I didn't move from the floor of the attic for a long time. Instead, I spent hours thumbing through all the names and notes on the tarnished pages just like I'd done back in the office when we'd closed up High Hopes. I even ran my fingertips over my old handwriting from when I had recorded some of the information in the first place. I noticed that the paper still smelled like South Vietnam, a tinge of must combined with the distinct odor of diesel fuel and burning feces.

Suddenly, my lonely reminiscing was interrupted by a startling realization. I held the old folder close to my chest, hustled down the wooden steps from the attic, and ran to my computer. During the next twenty-four hours I was glued to the internet website provided by The Wall – USA. I compared each one of my 91G20 cohorts and each one of the two hundred fifty-six guys who were listed in the ledger between October of 1971 and April of 1972 against the names of persons who were listed on the Wall as casualties of the War. I was urgent to learn just one truth…How many of the guys we met at High Hopes made it home from the War? As I checked out each name, one by one by one, I was still weary of what I would discover. I was also sickened to consider all the thousands of young people whose names on the Wall appear to be almost all that is left of them.

The results of my search showed up gradually, but I couldn't get my computer to work any faster. Initially, I was pleased to see that Caine, all fifteen of my Psychiatric Social Work friends, the Doc, Captain Brinkman, and Sergeant Cluster were not listed on the Wall. That being the case, I suspected that many of them had probably spent more time than they would have liked over the last four decades wondering the same thing that I was. Did we do any good?

As it turns out, my internet search produced some wonderful and somewhat unexpected results that have certainly contributed to breaking my silence. Most importantly, of all two hundred fifty-six guys we saw at High Hopes, only one young kid - the Mormon's friend - did not make it home from the War. Taken in terms of a percentage, the mortality rate among the group of guys we saw actually may have been lower than that for all those who served.

Obviously, I was surprised and thrilled by this finding and I suspect that my friends and many others may feel similarly. Bottom line is that it appears that we Psychiatric Social Workers may have done some good...maybe even saved a few lives. After all these years, the nagging fears or concerns we may have had related to other inadvertent heroin overdoses or deadly performance errors among those we saw at High Hopes can be put to rest. My relief is so welcome I find myself repeating it over and over just so it can fully sink in. Unfortunately however, just like all the thousands of others doing heroin in Vietnam who we never saw, I am still disappointed to say that there is no telling what became of them.

Although I'd never understood exactly how or why it would matter, I now believe that there could be some benefit forthcoming from my spontaneous act of protecting the legacy of High Hopes. Of course, I hope it provides my cohorts with relief from any pain of the unknown that they may have experienced over the years. However, I also wonder if the findings could provide some impetus for further research or a long-term follow-up study of this group of young people who fell into the clutches of heroin abuse and disillusionment in South Vietnam. Finally, I am hopeful that it provides a focal point, educational prop, or poignant reminder to others regarding this pervasive, largely undocumented, and seemingly long-forgotten outcome of the War. Young kids are still making life-altering decisions to join the military every day. And considering that many of them are currently involved in another unpopular and prolonged conflict in the poppy capital of the world, perhaps it is time to jog a few memories regarding the impact of war and drugs on young lives.

So, after nearly forty years as a Veteran of the 1960's and the War, I continue to consider what I've learned, how the experiences helped shape my life, and of what value they might be to anyone else. For now, what follows is the best I can do.

In many ways, although I am now nearly three times older than I was, I continue to think of myself as a toddler in this life…continually catching up with wherever my little feet carry me. Similarly, as children of the sixties, I think that many of us sensed that growing up, being alive, existing, was not really a matter of thinking ahead and planning out what would happen to us next. So many times we had no way of guessing what that might have been.

Reading about assassinations, waiting for rides on the sides of highways, hopping in cars with strangers, listening to wild new music, sitting through the Draft Lottery, carrying signs against the War, doing drugs, hanging out at rock festivals, joining the Army, touching down at Cam Ranh Bay, and treating young heroin addicts represented some pretty remarkable ways for me to get exposed to the world. But they were not unlike the experiences of a generation of young people who were growing up at the time. I believe that *living* was at least partially a matter of finding ourselves in novel situations, acting, and then deciphering how in the world we ever made it through.

So many children of the sixties experienced things first and then looked for the relevance in their lives later. Sometimes we enjoyed the experiences and went searching for more and better. Sometimes they frightened us and we veered off in other directions. In retrospect, it seems as though it truly was a matter of being moved by the things that happened around us. Cosmo responded one way, I responded another. Smutz responded one way, I responded another. I'm not sure any of us could precisely explain why, but there were always reasons…some of which we may never know.

In the process of being bombarded by novelty many of us were afforded powerful opportunities to begin to understand how our experience of "being free" was somehow related to abandoning the self-aggrandizing and illusory sense that we were somehow in command of whatever happened. So many of us just went along for the ride. Yet although we may have interpreted our actions as being free, and that was often a suitable interpretation at the time, I now believe there was much more to it. My journey suggests that the world changed us a whole lot more than any one of us ever changed it. And in the years that have followed I have realized that it continues to move us all the time.

The truth is that I believe I learned something very important from my young adult years that has become increasingly relevant for me as I have aged. Put as simply as I can, I think the 1960's taught me how to *watch* my life as it was unfolding in front of me. For me, this sort of *observing* started with the recognition that *living* was not something I controlled or something I could think, feel, or act my way through. With time, this recognition led to a deeper understanding that I had been influenced by things that happened around me, that I continued to be moved by an incomprehensible synthesis of those things, and that I responded to new things in exactly the only way I could have possibly responded to them given everything else that had already taken place.

As a result, I am now convinced that there were no mistakes along the way and there is nothing for me or anyone else to apologize for. In fact, it seems inaccurate to claim or discard personal responsibility for anything that has happened. I can now see that those things were simply the result of my emerging relationship and connection with the world around me.

Everything that has happened creates a stage for whatever happens next. For me, watching for what moves me and attending to what I am moved to do has gradually become a much bigger part of what my life is about. I recognize that labeling things as "good" or "bad" is arbitrary and broadly imprecise because things have been (and will continue to be) driven by other things that are much more powerful than any of our individual opinions. The 1960's helped me begin to question much of what I had been taught and transcend my fear about giving up my illogical ideas about freedom, ownership, internal control, and personal autonomy. As a result, my tendency to blame others has dissipated and I appreciate people much more...regardless of the things they do. Similarly, my personal experiences of guilt and self-doubt have lessened and I can more fully appreciate this thing I still refer to as my "self."

I have been just who I have been, we are just who we are, and we will be whoever we will be. I am now pleased to share things that have happened along my way and can imagine that readers of this book may be better prepared as well. There will be no need to climb stone steps on our knees. Far from it.

Experiencing whatever happens next as a *Spectator* in one's own existence can be an extremely interesting, fascinating, and potentially exhilarating journey - perhaps, the greatest show on earth. And thanks to the 1960's I can't wait to see what happens next.

About the Author

Marty McMorrow dropped out of college in 1971 and, shortly thereafter, found himself in the Army treating young soldiers who were addicted to heroin in Vietnam. Following his military experience, he completed a Master's degree in Behavior Analysis and Therapy at Southern Illinois University in Carbondale and has now spent 39 years participating in the lives of persons who are considered to be mentally ill, intellectually disabled, or brain injured. He has authored or co-authored more than 60 professional papers, as well as the specialty books *Stacking the Deck* (Research Press, 1983), *Looking for the Words* (Research Press, 1983), *Getting Ready to Help* (Paul Brookes Publishing, 2003), and *The Helping Exchange: PEARL* (Lash and Associates, 2005).

Since 2008 Marty has branched out to explore other "roads not taken" earlier in his life. *Phoenix to LA* represents his first work in novel form and is likely to be followed shortly by another entitled *Spectating: A Behavioral Pathway to Bits of Heaven on Earth* in which he will invite readers to consider a radically behavioral view of existence in the name of personal and interpersonal wellness.

In his spare time, Marty plays guitar in a low-key local band, enjoys traveling with his wife, watches stock car races, collects antiques, and does his best to keep his old tractors running.

LaVergne, TN USA
28 July 2010
191210LV00003B/3/P

9 781609 101879